'The King's Irish'

The Royalist Anglo-Irish Foot of the
English Civil War

John Barratt

Helion & Company

The Series Editor would like to thank Serena Jones and Jonathan Worton for the help with images for this book

Helion & Company Limited
Unit 8 Amherst Business Centre
Budbrooke Road
Warwick
CV34 5WE
England
Tel. 01926 499 619
Email: info@helion.co.uk
Website: www.helion.co.uk
Twitter: @helionbooks

Published by Helion & Company 2019
Designed and typeset by Mach 3 Solutions Ltd (www.mach3solutions.co.uk)
Cover designed by Paul Hewitt, Battlefield Design (www.battlefield-design.co.uk)

Text © John Barratt 2019
Black and white illustrations © as individually credited
Colour artwork by Seán Ó Brógain © Helion & Company 2019
Maps drawn by Alan Turton © Helion & Company 2019

ISBN 978-1-912866-53-3

British Library Cataloguing-in-Publication Data.
A catalogue record for this book is available from the British Library.

For details of other military history titles published by Helion & Company Limited contact the above address, or visit our website: http://www.helion.co.uk.

We always welcome receiving book proposals from prospective authors.

Contents

List of Illustrations

List of Maps

Chronology

1641

22 October	Outbreak of rebellion in Ulster
1 November	Parliament resolves to raise troops in England to suppress Irish rebellion
30 December	First troops under Sir Simon Harcourt reach Dublin

1642

Feb–April	Further troops from England Wales reach Ireland
15 April	Ormonde defeats rebels at Kilrush
July	Inchiquin defeats Irish at Liscarroll
24 October	Irish Confederacy established

1643

14 September	Cessation agreed between Ormonde and Irish Confederates
October	Regiments of Sir Charles Vavasour and Lord Paulet arrive in Bristol and Minehead
November	Regiments of Sir William St Leger and Nicholas Mynne land at Bristol
November	First 'wave' of approximately 1,800 troops from Leinster land at Mostyn, North Wales
December	Second 'wave' of 1,500 troops from Leinster reach Neston in Wirral
12 December	Anglo-Irish troops under Lord Byron take Beeston Castle
23 December	'Massacre' at Bartholmley Church
26 December	Anglo-Irish victory at Middlewich

1644

January	Royalists close in on Nantwich
18 January	Royalist assault on Nantwich repulsed
January/February	Regiments of Henry Tillier, Robert Broughton and William Vaughan land in North Wales and at Neston
January	Regiments of Lords Inchiquin and Broghill land at Weymouth
25 January	Byron defeated at Nantwich
21 March	Relief of Newark
29 March	Battle of Cheriton
April-May	Royalists consolidate position on Welsh border
28 May	'Bolton Massacre'
7–14 June	Siege of Liverpool
2 July	Battle of Marston Moor
7 August?	Mynne killed at Redmarley
18 September	Battle of Montgomery
October–November	Siege of Liverpool
27 October	Second Battle of Newbury

1645

18 January	Action at Chrisleton
14 June	Battle of Naseby
10 July	Battle of Langport

1646

3 February	Fall of Chester
21 March	Battle of Stow-on-the-Wold
August	Capture of town of Conway: destruction of Lord Byron's Regiment of Foot

Introduction

The use of troops from Ireland by King Charles is one of the most controversial episodes of the Civil War. Both the numbers involved, and the proportions of English, Welsh, Mainland settlers in Ireland 'native Irish' were the subject of fierce propaganda at the time and debate ever since.

Equally controversial was the part played by the forces from Ireland in the war, and whether the King actually benefited or lost support through their use.

This book examines the composition of 'The King's Irish', the mainly infantry forces which were despatched to support the Royalists in 1643/44. By tracing their campaigns it attempts to assess their impact on the war, especially in 1644 in the key operations in the Welsh Marches and the north of England.

Although this book aims to deal mainly with the foot from Ireland, I have included a brief summary of Sir William Vaughan's Regiment of Horse, a colourful story deserving one day of a fuller account.

Thanks are extended as always to various libraries and archives, including the British Library, the Bodleian Library, Shropshire Archives and the long-suffering staff of Ludlow Library.

As ever, the team at Helion have been generous in their suggestions and support.

John Barratt
Ludlow
April 2019

1

The Irish Rising

After more than 30 years of relative peace following the end of Tyrone's war, the outbreak of rebellion in Ireland in October 1641 came as a complete surprise to the authorities. It had a number of causes, chief among them in the province of Ulster, where unrest first began, were economic, social and religious fears, fuelled by the plantation policy which brought in large numbers of English and Scottish settlers, with an English-style economic system which alienated and threatened many Catholic landowners. Added to this was a run of bad harvests across Ireland, and the opportunity to take advantage of the political distractions afflicting Scotland and England.

Equally influential was the example of the successful defiance of the King by the Scottish Covenanting regime. As Clarendon complained: 'though Scotland blew the first trumpet it was Ireland that drew the first blood'.[1]

Although an attempt by the rebels to surprise Dublin failed, rebellion spread rapidly. On 21 November the rebels laid siege to the town of Drogheda, and by the end of the year insurrection had spread to much of the eastern and northern parts of the country, with the province of Munster following suit early in 1642.

English government in Ireland was exercised in theory by the Lord Lieutenant, at this time the Earl of Leicester, who remained in England, and the Lord Justice in Dublin. Militarily the English government was very weak. The largely Irish Catholic 'New Army' established by Thomas Wentworth, Earl of Strafford, the previous Lord Lieutenant, had been disbanded in the spring of 1641, and the only troops available were the 2,297 foot and 943 horse of the old Protestant army, clearly totally inadequate to meet the growing threat.

On 3 November, as news of the rebellion reached London, Parliament called for volunteers, initially 6,000 foot and 2,000 horse to be sent to Ireland. This call was rapidly increased to 10,000 foot.

But from the start efforts were crippled by mistrust between King and Parliament. Memories of the Scots Wars and the recent alleged Army Plots by Royalist supporters to use the troops raised for the Second Bishops' War

---

1   Earl of Clarendon, *The History of the Rebellion and Civil Wars in England* (Oxford: Clarendon Press, 1888), vol. VI, p. 2.

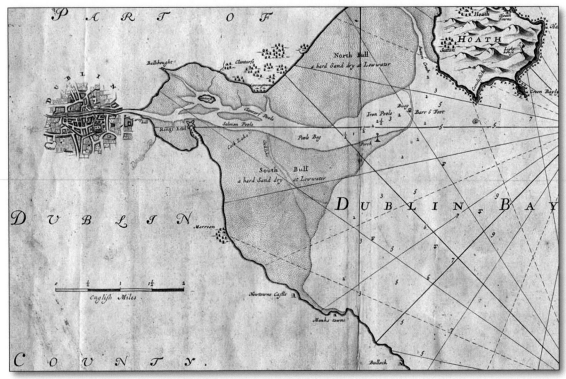

1 Contemporary map of Dublin and Dublin Bay. The City was the primary objective of the 1641 Rebellion and a principal port for the disembarkation of the newly raised government forces. (Map of Dublin Bay from Portmarnock to Dunleary, Captain G. Collins, 1693)

to suppress the King's opponents in England were fresh, and neither was prepared to agree to the other having control of the troops sent to Ireland. There were claims by some of the King's opponents that he was secretly in league with the rebels, and urged on by Queen Henrietta Maria, plotting to impose Catholicism on the whole nation with Irish rebel support.

Fears were intensified by reports of large-scale atrocities and massacres of Protestant settlers by the rebels. In March 1642 the Lords Justices would claim that 154,000 Protestants had been killed, although modern research suggests the real total was around 4,000.[2] But English settlers were certainly dispossessed of their lands, property and livestock, often with considerable violence, and thousands of refugees fled not only to Dublin and other towns still in English hands, but also across the Irish Sea to the mainland, carrying with them tales of the horrors they had alleged witnessed or experienced. A modern writer has summed up the wave of fear and alarm which spread across England Scotland: 'not every beggar woman in the streets of Dublin, Bristol or Chester who claimed to have seen her husband's throat cut by the Irish was telling the truth, but some of them were.'[3]

Whilst troops were recruited in England Wales and Scotland, resistance to the rebels rested with forces raised locally. In Munster Roger Boyle, Earl of Cork, spent large sums of money buying munitions and organising the local

---

2   John Kenyon and Jane Ohlmeyer, *The Civil Wars: A Military History of England, Scotland Ireland 1638–1660* (Oxford: Oxford University Press, 1998), p. 74.

3   C.V. Wedgwood, *The King's War* (London: Collins, 1958), p. 78.

Companyes of the Rebells meeting with the English flyinge for their liues falling downe before them cryinge for mercy thrust theire into their Childrens bellyes & threw them into the water.

X

2 One of many depictions of alleged atrocities in Ireland, as depicted in this contemporary illustration attributed to Wenceslaus Hollar. These exaggerated images caused panic throughout Britain. (From *The Teares of Ireland*, James Cranford, 1642)

defences. By 1643 Protestant landlords in Ulster had raised over 10,000 men from the local settlers.

On the mainland enthusiasm for service in Ireland varied. In general recruits seem to have been found more easily in areas such as Cheshire and North Wales which had closer links with the settlers in Ireland. Sir Simon Harcourt raised his regiment rapidly in Cheshire and North Wales, but in the South West Sir Charles Vavasour made slow progress. The Venetian Ambassador noted that 'the reluctance of the people to go there [Ireland] makes progress slow.'[4] The suspicion between King and Parliament regarding the deployment of the troops also dampened enthusiasm.

The continued absence of the Lord Lieutenant, the Earl of Leicester, hindered action in Ireland. In November James Butler, Earl of Ormonde, was appointed Lieutenant General. Ormonde, who had no military experience and would prove a better administrator than commander in the field, also commanded military units in Leinster. The army, such as it was, was divided into four commands, corresponding to the four provinces of Leinster, Ulster, Munster and Connaught. Ulster was in practice largely the responsibility of the forces despatched from Scotland under the Earl of Leven. Lord Inchiquin was responsible for operations in Munster, whilst Lord Ranelagh presided in the remoter province of Connaught. In the nine regiments eventually sent from England to Ireland, 55 percent of the officers had served in the Bishops'

---

4   *Calendar of State Papers, Venice*, 1640–1642, ed. A.B. Hinds (London: HMSO, 1923–24), p.285.

Wars; others, particularly if suspected of involvement with the Army Plots, were rejected by Parliament.

On 10 November Parliament in Westminster ordered that 'one regiment shall be with all possible speed transported into Ireland under command of some worthy person.' The choice was Sir Simon Harcourt, a competent professional soldier, who by mid December had raised 1,100 men in Cheshire and transported them over from Chester along with 400 extra volunteers. However Harcourt only had sufficient weapons for his own regiment. His career was brief, for on 27 March he was mortally wounded at the siege of Carrickmines. He was replaced by his lieutenant-colonel, Richard Gibson, another professional soldier who would make a name for himself in the Irish campaigns.

On 24 January another 12 companies of foot, forming the Lord Lieutenant's Regiment, under the command of Lieutenant-Colonel George Monck, reached Chester. Along with them came four companies of firelocks, one of them under Captain Thomas Sandford, a colourful character from a minor Shropshire gentry family, who had been a quartermaster in the Second Bishops' War. He quickly made his presence felt in Chester, with complaints about the provision made for his firelocks.[5]

Lord Lisle was to raise a regiment of horse, 600 strong. The first contingent, 300 men under Major Richard Grenvile, consisting of four troops – his own, Lisle's, William Vaughan's and John Marrow's – reached Chester early in January, though lack of shipping meant that neither Monck's nor Grenvile's men reached Dublin until 20/21 February. The horses of Lisle's Regiment were shipped from Chester and Liverpool in numbers which ranged from 16 to 30 per ship.[6] The 400 firelocks arrived in Dublin between 27 February and 31 March. The second half of Lord Lisle's Regiment, and 300 dragoons, arrived in Dublin between 14 and 19 April.

The large numbers of troops who stayed in Chester, sometimes for relatively long periods, caused a good deal of dissatisfaction among the citizens, and the town councillors complained that 'divers persons calling themselves soldiers for the Irish service, do commit divers insolencies and robberies banding themselves by tens and twenties in a troop without conductor or officer.'[7]

In late January and early February Sir Michael Earnley and William Cromwell were appointed as colonels of foot regiments to be raised. A little later another provisional soldier, Sir Fulke Hunckes, was commissioned to raise a foot regiment, at least partly in Yorkshire. Earnley's men were recruited in Cheshire and North Wales.

The regiments of Lord Ranelagh and Sir Fulke Hunckes were destined for Connaught, whilst Earnley and Cromwell reinforced the troops in Leinster and Dublin, arriving by early June.

Sir Charles Vavasour's Regiment was intended for Munster. The original intention was to raise half its strength in the West Country and half in Munster,

---

5   HMC. Portland MS, I., p. 84.
6   Ian Ryder, *An English Army For Ireland* (Partizan Press: Leigh-on-Sea, 1987), p. 7.
7   Quoted in R.H. Morris and P.H. Lawson, *The Siege of Chester* (Chester: G.R. Griffith, 1923), p. 1.

but then it was proposed that the whole regiment be raised in England, half in Devon and Cornwall. Recruits came in slowly, and it was the end of February before Vavasour sailed from Bristol and Minehead with 1,500 men, including 500 intended to reinforce troops under Sir William St Leger.

The Earl of Cork was raising troops in Munster including four companies of foot and two troops of horse under his sons Lord Kinalmeaky and Lord Broghill. A consignment of 500 arms for St Leger's men reached Ireland at the end of December 1641, and eventually it was decided that his entire Regiment should be raised in Munster, incorporating the independent companies already raised there, with Sir Hardress Waller as its lieutenant-colonel.

In January Parliament agreed on another two regiments to be raised in England for service in Munster under Sir John Paulet and Sir William Ogle. They arrived in Munster by the end of May 1642.

Vavasour's men may have arrived unarmed, as Lord Inchiquin complained that he had had to issue 1,000 foot arms out of the 4,000 sent him theoretically for the troops raised in Munster.

Almost from the beginning the attrition among the troops sent from England was alarming. By August 1642 out of a theoretical total of 3,000 men comprising Paulet's and Ogle's regiments, there were only '1,200 able and serviceable men through fluxes, smallpox, fevers and with long marches and lying upon cold ground'.[8]

Despite arriving in such a piecemeal and dispersed fashion, the troops from England sufficed to allow the Irish authorities to survive perhaps the most acute phase of the Rebellion. Though the Irish Confederates, as they would be known after the formation of the Confederacy in May 1642, in theory had four regional armies each of 6,000 men, and a 'flying army' of 2,000 foot and 200 horse, none of these forces were up to strength. The Confederates somewhat outdated tactics also proved ineffective, and they favoured a war of raids and sieges to large formal battles, which were relatively rare occurrences. Neither did either side have any clear strategy.

During the winter of 1641–42 Ormonde organised a series of raids into areas of Leinster. Both sides quickly adopted scorched earth tactics, and commanders such as Richard Gibson and Richard Grenvile had no hesitation in burning villages and farms and killing any regarded as rebels or rebel sympathisers. Men were hanged, women and sometimes children drowned. Crops were burned, often along with those 'native Irish' hiding in them. If such measures were regularly adopted in Leinster, where Ormonde was regarded as relatively moderate, reprisals elsewhere were even more severe. Inchiquin earned the nickname given him by the Irish: 'Murragh of the Burnings'.

Increasingly starved of supplies as the political crisis in England mounted, the troops suffered considerable neglect.

---

8   *Calendar of the Manuscripts of the Marquis of Ormonde, [formerly] preserved at the castle, Kilkenny. New Series.* Royal Commission on Historical Manuscripts, 36 (1902-20), 1896, p.126.

Early in the summer of 1642 William Jephson wrote to the Speaker of the Westminster Parliament of '… soldiers now languishing in rags. Languishing for want of natural food, whom I lately saw behave so gallantly in the field, till all the officers wished them in scarlet.'[9]

In February 1642 the London Merchant Adventurers Company made an offer to Parliament to raise an expeditionary force paid for out of funds raised against the two and a half million acres of land due to be confiscated from alleged rebels in Ireland. They insisted that the first five 'adventurer' regiments to be raised should be sent to Munster, though the first contingent of 1,000 men despatched operated independently from Inchiquin around Kinsale and Galway. A second force of 2,000 men were present in September 1642 under Lord Kerry, from Bristol and Minehead, without arms. Inchiquin commented of them that instead of 'assistance to withstand our enemies, those of my Lord of Kerry's regiment come to starve us.'[10]

Lord Ranelagh and Sir Michael Earnley's Regiments were sent to Connaught, where they struggled to maintain control even with the assistance of the locally raised forces of Sir Francis Willoughby and his son Anthony.

In August 1642, theoretical strengths of government forces, apart from those in Ulster, were: Leinster 11,800 foot, 1,500 horse; Connaught 3,000 foot, 300 horse; Munster 4,600 foot, 600 horse.[11]

Logistics

It was intended that the English regiments should be armed on a 2:1 musket/pike ratio. Each musketeer was to be issued with a bandolier and rest, though apparently not a sword.[12]

Pikemen received a sword, although helmets and corselets were evidently not issued. Regimental colours seem to been the responsibility of individual colonels.

The pay rate of the ordinary soldier is not clearly given, but can be determined as being 8d a day. This, of course, was not what they actually received, the usual deductions being made for food and clothing; even the generally better-furnished soldiers of the Dublin garrison received only 1/- after deductions. The Lords Justices admitted that the common soldier as a result 'doth extremely suffer'. Soldiers frequently sold part of their rations, and clothing, for a few extra pence. These shortages increased the widespread looting which was a common feature of operations in the field, although the increasingly ravaged nature of the countryside meant that needs were never satisfied by it. The Lords Justice complained that even the officers had been forced gradually to 'sell their clothes and all they have to keep them alive'.[13]

---

9   HMC 10th Report, I, p. 88.
10   Thomas Carte, *A History of the Life of James Duke of Ormonde*, 6 vols (Oxford: Oxford University Press, 1851), vol. III, p. 112.
11   Ryder, p. 14.
12   *Ibid.*, pp. 19, 21.
13   J. Hogan, *Letters and Papers Relating to the Irish Rebellion between 1642–1646* (Dublin: The Stationery Office, 1935), p. 108.

Basic rations consisted of the usual staples of salt beef, herrings, cheese, butter and biscuit. Occasional provision of mutton was greatly welcomed by the men. In theory each man was to be provided daily with a pound of bread, a pound of beef, or in lieu half a pound of cheese or fish and a quarter pound of butter. Peas, beans, oats, wheat and rye were also issued frequently. Cheese was viewed as being particularly essential, for without it, the Lords Justice said, 'the soldier cannot well march abroad'.[14]

Equally vital was biscuit or bread. Biscuit, because of its easier transport and longer preservation, was particularly important, and occasionally provided the only rations available. If cheese was not available then 'one pound more of biscuit is needful for each man per day, preferably supplemented by salt'.[15]

It is not surprising that lack of adequate rations was a major factor in deaths and sickness amongst the troops. The Earl of Cork would remark later that the type of rations issued made for a 'rich churchyard and weak garrison'.[16]

The quality of clothing issued to the troops caused constant complaints. In theory it was to be supplied from England, and the Lords Justices were soon complaining that 'Many of [the soldiers] especially the English, fall sick daily through cold for want of clothes and shoes'. Even when it arrived, the clothing was usually of very poor quality. Six thousand suits and caps (probably Monmouth caps) arrived in September 1642, but the Lords Justices commented that:

> The cloth is very bad, the suits ill and slightly made up, the cassocks not lined, the lining of the breeches very bad cloth, the caps so little as they cannot be useful for the soldiers and such of them as were brought to this board are so little as they can hardly cover the head of a child.[17]

Other coats were too short and without lining. In an attempt to improve the quality of the clothes issued, Ormonde obtained supplies of cloth and had it made up by the female Protestant refugees in Dublin, though it is unclear if the situation improved.

In September 1642 the Lords Justice fixed 10d as the weekly deduction from a soldier's pay for his clothing. In theory a soldier was to be provided with 'a good suit of clothes', normally coat or cassock and breeches. He was also to have two shirts, three pairs of stockings, three pairs of shoes and a hat, more usually described as a 'cap'.

Shoes were generally the items in shortest supply, and the subject of numerous complaints: 'Their want of shoes exceeds clothes, and is general, without which they are neither able to march nor do any service at all.'[18]

---

14 *Ibid.*, p. 135.
15 *Ibid.*, p. 119.
16 *Ibid.*, p. 135.
17 *Ibid.*, p. 72.
18 *Ibid.*, p. 84.

The Nature of the War

Both sides displayed considerable brutality in what was basically a guerrilla war interspersed with sieges and a small number of larger engagements. As mentioned earlier, neither had a clear strategy, nor sufficient strength to force a decision. Both sides attempted to deny their opponents any support from the countryside, killing and carrying off livestock and burning crops and villages, regardless of the fate of non-combatants caught up in the destruction. Some English garrisons were particularly notorious for their actions. One such was Trim, where Richard Grenvile and Colonel Richard Gibson were noted for the brutality with which they enforced 'Trim Law' on the surrounding countryside.

Often the government soldiers suffered more hardship on campaign than their opponents did. In 1642 Lord Ranelagh and Sir Michael Earnley's Regiments in Connaught took part in one such operation:

The next day I [Earnley] received order from his lordship [Ranelagh] to meet him at Kanesdown Castle five miles distant from Athlone … His Lordship directed I should stay near the castle at any place most for advantage, and that his Lordship would bring the artillery with him.

I came according unto the orders, and found the castle quitted; but his Lordship brought not the artillery, without which (if that castle had not been deserted,) it could not have been taken. From thence we marched unto Portleeke and Killenure, both which places were upon our march towards them quitted, where we were quartered some three weeks, during which time we had not above five pounds of bread for each man and no salt, which occasioned the sickness of many of our men, and made them unserviceable; and we were not drawn forth upon any service. Two companies, Captain Tyringham of my Lord/s regiment, and Captain Bertie [Francis Bertie, son of the Earl of Lindsey] of my regiment were quartered at the Nunnery, a place too far distant from the rest of the men; near the enemy and contrary unto my advice, who much disliked it, as full of danger; but the Lord President assured me, with many protestations, that they were free from all danger and safe as in Whitehall or in the castle of Athlone, for that we were in a friend's country and had orders to touch nothing; yet the enemy fell hotly upon the those two companies, being remote from the army, and cut off Captain Bertie and all his officers, with the greatest part of his company, and Captain Tyringham lost his lieutenant and many of his men. Then we came to Athlone, whence we were drawn forth every day to look about us without doing anything, and his Lordship being importuned by Sir Charles Coote, myself, and the field officers, to attempt some considerable service, his Lordship replied that the men sent unto him were rogues and gaolbirds in England, and such as he durst in no ways trust to fight, and wished that he had a commission to raise men of his own country; and that he desired no men of our nation, but his own countrymen. And now our men began through want of bread to weaken and famish, so that half of them were unserviceable, notwithstanding that there was corn enough in the country, and his Lordship suffered the corn in the deserted places to be embezzled, contrary unto my advice and the advice of others; there being then even in one house, the widow Dillon's as much corn as would serve two thousand men for two months …

His Lordship being solicited by Sir Charles Coote, myself, and others, to attempt some service before the loss of all our men, his Lordship pretended he wanted bread. Sir Charles Coote gave him ten days' bread, and procured others bread for ten days more at his own charge, for the furtherance of the service. Then we were drawn down unto the Ballagh, a place of great strength, but of no consequence in regard as the place was of no annoyance, no considerable persons or goods in it; where we had hurt and killed between fifty and sixty of our men. And having with that loss forced, that place, we moved his Lordship that the hut men might be sent unto some place where order might be taken for their recovery, I said I supposed that hardly some of them would. His Lordship replied that it was then better to leave them there unto the power of the enemy …[19]

Such were the characteristics of much of the fighting in Ireland, with few pitched battles. They normally resulted in government victories, particularly in Leinster where Ormonde, though having no great military ability, was able to score some successes with the troops from England, especially the horse. But the Irish were resilient. The constant operations took a high toll, even when successful, such as the mission which cost the life of Sir Simon Harcourt:

Sir Simon Harcourt (who loved always to be in action) the 26th. of March, 1642. took a small Party of men, and went out towards the County of Wickloe, where he found the Rebels had possessed themselves of a Castle, called Carrickmain, within four miles of Dublin; and seeing him draw near to it with those small Forces, and finding him to have no Artillery, so as their Walls were of sufficient strength to bear them out against any attempts he could make, they began to brave him from within, and to use reproachful signs from the top of the Castle, thereby to express their contempt and scorn of him. This his spirit was not well able to brook; and considering the Castle was not invincible, and that it would be very great advantage to the City of Dublin to remove so ill a Neighbour; and that with two Pieces of Battery he could take it (in some few hours) he sent presently away to the Lords Justices to acquaint them with his Design, and to desire them to send unto him the two Great Guns for the effecting of it. They very well approv'd his Design, and gave present order for the carying them out, together with all necessaries and provisions fitting for the service. In the mean time, he took special care for the surrounding of the Castle, and disposing of his Men so, as they might prevent the Rebels issuing out: In which Service, Serjeant Major Berry (with 200 Fire-locks, viewing the Castle) was shot in his side, though he died not till eight days after of a Feaver. All things being put in order, whilst they attended the coming of the Great Pieces, (now on their way) Sir Simon Harcourt with some of the Commanders, laid themselves down under the side of a little thatch'd house, standing near the Castle, (which they took as a shelter to keep off the Enemies bullets) from whence he suddenly rose up to call to the Souldiers, to stand carefully to their Arms, and to their Duties, in their several Stations; Which one of the Rebels (from within) perceiving, discharged his Piece at him, and shot

---

19 Sir J.T. Gilbert, *History of the Irish Confederation and the War in Ireland 1641–1643* (Dublin: M.H. Gill, 1882), vol. I, pp. 134–5.

him into his right breast, under the neck bone; and being so wounded, he was carried off, expressing his submission to the good hand of God, and much joy'd to pour out his last blood in that Cause; The pain of his Wound was so great, as they could not bring him to Dublin, but carried him to Mirian, a house of the Lord Fitz-Williams where the next day he died, to the great grief of the English, and the prejudice of the Service. His Lieutenant-Colonel Gibson took the Command of that Party, and the great Guns being come, within the space of very few hours, made a breach sufficient for the Souldiers to enter, who, being mightily enraged with the loss of their most beloved Colonel, entred with great fury putting all to the Sword, sparing neither Man, Woman, or Child.[20]

Ormonde's Leinster forces won a significant victory in an action at Kilrush on 15 April:

The Rebels having gathered their Forces from Wickloe, Wexford, Caterlagh, Kildare, Queen's County, Kilkenny, Tipperary, and West-Meath, on Easter Sunday, the 10th. of April, they displayed 40 Colours, within two miles of Athy, near the Barrow, (of which Colonel Crafford gave speedy intelligence) under the Command of the Lord Viscount Mountgarret, the Lieutenant General's great Unkle, making of the old English and Irish near 10000 men, Horse and Foot; which the Lieutenant General perceiving, on the other side of the River of the Barrow, to have sent out some Horse near Tankardstown, over against Grangemellain; His Lordship return'd to Athy, giving out he would fight them the next day; but their numbers vastly exceeding his, and he, having done the service he went out for, thought it as honourable to retire to Dublin, in the face of them, with Sir John Bowen, Fitz-Girrald of Timoga, Richard Grace of Marryburrough, and Captain Crosby, Prisoners. But when they came to Black-hale-heath, between Kilrush and Rathmore, about 20 miles from Dublin, the Army of the Rebels drew up in a place of advantage, to hinder the passage of the English Army, having two great Ditches on each Wing, so high that we could see no more then the heads of their Pikes, and with such a hill before, (betwixt them and us) that we could scarce see their Colours, the wind also on their backs, and a great Bog a mile behind them. However the Lieutenant General called a Councel under a thorn hedge, (being loath to venture so gallant an Army on such disadvantages) but the English Commanders were all of opinion, they should be fought with, numbers making no difference, where the Cause was so good: in as much as Sir Charles Coote told them in few words, that he discern'd fear in the Rebels faces, as well as Guilt in their Persons, and that he thought they would hardly stay, till his Lordship had put his men in order for the battle, and therefore desired they might have presently Command to fall on, which indeed he was ever ready to obey before the Word was given, neither the matter nor the time now admitting of debate. Whereupon, Friday the 15th. of April, about 7 in the morning, the English Army marching, as if they would force their way to Dublin, leaving in and about Athy, Captain Erasmus Burrows, Captain Grimes, Captain Thomas Welden, and the two Captain Piggots, with their

---

20 *Ibid.*, pp. 182–3.

Companies, 300 whereof was part of our Army, which made ever now and then (as the Enemy halted) an halt, and resolving to fight the Enemy, drew up in that sort as did best agree with the Ground; Sir Charles Coote (who commanded in chief under his Lordship) had the ordering of the Foot; Sir Thomas Lucas of the right Wing of Horse, and Sir Richard Greenvile of the left; The Lieutenant-General having many Gentlemen with him, (who voluntarily followed him in that expedition) put them all in a Troop, under the Command of Major Ogle, a Reformade, (a worthy Person) and himself in the midst of the first rank of them, and so attended the Encounter; the Ordnance first began to play, but without much effect; The Rebels Army led by Mountgarret, Purcel Baron of Loghmo, Hugh-mac Phelim Birn, Lieutenant of the Leinster Forces, Colonel Toole, Sir Morgan Cavenagh, Colonel Morris Cavenagh, Arthur Cavanaugh, Colonel Bagnall, the Lord Dunboyne, Colonel Roger Moore, was drawn up (as I have said) in a place of great advantage, upon the top of a hill, where there were but too narrow passages to come at them; yet our forlorn Hope (commanded by Captain Rochford) consisting of 150 Musketiers, making up the hill fiercely, discharged upon the Rebels, and was seconded by Captain Sandford, with his Fire-locks, Sir Charles Coote leading up the rest of the Foot with great celerity; Colonel Crafford in the Van, and Serjeant Major Pigot, excellently well discharging their Commands. But before these could come near them, our Horse both under Sir Thomas Lucas, and Sir Richard Greenvile, (one charging at one of the passages, the other at the other) fell in upon them, who would not stand the first shock, but fled presently, taking their flight to a great Bog not far from them, (a Sanctuary which the Irish in all their flights, chuse commonly to provide for themselves, and seldom fail to make use of it) and so the English gain'd this Victory without any considerable loss, or much hazard; whilst a body of 2000 Rebels, led by the Lord Viscount Mountgarret, and General Hugh Birn, wheeling about, thought to possess themselves of our Ordnance, Carriage, and Ammunition, which my Lord of Ormond perceiving, drew out one of his Divisions to attend that great Body, and with them and some Voluntier Horse, to the number of 30. which were then with his Lordship, (the rest following the execution) he faced that Body, and within a short time put them to rout: there were not above 600. some write 300, of the Irish slain, amongst which, there was the Lord of Dunboyn's Brothers, the Lord of Ikernis Sons, and Colonel Cavenagh's Heads, brought by the Souldiers to the Lieutenant General. The Enemy lost twenty Colours, many Drums, all their Powder and Ammunition, the Lord Mountgarrets Wain, drawn by 8 Oxen, where all his Provision was, his Sumpture, and the Lord of Ikernis Sumpture. Colonel Monk, who (by the quick flight of the Irish) was prevented from doing that service in the field he intended, followed with a Party of his Regiment, to the Bog which the Rebels had taken, which looked even black, (for their Apparel was generally black) being all cover'd over with them, and there began to fall upon them, as resolving upon a severe execution; But he was commanded to retire, having got Honour enough that day, and so the Army marched off the field confusedly, whereas that Victory (how just soever) is ill gloried in, which is the loss of Subjects. The Van of our Army lay that night at old Connel, the rest on the Corrough of Kildare, all in open field; arriving at Dublin the 17th. of April, where they were receiv'd by the Lords Justices and Council, with all imaginable demonstrations of Joy and Honour.'[21]

Not all expeditions were as successful:

About the beginning of June, 1642. came over some Regiments, under the Conduct of Sir Foulk Hunks, and Lieutenant-colonel Kirk, who brought over the Regiment design'd for the Lord Rannelagh; whereupon two Regiments were immediately dispatch'd for Connaght, and accompanied thither by the Lord Lieutenant, who in that Expedition, took by storm, Knocklinch, a strong Castle of Mr. Linches, the besieged, except Women, (not accepting of Quarter) were put to the sword; and Trimbleston, a Castle of the Lord Trimbleston's, quitted on the former's success, as Kymkelf, a fair Castle of the Lord Nettervile's, and divers other Castles: And upon his approach towards Athlone, Sir James Dillon (who had besieged it ever since Christmas) ran away; so that the Lord President, with about 50 Horse, and some 200 Foot, met the Lieutenant General 5 miles from Athlone; and after an hour or two's stay in the Field, the Earl of Ormond took leave of the Lord President, leaving at his departure a Regiment for the President himself, and another under Sir Michael Earnly, Sir Abraham Shipman, and Sir Bernard Ashley, and two Troops of Horse, with which Forces the Lord President might have subdued all Connaught, except Galloway. But he, instead of imploying such brave Men abroad, while the Summer lasted, kept them at home on short and rotten Commons, whereby most of them were famish'd, or contracted mortal Diseases, and were presently so enfeebled, that the tenth Man was hardly able to march. In the mean time, all almost that had fought against him of his Neighbours, were receiv'd under Contribution, which was never paid, nor Victuals brought in for his Men, though the Countrey yet abounded in Corn and Cattle; so that the Garrison of Castle-Coot, for meer pity, baked Bread, and sent them many Cart-fulls thereof, bringing away in their empty Carts many of their sick Men, that they might not perish. And yet at last the General (the Lord President) was perswaded to draw out his Men to service, besieging Ballagh Castle, in the mid-way between Roscommon and Athlone, wherein he made a breach, and commanded a Party to storm it. The Rebels killed many of our Men that day by shot, besides what perish'd by Stones, and other Materials thrown from the top of the Castle; the Night afterwards the Rebels stole to a Bog, not far distant, through the negligence of our Guards, and left us the Castle. The next Exploit of my Lord President, was (with the remnant of the two English Regiments, and what could be spared out of our Garrisons thereabouts) a March towards Balintober, to which he was provoked by the Enemy, and stimulated on by his own Party, impatient of further delays. O Conner Dun of Balintober, ever since his Son was taken, till now, (that is the middle of July, 1642.) had acted nothing, though the tacit Votes of the Province did seem to own him as their King, Prince, or what Name of Supremacy in that Province could be greatest; who seeing that those Forces which were sent from England, to the Lord President, to subdue that Province, (which at first much frighted the Rebels) had done nothing of moment, through a supine negligence,

---

21 *Ibid.*, pp. 74–5.

if not worse, and were much less considerable than those Forces which we had before, he began to awake out of his Ale and Aqua-vitae, and to call in Subjects to help him, out of all the Parts of Connaght; but above all that came to joyn with him, none were more forward, or came in greater numbers, than the County of Maio-Men, and the rather, because in all the Conflicts of Connaght with the English, few of that great County came to fight with us. They drew together 1800 or 2000 Foot, and 160 Horse, and more had joyn'd with them, if we had defer'd to visit them. It was therefore adjudged necessary by the Lord President, Sir Charles Coot, Sir Mich. Earnly, Sir Abraham Shipman, Sir Edw. Povey, Sir Bernard Ashley, and others of the Council of War, That we should draw out all the Men, sick or sound, that were able to march, and march to Balintober. It was a wonder to see with what alacrity and courage, our new-come English put themselves on this service, even they that were ready to die, (as divers of them did on the way) rejoycing that they might expire, doing their Countrey the best service they could, as Souldiers, and not as Dogs on a Dunghil. Our March that day was from Roscommon, through Molinterim, and over the Hill of Oran, near Clalby, which is little more than 2 miles from Balintober; from thence we might see the Enemy coming with all speed to meet us. The Lord President was of opinion that our Forces should retreat, and commanded it; but the rest were otherwise resolv'd, and without his Orders drew on towards the Rebels, whilst he washed his hands from what evil might accrew. Our Commanders as they march'd, agreed how to order their Men, and on what piece of Ground; but the Enemy came on so fast, that they could not gain the Ground desired, which made the Work on our part more difficult, for all the way on that Hill, till we come near Balintober, is boggy, with great long Heath in all places, very unfit for Horse-service. However, when the Rebels came near us, Captain Rob. King with his Troop (well mounted, and well arm'd with Back and Brest, and as well disciplin'd as any in Ireland) was commanded to pass by their Front to their left Flank, as Sir Charles Coot, and Sir Edw. Povey, with the rest of their Troops, being before, nearer to the top of that ridge of Ground, were almost past, that they might make way for our forlorn Hope of Musketiers, to play in the Front of their great Body of Pikes coming on. Captain Rob. King (an old Souldier) in executing of this, saw (by the badness of the Ground he march'd on, and by the Rebels haste to come up) that he should not, without disorder, get by the left Point of this Battalia, gave order to his Men to fire in flank all at once, when they should be close up with the Point of the Battalia, over one another's Horses Manes, which was a thing seldom heard of or practised, yet was no new thing either to him or his, for he had taught them this, amongst other Points of War he had long nurtur'd them in, which they exactly perform'd, when he was come within two Pikes lengths of the Enemy, with their Carbines. At which time our forlorn Hope of Foot being come up, fired with excellent success on that part of the Front that lay to the right hand; so that by this unexpected way of firing by the Horse, (timely assisted by the Foot) the Enemy was soon put into disorder, with the loss of many Men; which breach Captain King soon apprehending, and finding the Pikes of the fall'n Men to have intangled and galled others, he rush'd in with his Horse, and breaking the left corner of the Battalia, so amazed the Rebels, as they fell into disorder, who (quitting their Pikes all at once) made a great noise, and began to run; but before their running, (that was almost as soon as Captain King was got into their Front) Sir Charles Coot and

Sir Edward Povey charg'd them in the Flank with their Troops, with which they had kept the upper Ground, on purpose to encounter with the 160 Horse of the Rebels; and to them was Captain Robert King drawing to second them, or to fall into the Flank of this Battalia, (which he had new broken) but the Rebels Horse fled before they were able to come near, and therefore they had leisure to fall into the Flank of the Foot. This Battalia of Pikes was supposed to be 1200. They had 1000 Musketeers, which either by bad way, or staying longer than the other, for to receive Ammunition, were not come up to begin the Battel, but were within Musket-shot, who also ran for company. Our men pursued, and killed most of them, but were commanded not to come too near Balintober, where the Credulous were to believe, some had seen beyond the Castle another great Body of Men; so as not pursuing this Victory, we lost the benefit of it. In this Battel there was a young Gentleman on the Irish side, who very gallantly behav'd himself, after that his Party was fled, getting to the corner of a Ditch, where with his Pike he withstood the encounter of five Horse that had spent their shot, till a gantick Soldier of the English getting within him, slew him. And amongst the dead, one pulling a Mountero from the head of one, there fell down long Tresses of flaxen hair, who being further search'd, was found a Woman. After this, the President consider'd what was to be attempted; and it was resolv'd to go into the County of Galloway. But as in all other Designs, many Objections were alledg'd, and the Lord President with a few, accompani'd with the Marquis of Clanrickard, went to Galloway, before which the Lord Forbes (Lieutenant General under the Lord Brook) was come (the 9th. of August, 1642.) to besiege the Town with a Fleet; and having taken possession of the Abbey near adjoyning, landed many of his Battering Guns. But before he attempted any thing (according to his Commission) he first advised with the present Governour, (the Lord of Clanrickard) affectionate to his Majesties Service. As the Town seem'd to be placing his Majesties Colours on the top of their Tower, charging Captain Willoughby (Governour of the Fort) with the breach of Pacification, (an Agreement, it seems, assented to by the State) though in vindication of himself, he and Captain Ashley alledg'd much: Great straits he had been put to, though at length happily reliev'd by the Earl of Clanrickard, when he was closely Beleaguer'd, together with the Archbishop of Tuam (Richard Boyle) and his Family, besides 36 Ministers, 26 of which serv'd as Soldiers, and did their Duty. After all, the Lord Forbes being by the Town, the Earl of Clanrickard, and the President of Connaght (with whom he had had several ineffectual Conferences) daily delay'd in what he endeavour'd to give Captain Willoughby satisfaction in, prepar'd to make his approach to the Town; but not being strengthen'd by any supply he could get from the Lord President, or Sir Charles Coot, and disharten'd by Captain Willoughby, in that every House in the Town was a Fort, he drew off, being perswaded to a Composition to be paid in Money within two months, which he never got. And at the Lord Presidents return to Athlone, the Soldiers Mutini'd, both Officers and Soldiers offering to go to Dublin; but the Common Soldiers being very weak, not able to draw into a considerable Body, (the Irish Kerns killing all sick and fainty persons, that could not accompany the Body of the Army) that intent for the present was deferr'd.[22]

---

22 *Ibid.*, pp. 203–5.

Richard Grenvile was also earning a reputation:

> About the 20th. of January, 1642. Sir Richard Greenvile, with a Party of 200
> Horse and 1000 Foot, with 600 Suits of Cloaths, and Money, reliev'd Athlone.
> In his return, he was encounter'd at Raconnel by 5000 Rebels, which he routed,
> took their General Preston's Son Prisoner, killed many, gained 11 Colours, and
> surprized many Prisoners; for which service, Captain William Vaughan was by
> the Lords Justices (to whom he brought the News) Knighted. The Irish thought
> much of this Victory; for that there was an old Prophesie, That who got the Battle
> of Raconnel, should conquer all Ireland. The Army return'd to Dublin the 10th. of
> February, with the remnant of Sir Michael Earnley's Regiment.[23]

In the spring of 1642, Ormonde won another success at New Ross:

> March the 2d. 1642. the English Army march'd forth from Dublin toward
> Kilkenny, consisting of about 2500 Foot and 500 Horse, together with two Pieces
> of Battery, and four small brass Pieces, the Marquess of Ormond being Lieutenant
> General of the Army, and my Lord Lisle General of the Horse.
>
> The 3d. the Army being come nigh Castlemartin, the Rebels then possessing
> it, gave it up to the Lieutenant General, upon his promise of fair Quarter, which
> they accordingly had, to march away thence with the safety of their Lives, they
> being in number above 400 Men and Women; and the same day 3 Divisions of
> Foot were sent to Kildare, and a Castle called Tully, which the Rebels then quitted,
> and left unto us.
>
> The 4th. the Army came to Tymolin, where finding two Castles possest by
> some Rebels, our Cannon compell'd them to submit to mercy, very few of them
> escaping with their Lives, there being about 100 of them slain; and also of the
> English Army was slain Lieutenant Oliver, and about 12 Souldiers.
>
> The 11th. my Lord Lisle march'd from the Army at Temple-soul before day
> towards Ross, having with him Sir Richard Greenvile, Sir Thomas Lucas, and
> about 400 Horse, and also Sir Foulk Huncks, with about 600 Foot. Being come
> within two miles of Ross, our Horse took 4 Horsemen of the Rebels, Prisoners,
> who inform'd us, that the Army of the Rebels lay then about 3 miles distant
> thence, being near 4000 Men. Shortly after my Lord Lisle came before the Town
> of Ross, and by a Trumpeter he sent to the Town, to have some one of Quality
> therein to come to treat with him, concerning the surrender of the same to the
> King's use, which they refused to do. Then Sir Thomas Lucas, fearing the safety
> of the Army, (by reason he understood that the Rebel's Army lay the last night
> within 2 miles of the English Army) importuned my Lord Lisle to march back
> with all his Horse, to secure the Army, leaving Sir Foulk Hunks with his Division
> of Foot, to guard a Pass in that way. And then after a few miles riding further,
> the English Army appear'd at hand, which march'd on towards Ross, nigh before
> which that night a great part of our Horse and Foot lodged. And the next morning
> our Cannon were drawn and planted against the Town, and continued battering
> with two Pieces, on a part of the Town-Walls, about two days together, which

---

23 *Ibid.*, p. 198.

made a fair breach therein, which Sir Foulk Huncks undertook to assault with his Men, and attempted it, but were beaten back with some loss, which so much disheartned the Souldiers, that they would not be drawn on again; and finding that the besieged had both daily and nightly very many Men, and much Ammunition, and other Recruits, conveyed by Boats into the Town, and understanding that the Rebel's Army was grown very strong within few miles of ours, and our Lieutenant General finding Bread to be grown scarce in our Army, resolv'd to leave Ross as it was, and gain Honour by a Battle with the Irish.

The 18th. our Army being march'd away, about 2 miles distant from Ross, the Irish Army appear'd fairly in view, who hastned their Forces into Battalia, on a Ground of some advantage, nigh the way our Army was to pass. Whereupon our Commanders endeavour'd with all diligence to draw their Forces into Battalia, to confront the Rebels within the distance of Cannon-shot, our Cannon being plac'd at the Front of our Infantry, which was winged by our Horse-Troops, and advanc'd forwards before our Army, within Musket-shot of the Enemy's fore-Troops; Sir Richard Greenvile (having that day the Vauntguard of the Horse) had his Division for the right Wing of the Army; likewise my Lord Lisle's Division (having the Battle) had the left Wing of the Army; Sir Thomas Lucas's Division (having the Rearguard of the Horse) had the one half of his Division, appointed to stand for Reserves for both the Wings of Horse. Both Armies being order'd against one another, Sir Richard Greenvile sent forth towards the Rebels a forelorn Hope of 60 Horse, commanded by Lieutenant White, which advancing towards 2 Troops of the Rebels, they seem'd to shrink from. Then (our Cannon beginning to play) Captain Atkins, commanding a forelorn Hope of about 100 Musketiers, march'd forwards directly before our Foot-Army towards the Rebels, who had mann'd a Ditch in a High-way, lying right before their Army, with a great number of Musketiers; during which time, certain other Divisions of the English Foot followed orderly their forelorn Hope, Captain Atkins with his shot excellently performing his part, by exchanging shot with the Rebels that lay in ambush. Sir Richard Greenvile, with his Division on the right Wing, advanced to begin the Battle; in the interim whereof, Sir Thomas Lucas (being Major General of the Horse) came and took upon him the chief Command thereof; and so leading those Troops on towards the Enemy, being come past a deep High-way, that lay between both Armies, presently (at hand) advanc'd towards those Horse, a Division of Horse and Foot of the Rebels. Sir Richard Greenvile being then in the head of his own Troop, (which had the right hand of that Division) commanded his Men to keep together and charge home without wheeling; which was no sooner spoken, but immediately Sir Thomas Lucas call'd aloud to our Troop, to wheel to the left hand, which they presently performing, were gotten into a Lane in some disorder, and before they could get out of the same, and come into any good order again, a Troop of above 100 of the Rebel's Horse, all Gentlemen of Quality, and Commanders, led by Cullen, their Lieutenant General, charg'd our Horse on the left Flank. Whereupon Sir Richard Greenvile encouraged several of his Troops, by his example, to charge the Enemy, where meeting with Colonel Cullen in the head of his Troops, divers blows pass'd betwixt them; mean while my Lord Lisle with his Troops, gallantly charg'd Cullen's Troop, on his Flank and Rear, whereby they were so routed, that the Troops were all intermixed one with another, and the execution of both Parties continued violent, until about

20 of the Rebel's Horse escaped away together, leaving the rest of their Company to be killed and taken Prisoners, (as they were;) during which time, the Foot and Cannon performing well their parts, drove the Enemy to shift away to save themselves, which Captain Hermon seeing, pursued their Rear with some Horse, with which he did notable good execution; and, to say the truth, it is probable that most of the Rebels had that day been cut off, had not the un-passable deep High-way betwixt both Armies, hindred our left Wing of Horse from giving on upon their side, and also the disorder that happened to the right Wing of the Horse, by their unhappy wheeling to the left hand. But so soon as the Officers of those Troops could reduce their Men again into order, my Lord Lisle and Sir Richard Greenvile presently pursued the Enemy with 2 Troops, and sent Sir William Vaughan with 2 Troops more to pursue others, flying away to the right hand. And having followed the chase of them about 2 or 3 miles distant from the Army, (the Rebels having made their escape over Bogs, and un-passable Grounds for Horse) our Horse were fain to leave them, and return to the rest of the Army, where the Cannon stood. In which service were 300 of the Rebels slain, amongst which were a great number of their best Gentry and Commanders: There were of the Rebels taken Prisoners, Colonel Cullen their Lieutenant General, Major Butler, besides divers other Captains, and some of their Ensigns; of the English Forces were slain not full 20 Men: in which service, Sir Thomas Lucas unhappily received a very sore wound in his head. That night, the English Army lodged at Ballybeggan. After which time, the Army march'd without molestation of any Enemy, until they return'd to Dublin, whether the Rear of the Army came safe on Munday the 27th. of the same month, 1643.

Where they were again Quarter'd, even to the undoing and great desolation of that poor City, which had now suffered so much, and so long, under the burden and insolencies of unpaid, wanting Soldiers, as they were unable to bear it longer, and with loud cries and complaints made known their Grievances to the Lords Justices and Council, wholely unable to relieve them. And indeed, such was the posture of the present affairs at that time, as every thing tended to bring on a Cessation; yet for the present, the Lieutenant General (that the Soldiers might be quieted) publish'd a strict Edict, Prohibiting all Soldiers to offer the least violence to any who brought Provision to the Market, or any Inhabitants of the Town, under the severest Penalties of the Marshals Court; which, for a time, begat an obedience. But the Army being ill Cloath'd, meanly Victuall'd, worse Paid, and seldom employ'd in service, necessity enforc'd them to those outrages Humanity could not take notice of, many of them being the effects of a very pinching want; though the Lords Justices and Council (to the great dislike of the Army) pursued some of the Offenders with exemplary Justice: A sense of which, with the Meagre return which Serjeant Major Warren brought out of England, on his sollicitation for the Soldiers Pay, and the dissatisfaction that thence arose; some of the Officers, not all, (there was a Party that presum'd they might have gone through with the work, had there not been another in the Loom) afterwards presented the State, the 4th. of April, 1643. with a Paper, in such a stile, threatening so much danger, as the Lords Justices and Council remitted the Copy of it to the Parliament of England.[24]

24 *Ibid.*, pp. 224–28.

The King had been pressing Ormonde to seek a truce with the Confederates since the previous autumn, and urgency was heightened by a number of military reverses.

By the summer of 1643, the military situation as effectively one of stalemate. The troops from England had denied the Confederates total victory, but they were inadequate to defeat them. Ormonde and his Council were aware that with few supplies now reaching them from England, their position was bound to deteriorate. For both sides a cessation of hostilities offered advantages. Ormonde did, however, face opposition from pro-Parliamentarian members of the Privy Council, though he effectively silenced them by offering to continue the war if they could find supplies for the troops – a clearly impossible task.

Negotiations were made easier after the formation by the Confederates of their General Assembly at Kilkenny, providing a cohesive body with which Ormonde could make terms.

The King had few qualms about what terms Ormonde would make, provided that a truce to release the army was reached quickly. On 23 April he authorised Ormonde to treat for a cessation of one year, and then to 'bring over the Irish Army to Chester' as quickly as possible.[25]

The Cessation was duly agreed on 15 September. It remained to be seen what impact the hardened troops from Ireland would have on the war in England.

---

25 *Ibid.*, p. 266.

2

An Army From Ireland

With the Cessation concluded, Ormonde now had to deal with the practical problems of transporting as many as possible of his troops to the mainland. On 7 September, a week before the Cessation was actually agreed, the King sent his instructions to Ormonde and the Lords Justices:

> That you agree upon what number of our army will be necessary to be kept in garrisons there, for the maintenance of the same, during the time of the cessation, and what soldiers they shall be, and what persons shall command the same; and that you settle them accordingly in that manner as shall appear to your discretions to be most conducing to our service.
>
> That you do consider and advise of the best means of transporting the rest of our army in that our province of Leinster (excepting such as are to be kept in garrisons) into our kingdoms of England: and to that end we hereby give you, or any one of you, full power and authority to seize upon all ships, barks, or vessels whatsoever, and to treat with any persons whatsoever for the loan, hire or sale of any ships, barks or vessels, upon such conditions as you, or any one of you, shall agree upon with them.
>
> That in such time and manner as to you shall seem meet, you communicate unto the officers and soldiers of that our army this our intention, to make use of their known courage and fidelity to the defence of our person and crown, against the unnatural rebellion raised against us in this our kingdom, and against the like, laboured by the rebels here, to be raised against us in our kingdom of Scotland.
>
> That you signify unto them, that we are the more moved and necessitated unto this course, for as much as it is resolved, by some ill-affected persons in that our kingdom of Scotland, to call over the army of our Scottish subjects out of our kingdom of Ireland, to the end to make use of them for the invasion of us and of our good subjects of England. And forasmuch as this rebellion against us, under colour of the authority of our two houses of parliament, hath exhausted the means appointed by the concurrence of our royal authority for the sustenation of that our army there; and by force hath seized and taken from us all those our revenues, which might have enabled us to have supported them in that our kingdom; so that we ought in reason (beside the bond of their allegiance) to expect their ready concurrence against those persons, who are as well the causes of all the miseries they have endured, as of all the miseries we have suffered.

That you assure them, both officers and soldiers, that upon their landing here, they shall immediately receive our pay in the same proportion and manner with the rest of our army here. And you are to assure the soldiers, that all care shall be taken that clothes, shoes, and other necessaries be forthwith provided for them, after they are landed here; and that care shall be taken for the provision of all such as shall happen to be maimed here in our service; and for the payment of all the arrears that shall be due to any of them, that shall happen to be killed in the same, to wives, children or nearest friends.

And you are to assure both officers and soldiers, that we will take especial care to reward all such according to their merit and quality, that shall do us any eminent service in this our war against this odious and most unnatural rebellion.

We will and require, and do hereby authorise you, to use your utmost interest and industry for the speedy transportation of this forementioned part of our army; with their arms, horses, and such ammunition, and the like, as you shall think fit, into our kingdom of England, and particularly, if it may be, to the port of our city of Chester, or to the most commodious haven in North Wales …[1]

Ormonde's first task was to select the forces to be sent in response to the King's orders. These were to be a mix of existing regiments, those of Richard Gibson (700 men), Sir Fulke Hunckes (400 men), Sir Michael Earnley (his own and Lord Ranelagh's Regiments combined 400 men), Sir Robert Byron's (most probably a composite all- musketeer unit with detachments from a number of regiments, about 900 men), Henry Warren (the Lord Lieutenant's Regiment (about 800 men), Robert Broughton (about 800 men), and Henry Tillier (a composite unit of 800 men, possibly all musketeers). There were to be two companies of firelocks, each about 60 strong under Captains Thomas Sandford and Francis Langley, and three troops of horse, perhaps 150 troopers from Lord Lisle's Regiment, under the command of Sir William Vaughan.[2]

The intention had been that the whole contingent should be despatched at the same time, but it quickly became apparent that this would not be possible. The Royalists had been given what might well be a brief window of opportunity by a temporary reduction of the normally powerful Parliamentarian naval presence in the Irish Sea. The naval vessels known as the Irish Guard, under the command of Richard Swanley, were for the moment preoccupied by a Royalist threat to Milford Haven. This left only a force known as the 'Liverpool ships' to contest the northern part of the Irish Sea. There were apparently six of these, mostly armed, merchantmen, with perhaps one sixth-rate warship with six guns.[3]

For the moment the most powerful warship in the northern Irish Sea was Royalist: the *Swan*, a fifth rate commanded by Captain John Bartlett, together with an armed merchantman, the *Providence*, under John's relative Thomas

1   Carte, *Life of Ormonde*, vol. V, pp. 465–6.
2   Ryder, p. 31.
3   R N. Dore, 'The Sea Approaches. The Importance of the Dee and Mersey in the Civil War in the North West', in Transactions of the Historic Society of Lancashire and Cheshire for the Year 1986 (Liverpool: printed for the society, 1986), vol. 136, p. 5.

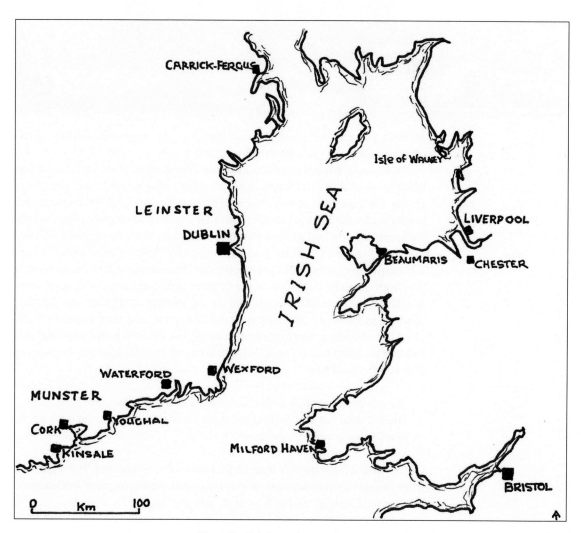

Map 1 The Irish Sea and principal ports on it.

3 Chester Castle, from a 1747 engraving by Samuel and Nathaniel Buck.

Bartlett. These would be able to command the crossing to North Wales and Chester unless the enemy were reinforced.

There were a number of reasons why a landing in the Chester area was thought desirable. The immediate concern, which would be reinforced by the advance into North Wales early in November by Parliamentarian troops under Sir William Brereton and Sir Thomas Myddelton, was that the Parliamentarians had gained the upper hand in the campaigning of 1643 in Lancashire and Cheshire, and Chester itself might soon be under threat. Although the exact use of the troops from Ireland had still to be decided, if they were initially deployed in the Chester area a number of options were available. They could be employed in an attempt to restore the Royalist position in Cheshire, and perhaps take Liverpool, and they would be well-placed to counter a Scottish advance along the western route into England. Indeed this was a major consideration, for as Ormonde's agent at the court in Oxford informed him:

> The expectation of the English-Irish aid is the daily prayer and almost the daily bread of them that love the King and is put into the dispensatory and medicine book of state as a cure for the Scotch.[4]

Or they could fairly quickly be deployed elsewhere as required. The regiments from Munster, partly because of shipping considerations, were intended for the West of England, and will be dealt with in Chapter 7.

However obtaining sufficient shipping was a major problem. The King had tasked an influential local Royalist, Orlando Bridgeman, with making preparations for the reception of the Irish troops in Chester and North Wales, and on 19 October Ormonde told Bridgenan that he had procured from his stores four demi-culverin and two whole culverin 'all iron, mounted with their appurtenances to load and discharge them, together with 200 culverin and 400 demi-culverin shot', which he was sending via Captain Thomas

---

4   Carte, *Life of Ormonde*, vol. V, p. 521.

Bartlett to strengthen the defences of the North Wales harbours. He then moved on to his main concerns:

> And now I am to inform you that by his majesty's command, I am preparing to transport part of his army here to his service there; and I trust it will be to the number of 3,000 foot at least and 300 horse. The main difficulty I find in the work is shipping to transport and safely to convey them to that port of Chester, whither, by the King's command, I am directed. This want is much increased, and our supply thereof made almost impossible, by the coming hither and lying here certain parliament ships, who hinder the coming of vessels, and the relief they would bring us, not only to the difficulting of his service, but to the destruction of his majesty's protestant subjects here. Which forseeing might happen, I humbly besought his majesty in two former despatches and do now again renew it, that he would immediately command hither some ships of force, for the security of this harbour, and the wastage of that part of his army. And this was promised by letters of the 8th of September from Sudeley, but yet we hear nothing of them.
>
> In these former despatches I expressed, as neat as words could do it, at least any of mine, the miserable wants the soldier had sustained here, and how absolutely necessary it would be to have provision in good measure made for them of victual, money, clothes, shoes and stockings; without which they would not only be unserviceable, but very seducable, by those that doubtless will attempt to corrupt both them and officers from their allegiance. Which I inform you of, because I understand you are principally and deservedly trusted by his majesty in these parts: and to the end you may set the uttermost of your endeavours a work to prevent the danger the wants of the army when it shall arrive (if it so please God) on that side may bring upon his majesty's service...[5]

Ormonde wrote in similar vein to John Williams, Archbishop of York, currently in 'exile' in his native North Wales, where he claimed to have considerable influence. Ormonde explained the King's instructions to despatch the bulk of his troops to England, complaining of his lack of shipping, and adding that:

> To his service in England ... I find a ready inclination in the best and most considerable part of the army, though there has been, and is still, great industry used to corrupt the officers and debauch the soldiers. But the greatest difficulty I meet with, is the want of shipping for their transportation, and the greatest danger I fear, when they are landed on the other side, is that if provision of shoes, stockings, and clothes, and money be not instantly with them, it will be easy to seduce them with likely promises of having these wants supplied. And I make little doubt but the rebels there will promise all this, and perform as much as they can of it; which if not prevented, by timely provision to be made for officers and soldiers by his majesty's servants, this part of the army will not only be useless to his majesty but perhaps be drawn in a great part to fight against him...

---

5 *Ibid.*, pp. 478–9.

He asked for Williams' assistance in meeting the needs of the soldiers.[6]

The King meanwhile gave responsibility for liaising with Ormonde to the ambitious and frequently unrealistic George Lord Digby, newly created a Secretary of State. On 2 November Digby demonstrated his over-optimistic outlook by telling Ormonde: 'I hope … that the Leinster forces are ready to come to Beaumaris, even without ships from hence, by the help of the Irish ships. In case that fail, you will have some at Dublin quickly from Bristol…'[7] On 10 November he assured Ormonde that:

> I hope … that there is such a proportion of ships procured from the Irish, as with the help of those twelve or thirteen sent from Bristol above a week since, will suffice for the transportation of the Leinster forces to Beaumaris, for the good reception of which, and refreshment with money, clothes, shoes, stockings and other provisions, there is all possible order taken in those parts, the business being principally recommended to my lord of York and Mr Bridgeman'.
>
> We are in hopes that we shall soon have a good party on foot in Lancashire to join with them.
>
> The report of so considerable a power to come into those parts from Ireland, hath already struck a great terror among the rebels, and I am advertised that they are bending their chief forces of the northern parts toward Chester, in hopes to prevent those forces, if not of landing, yet of those advantages and supplies that may be intended there…[8]

Digby was at least partly correct: on 7 November Cheshire Parliamentarian troops under Sir William Brereton, together with a detachment led by Sir Thomas Myddelton, nominally Parliament's commander in North Wales, forced the crossing of the River Dee at Holt Bridge. The local Royalist forces dissolved before their advance, and the Parliamentarians occupied Wrexham, Hawarden Castle and pushed on into Flintshire. North-east Wales had been lost to the Royalists, and Chester threatened with isolation.

The debacle occurred in part as a result of the shortcomings of the King's Lieutenant General in North Wales and the northern Marches, Lord Arthur Capel. Capel was a loyal servant of the King, but an indifferent soldier, and the failure of his campaign in October to take the Parliamentarian garrison at Wem forced his battered army to retreat to south Shropshire, leaving the way clear for Brereton and Myddelton to take the initiative.

Archbishop Williams wrote to Ormonde on 13 November in tones of near panic, telling him that:

> The enemies are possessed of Wirral, where your excellency intended to land, are entered into Denbighshire, have taken Wrexham and Ruthin … plunder up and down the whole country without resistance; and whether with a resolution to fortify here, or to return again and besiege Chester, upon the Welsh as well as the English side, I am not able to conjecture …

---

6   *Ibid.*, pp. 480–1.
7   *Ibid.*, p. 502.
8   *Ibid.*, pp. 503–4.

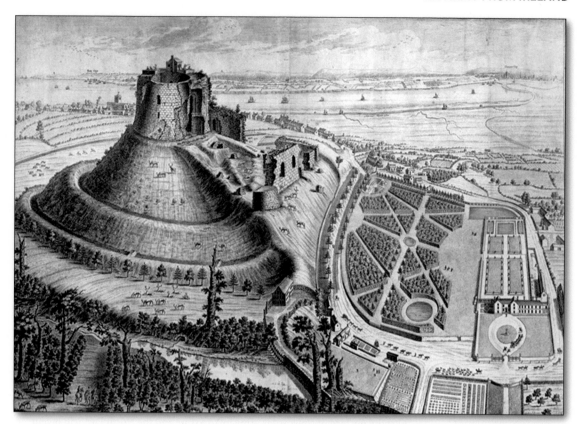

4 Hawarden Castle, regained from Parliament after a short siege. (Engraving by W.H. Toms, c. 1700–c. 1750)

Williams feared that the forces from Ireland would have to land at Holyhead or the harbours at Conway and Beaumaris, none of them ideal for the purpose, whilst Capel was 'hiding himself in Shrewsbury, and not daring to take the field, lest he be shut out from that town, the citizens whereof, with the inhabitants of that shire, having not only a mean, but malignant estimation of his lordship.'[9]

Capel's latest failure reinforced dissatisfaction with him in the Royalist high command, and it was clear that he must be replaced. The initial reaction, as we shall see, was to bring Ormonde himself over to replace Capel, including in his command the troops from Ireland. But Prince Rupert was also a possible candidate, and until a decision was reached, there was an effective power vacuum on the Welsh Marches. Into this stepped the energetic and ruthless John, Lord Byron.

Byron (born *c.* 1600), of Newstead Abbey, Nottinghamshire, was head of a strongly Royalist family, his six brothers and uncle all serving in the King's forces. Byron, who apparently had military experience in Europe, was colonel of the first Royalist regiment of horse to be completed in 1642, and proved himself a capable cavalry commander, distinguishing himself at Roundway Down and most recently at the First Battle of Newbury. In October he was serving with his brigade in Buckinghamshire.

---

9 *Ibid.*, p. 507.

5 Lord John Byron. This energetic and ruthless officer was eventually placed in command of the troops from Leinster. (Artist: Samuel de Wilde (1766–1832); engraver P. Paul)

During the spring and summer the Earl of Derby and the Lancashire Royalists had suffered a series of reverses, and it was clear that reinforcements were needed if the situation was to be restored. Serving with the Oxford Army were four much-reduced regiments from Lancashire, Richard Lord Molyneux's regiments of horse and foot, and those of Sir Thomas Tyldesley. Their departure from Lancashire had been a factor in Derby's reverses, and it was decided that they should return in an attempt to regain the Royalist initiative there. It was also felt that they should return under a competent commander. The choice fell on Lord Byron.

On 6 November, the King's senior secretary of state, Sir Edward Nicholas, wrote to Prince Rupert, under whose command Byron then was, saying that he was:

… very glad that your Highness' judgement concurs with us concerning the Lancashire propositions … therefore his Majesty desires you to send my Lord Byron presently to him if your Highness can presently spare him, that this great design may be presently adjusted, for his Majesty thinks it of that weight, that without it not only those counties will be in hazard to be irrevocably lost, but likewise my lord of Newcastle's army in Yorkshire and the North East will be put into very great disadvantage, if this design be not effectually pursued.[10]

Next day Byron wrote effusively to Rupert:

Though I despair of ever doing it to my own satisfaction, yet I shall never (so long as I have life) leave endeavouring to merit the great obligations your Highness is pleased to lay upon me, both in the behalf of my regiment and my own particular. As for the employment of Lancashire, (which your Highness is pleased so nobly to offer unto me)so that county will agree to such conditions as may make me capable of doing that service which will be expected from me, and that I may have the sole command of all the forces that are to be employed there (under your Highness) both horse and foot, I shall cheerfully and willingly undertake it, only I shall desire some convenient time, to put my regiment in a condition to make so long a march. One thing more, Sir, I shall humbly offer to your Highness's consideration which is this, I am told by some of my very good friends, that there is some intention to make me governor to the Prince of Wales, instead of my lord of Hertford, who is now removed to another place about the King. I shall humbly desire your Highness to be a means to make that sure to me before I go, this being

---

10 Eliot Warburton, *Memoirs of Prince Rupert and the Cavaliers* (London: Bentley, 1849), vol. II, p. 327.

but a temporary, that an employment likely to continue to my advantage when this war is ended…[11]

Byron's concerns regarding his area of responsibility were no doubt occasioned because Lord Derby was still technically in command of Royalist forces in Lancashire, although currently in the Isle of Man and Chester, whilst Lancashire was theoretically part of Newcastle's responsibility. His request regarding the governorship of the Prince of Wales, an appointment which he did not receive, illustrates Byron's fierce ambition and desire to make a name for himself, which would have fateful consequences.

On 14 November Byron's appointment was confirmed by the King:

> Charles R,
>
> Right trusty and right entirely beloved nephew, we greet you well. Whereas we have newly received information of the hazardous condition of our affairs in Cheshire and Lancashire, unless some speedy supply of some fresh forces be sent thither we having formerly designed our right trusty etc the lord Byron unto this employment, Our will and pleasure is that immediately upon sight of hereof, you give order for the said Lord Byron to march with his regiment toward our City of Chester, we having likewise recommended all the other Lancashire regiments to march away with all expedition to join themselves under the said Lord Byron at such place as he shall judge fit to appoint.
>
> Given at our Court at Oxford this eleventh of November 1643, by his Majesty's command.
>
> George Digby[12]

News of the latest reverses in North Wales had of course not yet reached Oxford, but already the exact extent of Byron's responsibility was becoming less clear. But he would not reach the area, with 1,000 foot and 300 horse, for some days, and meanwhile the situation was changing rapidly.

On 16 November Ormonde told the Earl of Clanricarde that 'above 2,000 foot are now aboard and I hope will be under sail by tomorrow noon.'[13]

It was also apparent that the feeling was growing among the King's advisers that Ormonde's continued presence in Ireland was indispensable. On 7 November he was appointed Lord Lieutenant, and on 17 November Digby told Ormonde, somewhat tentatively, that:

> … you are conceived so personally necessary … to the support of his Majesty's affairs [in Ireland] that his Majesty, nor all his ministers … are not able at all to determine whether your presence be most essential in this kingdom [England] or in that [Ireland] nor can they at all advise to which way your lordship should apply yourself for the most advantage of his majesty's service. And therefore his majesty hath commanded me barely to state unto you without opinion the arguments on

---

11 *Ibid.*, p. 328.
12 *Ibid.*, pp. 329–30.
13 Carte, *Life of Ormonde*, vol. V, p. 510.

both sides, leaving it absolutely free to your judgement and election, to choose which you will do.[14]

After pointing out the need to preserve the fragile truce in Ireland and deal with a very volatile political situation there, a task which perhaps only Ormonde could deal with, Digby went on, somewhat breathlessly, to discuss the troops being sent over:

… the army that is transporting hither considered as fatal to the rebels here, in case it come over and continue with hearty and entire affections, but fully as fatal to his majesty's affairs in case it should revolt; the temptations also considered to such a revolt by insinuations and practises upon their affections there, and the same or greater arts which probably may be used here at their landings to debauch them, when possibly the concurrences of things in these parts where they are to land may be of more dangerous force than arguments and insinuations, as namely, an impossibility perhaps of their meeting with so good refreshment and accommodation at their landings as they may promise themselves, though, in truth, all care imaginable is taken in that point; a strong power of the rebels in those parts likely soon to face them, and either to invite them to join, or to interrupt their hoped for refreshment with a necessity to fight so much sooner than they expected; for the truth is, his majesty's affairs, though extremely prosperous, God be thanked, in more vital parts, have lately received a very great declination in those. These temptations, I say, considered and your lordship's person at the head of that army considered also as the only sure means to frustrate their effect by the power and affection whereby you have submitted that army to an exact obedience, and contained it therein, when pressed with greater difficulties than these, your personal presence here for some time cannot but be looked upon by all prudent men as of an importance and moment hardly to be outweighed.[15]

However, and probably reflecting the King's real opinion, Digby pointed out that:

… your coming over hither seems clogged with many impediments, besides the importance of your being there: as first, since it hath been necessary to divide the Irish army, and to distribute one part of it to several differing employments, whether the Leinster forces will still be an army fit for your honour and quality to command in person here; but this objection will be in some part solved by submitting unto you, when you come over, all other forces and commands in those parts of England, which are not inconsiderable, though for the present somewhat overborne by some late success of the rebels.[16]

Also, Digby said, the effects in Ireland of any military reverse which Ormonde might suffer needed to be considered:

---

14 *Ibid.*, p. 511.
15 *Ibid.*, p. 512.
16 *Ibid.*

[And] whether your lordship giving out that you will come over, the good affections of the officers you send over with the army, and the fitting choice here of my Lord Byron to command them in chief, in case you do not come, may not suffice in some good measure to continue them, and to prevent their apprehended debauching.[17]

The growing crisis in North Wales had led it seems to a last minute change in Byron's orders. Whilst Capel still waited in uneasy limbo at Shrewsbury, Byron had been appointed 'Field Marshal General in North Wales and those Parts', including Cheshire, Shropshire and Lancashire, to deputise until whoever was eventually appointed to supreme command arrived.

Digby pointed out that if Ormonde did decide to assume command, the troops would have to be sent ahead of him, 'for the least delay of that supply is as ruinous to those countries of Lancashire, Cheshire Shropshire and North Wales as if, when they did come, a good part of them should revolt, his majesty, by relying upon that relief, having provided for no other.'[18]

The Archbishop of York on 18 November reported to Ormonde that the situation in North Wales and the Marches had grown worse: 'The people of Denbighshire and Flintshire being disunited amongst themselves and ill-united under an unfortunate commander, [Capel] who never led them in any action, but when they were entered upon the same, retired, and now the enemy is entered these parts, dare not show his head...' He went on to say that Brereton and Myddelton only had about 1,500 men in all, plus some of the Cheshire Trained Bands at Mold and Holt, 'and by these contemptible numbers, these great and populous counties, for want of a head and arms and ammunition, are quite routed and mastered up and down these mountainous countries.' He reported, however, that the enemy were so thinly scattered that not only the remaining North Wales coastal ports, but Wirral were open for the troops to disembark.[19]

On 21 November Arthur Trevor, Ormonde's gossipy and not always totally reliable informant in Oxford, told him:

The expectation of the English Irish aids is the daily prayers, and almost the daily bread of them that love the King and his business, and is put into the dispensatory and medicinebook of state as a cure for the Scotch. The obstruction now made in North Wales makes many doubtful, all fearful of some distress that may befall them at their landing. My lord Byron marched this very day with 1000 horse and 300 foot to join with my lord Capel in the opening of the passage, and making one body with your lordship's aids: yet I am still fearful it will be a work of much trouble, as well by the interruption of the enemy, but chiefly by the unevenness of the way.[20]

In an effort to ensure the loyalty of the officers with the troops sent to England, Ormonde had required them to swear an oath of allegiance. Most

---

17 *Ibid.*, p. 513.
18 *Ibid.*
19 *Ibid.*, p. 515.
20 *Ibid.*, p. 518.

6 George Monck, who served originally as lieutenant-colonel in Warren's Regiment. ('George Monck, 1st Duke of Albemarle. From the original by Sir Peter Lely', G.P. Harding. Frontispiece, *Memoirs of George Monk, Duke of Albemarle* (London: Richard Bentley, 1838))

did so, especially as those among them who had wished to serve Parliament had already gone to England. However two expressed unease, one of them being George Monck, lieutenant-colonel of Henry Warren's Regiment. Ormonde was reluctant to lose such a capable officer, and sent him to Bristol, informing its governor, Sir Francis Hawley, that:

I have found cause to send colonel George Monk under safe custody to Bristol, where I must desire you in like manner to keep him, until you shall receive his majesty's pleasure concerning him, which I conceive you will in a short time after the letter I send you herewith comes in my Lord Digby's hands. In the meantime, I must assure you that colonel Monk is a person that hath very well deserved in the service of this kingdom, and that there is no unworthy thing laid to his charge, therefore I desire you to use him with all possible civility…[21]

Monck's doubts were eventually removed by a personal interview with the King in Oxford, and he would rejoin Warren's Regiment in time to be captured at the Battle of Nantwich.

Meanwhile Orlando Bridgeman was making preparations to receive the first contingent of troops at Chester. The mutiny which had occurred among the soldiers sent to Bristol had emphasised the need for adequate provision for the troops on their arrival:

… so that his majesty sent down letters to the several counties of North Wales, as also a gentleman, one colonel [Sir Thomas Tyldesley] to those of Lancashire, residing in these parts for a present supply of clothes, victuals and some proportion of money, to which there was a fair return of promises; but the enemy being fatally (whether through abominable cowardice or treachery or both, I cannot tell) forced a passage into Wales over Holt bridge, a place of great import within 5 miles of Chester, and dividing that shire from Denbighshire: where there were as many (these backed with a strong castle at Holt) to guard it as to assault it; by these means for the present forced them to lay aside their preparations for the public service, and provide for their own particulars. And by this means Chester itself being in a manner blocked up, they were forced to burn all that part of their suburbs which were on the Welsh side of the city.[22]

Bridgeman had been despatched to Chester from Oxford, and found on arrival that the situation had changed considerably for the better, as the first contingent of Ormonde's men had arrived. These were the troops who were

---

21 *Ibid.*, p. 525.
22 *Ibid.*, pp. 525–6.

embarked on 12 October, but prevented by contrary winds from sailing until the 14th. Ormonde had meanwhile written to the Mayor of Chester, telling him that:

> His Majesty having commanded me ... to take order for the transportation of part of his army in this kingdom to his Majesty's Kingdom of England, and particularly if it might be to the port of Chester. I am, therefore, to desire you, in his Majesty's name, by virtue of the said letters, that as you tender His Majesty's service you take care that the soldiers, under the command of Sir Fulke Hunckes, Sir Michael Earnley, Colonel Gibson and Colonel Byron, who shall land there, be conveniently quartered by you, and accommodated with such necessaries and provisions as are fit according to His Majesty's Royal intentions, whereby they may be the better enabled and encouraged in his Majesty's service.[23]

On 11 November, Ormonde had again expressed his concerns to Orlando Bridgeman:

> I have been since the 7 of this month (the day that his majesty's fleet under the command of Captain Wake, consisting of 2 ships and 5 barks, arrived here) in continual thought how to transport of this army (according to His Majesty's command) to the port of Chester; and I am now in that forwardness, that I hope a few days with a good wind will bring them thither to the number of about 3,000 foot, as the lists are given me by the officers, and that is the only way of muster that will now be endured. The horse, artillery, and some more men I intend shall follow, according to means of transportation and other important things shall admit of my own departing hence.
>
> In the meantime, I hold it necessary by these to second my former letter sent you by Captain Bartlett, dated the 25 of October, and to desire you that all possible provision be made for the good entertainment of the officers and soldiers, who are in the greatest want that can be imagined, and in such distemper by reason thereof, that I much fear great inconveniences will unavoidably fall upon the King's service, if they find not their condition much mended upon the instant of their landing. And if the case be such, that plentiful provision cannot be instantly ready, it is absolutely needful that a competent strength of horse and foot, of whose affections you are confident, should be in readiness by force to keep the common soldier in awe. And whatever provision is made for them, this will not be amiss; for they have gotten such a head, and punishment hath been so moderately inflicted on them, by reason of their extreme sufferings, that they will be apt to fall into disorders and will think themselves delivered from prison, when they come on English ground, and that they may make use of their liberty to go whither they will.
>
> There cannot go much ammunition with them this time, 10 or 12 barrels will be the most, and therefore if they be suddenly put upon service, which I could wish they might be, preparation must be made accordingly; nor is there much more to expected when I go, so empty our stores are.[24]

---

23 *Ibid.*, p. 501.
24 *Ibid.*, pp. 525–6.

These men were commanded by Sir Michael Earnley and arrived off Mostyn in Flintshire on 15 November, and disembarked, without opposition, the next day. They consisted of approximately 1,800 men, comprising the foot regiments of Richard Gibson (formerly Sir Simon Harcourt, raised in Cheshire and North Wales, 1641), 700 men; Sir Fulke Hunckes (raised Yorkshire, 1641), 400 men; Sir Michael Earnley (a composite unit from the Dublin garrison, including men from his own and Lord Ranelagh's Regiments (raised in Cheshire and North Wales, 1641), 400 men; and a detachment of Robert Byron's Regiment (a composite all-musketeer unit drawn from various regiments in the Leinster forces), 250 men under Lieutenant-Colonel Sir Francis Butler. In addition there were two companies of firelocks, each 50 strong, under Captains Francis Langley and Thomas Sandford. Most of Sandford's men, like their commander, probably came from north Shropshire.

On 15 November Ormonde had explained to the King:

> … by the list sent herewith, your majesty will see in what proportion the lords justice and I have been able for the present to fulfil your commands for the transportation of part of your Leinster army in England, By that time it shall please God and your majesty to send back such parts of this fleet as fitted to come, I shall endeavour to have all the remainder of horse and foot that can be spared from the necessary defence of this part of the kingdom to a readiness to follow them.
>
> For the present it falls to Sir Michael Earnley to command these men, who is a person that hath eminently deserved in your majesty's service here. I am confident his affections are as good to serve you in England, which he had long since manifested there, but that I found his assistance hereof so great use towards the bringing to this pass the service he is now employed in, that notwithstanding he had obtained your commands to me to licence his going hence, I persuaded him to stay til now.
>
> I send your majesty herewith the oath, first taken by myself, and then very cheerfully in my presence by all the officers that go, and voluntarily by many of those that stay. It will be administered, and I doubt not, unanimously taken by the soldiers on shipboard.
>
> In the last place, I most humbly recommend to your majesty's royal favour and gracious acceptance the merits of all these officers and soldiers in your service of this kingdom, the exceeding and unwearied patience wherewith they have borne all kinds of wants therein; and last of all, their readiness to undertake this expedition, which is such as gives more than hopes of the services they will do your majesty in what you shall command them there.[25]

All three colonels, as we have already seen, were experienced soldiers. The senior colonel, who was to serve briefly as Lord Byron's major general of foot, was Sir Michael Earnley. From Canning in Wiltshire, Earnley was described as 'An unwearied man, night and day in armour about affairs either of the field or country, an old soldier, bred in the Low Countries.' A professional soldier, Earnley was knighted in 1638, during the First Bishops' War, when he

---

25 *Ibid.*, pp. 528–9.

was Governor of Berwick. But he contracted consumption whilst in Ireland, and recurrent ill-health would limit his role in England.

Richard Gibson, as we have seen, was an equally experienced soldier who had served capably under Ormonde. Hunckes, who claimed to have commanded large forces in Europe, was a noted disciplinarian who may have been severely tested by the unruly nature of some of his men.

At news of the landing of the 'Irish', potential Parliamentarian opposition melted away. Brereton had been aware of an imminent landing, but felt unable to face Earnley in battle. Hoping to encourage desertion among the troops, Brereton and his officers sent a letter to Earnley and his colonels:

> Being assured that amongst the Forces now arrived in Wales, your Regiments have likewise entered these parts, we have thought good, before there be further proceedings tending towards hostility, to apply ourselves to you in this way that so if it is possible you may rightly understand us and we not mistake you, and so happily you and we having formerly ventured our own persons in one and the same quarrel in England Ireland may not through mistaken or misinformation be divided, and we under the brand of Rebels and be made enemies. Now Sirs, give us leave to tell you, that we apprehend, and are assured your voyage in to Ireland was to fight against Popish Rebels and for the Protestant Religion wherein you have expressed great fidelity. We imagine you are not yet thoroughly informed of the cause of taking up Arms, or if you were, you could not be engaged against us. For this reason, we have tendered our respects unto you, and if you show yourselves the gentlemen we formerly knew you at your last departure out of this Kingdom, we doubt not but to procure satisfaction from the Parliament for the service you have done in Ireland with the like preferment here, and show yourselves as real here for the Protestant Religion, as you did there, which will engage us all to remain, Sirs,
> your affectionate and faithful friends to serve you,
>
> Will. Brereton   Jo. Booth
> Tho. Middleton   Peter Egerton
> G. Booth   Jo. Holcroft.[26]

Earnley and his officers were unimpressed; they replied on 20 November:

> Gentlemen
> We were not engaged in the service of Ireland otherwise than by the King's Commission; The service we have done there envy itself dares not extenuate. And although we are very sensible how unworthily we have been deserted by your pretended Parliament, yet we are not returned hither without His Majesty's special Commission and Authority. If you have the Commission from the King for the Arms you carry, we shall willingly treat with you. Otherwise you must give us leave to carry ourselves like Soldiers and Loyal Subjects
>
> Michael Earnele [sic]   Fran. Butler
> Rich. Gibson   Ed Hammond
> Geo. Wynne[27]

---

26 *Ibid.*, pp. 505–6.
27 *Ibid.* pp. 508–9.

Somewhat inconsistently, Brereton attempted to persuade the local population that the newcomers were in fact 'bloody Irish rebels'. Failing in this, and believing that up to 10,000 more troops from Ireland were on their way, the Parliamentarian force hastily retreated behind the Dee and the Lancashire troops headed for their own territory, whilst Brereton fell back on Nantwich, having rather pointlessly left a small garrison to hold Hawarden Castle.

The opening stages of operations by Earnley's contingent were described by Captain Harry Birch, an officer with the contingent, in a letter to Ormonde's Secretary:

> At our first landing we met with several disrespective warrants from Sir William Brereton, requiring all from 16 to 60 to be in arms to defend themselves from the invasion of 4,000 bloody Irish rebels. He could not have done us a greater courtesy, than telling so loud a lie. (The honest Welsh received us very courteously…) This was required to be published through Wales, that we were such, that is, so far as Sir Thomas Middleton's faction prevailed. This caused several religious Ministers that loved Conscience and the King, to withdraw themselves, and not few of the laity, though we found enough besides to bid us hearty welcome.
>
> At Holywell, the first place we came to, though the town were mostly Papists, we were told they [the Parliamentarians] pillaged none but the churches, (in want of linen) and the poor Curate. At Northop (thither we next) they took away the surplice again, and did no other harm. It was their time of probationship amongst disarmed people: and you must understand the Minister staid, and was a Scotchman. Thence to Hawarden we came, where our men besieged the castle there, (but lately and falsely betrayed by its owner a week before we came, a man intrusted much by the King and his officers the more is his sin, one Ravenscroft) where we stayed three days; in which time very happily we had but six men killed; for at no less a cost would our men believe that Englishmen would fight any Englishmen but Papists. And I cannot honestly conceal from you, that three of these were killed more basely than ever you heard of any killed by the rebels of Ireland; for while some called them unto them from the top of the wall upon pretence of old acquaintance, and promised them sacredly they should receive no harm by their approaching, others shot at them and missed not.[28]

Most of the garrison of Hawarden consisted of 120 men of Sir Thomas Myddelton's Regiment of Foot, together with a handful of deserters from Earnley's force, it probably being the latter who had lured their old comrades into a trap.

The bulk of the Anglo-Irish troops continued their march to Chester after three days, leaving about 1,000 of the North Wales trained band under Colonel Roger Mostyn, supported by Captain Thomas Sandford and his firelocks to maintain the siege. With them was Colonel John Marrow, another veteran of the war in Ireland, who is sometimes incorrectly claimed to have crossed with Earnley's contingent. In fact he had come over much earlier

---

28 *Ibid*, pp. 531–5.

in the year, and had taken command of Lord Cholmondeley's Regiment of Horse in Capel's army.

He summoned the Hawarden garrison to surrender, but this was rejected in a rambling reply which reminded the soldiers from Ireland of the atrocities supposedly committed by the rebels there, and that 'we desire (before you pass further) your thoughts may make a pause, lest you find that God of the Protestants against you whom you have hitherto found miraculously for you.'[29]

Marrow was unimpressed:

Gentlemen,

It is not for to hear you preach that I am sent here, but in his Majesty's name, to demand the Castle for his Majesty's use. As your allegiance binds you to be true to him, and not to inveigle those innocent souls that are within with you, so I desire your resolution, if you will deliver the Castle or No?[30]

This further summons, along with one which Earnley and Gibson had delivered on 22 October, was also rejected.

Throughout the next few weeks, the loquacious Captain Thomas Sandford, who had evidently taken over command of the siege from Marrow, took every opportunity to deliver colourful threats to the enemy, and Hawarden was no exception.

Gentlemen,

I presume you very well know, or have heard of [my] condition and disposition, and that I neither give nor take quarter. I am now with my firelocks (who never yet neglected opportunity to correct rebels) ready to use you as I have done the Irish, but loath I am to spill my countrymens' blood. Wherefore, by these I advise you, to your fealty and obedience towards his Majesty, and to show yourself faithful subjects, by delivering the Castle into my hands for his Majesty's use. In so doing you shall be received into mercy, otherwise, if you put me to the least trouble or loss of blood to force you, expect no quarter for Man, Woman or Child. I hear you have some of our late Irish army in your company – they very well know me, and that my firelocks use not to parley. Be not unadvised, but think of your liberty, for I vow all hopes of relief are taken from you. And our intents are not to starve you, but to batter and storm you, and then hang you all, and follow the rest of that rebel crew. I am now no bread-and- cheese rogue, but as ever, a loyalist, and will be whilst ever I can write my name.

Thomas Sandford

I expect your speedy answer this Tuesday night at Broadlane Hall, where I am now your near Neighbour.[31]

---

29 *Mercurius Aulicus*, Oxford 1643–1644. In Peter Thomas (ed.), *The English Revolution III: Newsbooks*, 4 vols (London: Cornmarket Press, 1971). Vol. 1, Oxford Royalist. Above quotation, p.684.

30 *Ibid.*

31 *Ibid.*, p. 693.

Though Sandford had a particularly colourful turn of phrase, his attitude seems to have reflected that of many of troops from Ireland, hardened by the brutal war there.

He quickly resumed his verbal bombardment:

> … if you like your present condition, remain where you are and feast your bodies with your boiled corn, and glad your souls with a draught of your unwholesome water, if you pleased to be informed that Relief cannot come to you, send out one of your Sergeants, who shall have a pass to and from Wrexham, of the truth to inform you.[32]

Although the defenders of Hawarden responded to Sandford's blandishments with the comment 'Big words do not take Castles', they had in reality no hope of relief, and on 4 December surrendered, being allowed to march out with half their arms, one colour and £25 worth of goods. 'Which articles were not performed as I could have wished; but our men profess they could not help it, but it was the fault of some of the Lord Cholmondeley's men, who bid them remember Reading. For which fact, they say, Captain Sandford hewed some of our own side sufficiently, and (which was more than the articles required) guarded them out of Wales…'[33]

It is unclear whether the Royalist deserters were also allowed to go free. So far desertion had not reached the levels Ormonde had feared. Perhaps 200 men left the colours, but some of them apparently returned.[34]

On 29 November Orlando Bridgeman sent a long situation report to Ormonde. After outlining the recent course of events, Bridgeman continued:

> … now your forces are at Chester, where we endeavour all that is possible for their accommodation, hitherto retarded by this unhappy eruption of the rebels into Wales. I have provided shoes and stockings for 1,000 or 1,200 of them already delivered, and the rest were in making, which I hope they have by this time I have got cloth and freize sufficient for them all, not yet made into apparel, but hastened it to Chester, where I hope to have it fitted up this week and the next. And I am now purposely in these parts to raise some proportion of monies for the officers and soldiers, and have gotten about £1000, which I shall distribute with their advice to the best advantage of his majesty's service.
>
> I am bold to give your excellency a more particular account of this business, both for my excuse in the unreadiness of these accommodations, which might justly have been expected, and to give your lordship an assurance, that I shall be so provided for those that are now to come over, that I shall have all the shoes and stockings, and I hope most, if not all the apparel, ready against their coming, if they be not above 2,000 men.
>
> And in truth all that can be done is little enough; for the rebels do so much tamper, and underhand infuse such dangerous notions into some of them, that were it not for the discretion, loyalty and moderation of the officers which

---

32 *Ibid.*
33 *Ibid.*, p. 694.
34 *Ibid.*

kept them in, many of them would turn to the enemy through hopes of their arrears, (which he hath cunningly promised them) though they would soon find themselves deceived, God be thanked, that treasury being now as empty as ours.

The sad condition of these parts (as they were before these forces landed) hath hastened down my lord Byron with 1200 horse and foot, most of Lancashire, he has advanced to Shrewsbury, and comes in the quality of field marshal of Cheshire, Shropshire, and North Wales, and so under my lord Capel, who is Lieut. General under the prince. My lord Byron's commission extends also to Lancashire, but when he is there, he is under the command of my lord of Newcastle; of which I thought it my duty to advertise your excellency, that, if you shall think fit to propose anything to his majesty concerning the commanding of these forces sent from Ireland, you may know their present condition. I conceived the King's intention was, (unless your excellency should advise any other course, which I am sure will be followed) that my lord Byron should command them; and that he should with all speed march into Lancashire and attack Liverpool, a place without any works or defence of the land side, and is near to Lathom, the earl of Derby's house, (a good retreat, if need be), and in the best affected part of all the county, which, I believe, upon appearance of our forces, will come unto us. Besides there are 2,000 men ready to fall in upon the north part of Lancashire, and we hope to keep that correspondence with my lord of Newcastle, that they will at the same time fall in from Halifax.

If we can clear that shire, we do not only spoil the design of the enemy, which is to bring in the Scots through Westmoreland into Lancashire, where they assure them (and as the case now is, may make it good) of many thousand assistants; but shall be able, God Willing, early in the spring to march up towards the King with as considerable force as most armies in the kingdom. And I am assured (though soever the ill manage of things have rendered Lancashire wholly under the obedience of the rebels) that they are generally (except about Manchester) as well affected as any.

My lord, this town of Liverpool is of great consequence, in the respect of the mutual intercourses of these kingdoms, and if it be taken away from the rebels, they have no port to bring in a new store of arms or ammunition. Besides, if we possess it, it is so near Chester, that upon any necessity we can relieve them. I shall therefore humbly offer it to your lordship, that if it be possible on the return of Captain Wake, we may have some of his ships assigned for that service. I hope a short time will despatch it, and the reward of their service will be answerable to their expectation. Captain Thomas Bartlett's ship and the King's pinnace, the *Swan* now at Chester, excellently fitted of all things, but some few ordnance wanting, joined to 2 or 3 others, are able to master all ships in Liverpool water; and if your Excellency please to confer with him about it (though he know nothing of the land design), I believe he will give you very good satisfaction; and (if you shall think fit, together with the soldiers, will bring over some smaller pieces of ordnance, such as are fit for that vessel; one of the best, as they say, in these seas) and I will take care she shall be ready to launch forth upon their arrival.[35]

---

35 Carte, *A Collection of Original Letters and Papers* (London, 1739), vol. V, pp. 526–28.

Bridgeman had outlined what would, in essence, be Royalist strategy in north-west England for the next six months.

On 1 December Ormonde wrote once more to the Mayor of Chester:

> Sir,
>
> There is now shipped from hence another part of his Majesty's army, under the command of Colonel Robert Byron and Colonel Henry Warren. With orders to land, if they can, at the port of Chester. I this time only recommend them to your care for their good accommodation, as I did those that were formerly transported from hence…[36]

He added next day:

> His Majesty's fleet returning hither very opportunely for the transportation of the rest of the men designed from hence to his service in England, I have now sent them, and directed their landing to be as near Chester as may be, to avoid the inconvenience that must unavoidably fall upon them, to the very great prejudice of his Majesty's service, if they should be landed at Beaumaris, or at any place where provision is not made for them, as I doubt not there is at Chester. On the other side, I am informed by the Commander of the Fleet, his victual is so near an end that unless he be supplied there it will not be in his power to pursue what is further directed, but must stay there to the loss of his time and great detriment to his Majesty's service. Wherefore I shall desire you to afford him all the assistance and furtherance you can towards his victualling…[37]

The new contingent of troops landed at the harbour at Neston in Wirral on 6 December. They consisted of 1,300 foot, the remaining 800 men of Robert Byron's Regiment and 500 of Henry Warren's. The latter had a somewhat chequered history. Sent to Ireland in 1641 as the Lord General's Regiment, it had been commanded by Lieutenant-Colonel George Monck, until the latter had been sent to England by Ormonde to resolve his doubts about the oath of allegiance to the King. In the interim the regiment was commanded by Colonel Henry Warren, and was probably the most unsettled of the units so far despatched. Also arriving were three companies of dragoons, totalling 140 men, under Captains Nathaniel Moyle, Radcliffe Duckenfield and Adam Pate.[38]

The men of the earlier contingent had now arrived in Chester, 'Faint, weary, and out of clothing.' Pending the delivery of the clothing Bridgeman had ordered the mayor 'sent through all the wards to get apparel of the citizens, who gave freely, some whole suits, some two, some doublets, others breeches, others shirts, shoes, stockings, and hats, to the apparelling of about 300.'[39]

---

36 *Ibid.*
37 Carte, *Life of Ormonde*, vol. V, pp. 526–8.
38 *Ibid.*
39 *Ibid.*, p. 529.

Ormonde had originally stated his intention of accompanying the second contingent of his men, but the details of command had still not been finalised. On 1 December Secretary of State Lord Digby told Ormonde:

> … there is a commission already drawn constituting you general, not only of the army which comes out of Ireland, but also of all his majesty's forces in the counties of Cheshire, Shropshire, Worcestershire and North Wales, it being thought necessary, whether your lordship come over or no, to hold up in the Irish army the name and opinion of your lordship being their general.[40]

However various difficulties and some second thoughts, were arising. On 14 December Sir George Radcliffe, entrusted at Oxford by the King to arrange the details of Ormonde's commission, reported that the promised commission to command if not actually executed 'was to remain with your lordship. As a badge of his majesty's favour', and, Sir George continued:

> In the soliciting of this business to get this commission dispatched, I found some stop and difficulty, in respect of the dispersing of the soldiers [from Ireland] into several places under several commanders. In conclusion it was resolved that your lordship should command in chief all his majesty's forces in north Wales, and in the counties of Chester, Shropshire, and Worcestershire (whether English or Irish) and have the like power there as Prince Maurice had in the west. When I saw the draught of your commission, I disliked the commission of some clauses (which I had seen heretofore in other commissions of like nature, and the manner of penning of others: wherein I moved some of the lords, and got directions to rectify them.) And then the King's learned counsel thought fit that Prince Maurice's commission should be altered accordingly; and so they should be made alike and passed together. All this spent some time, and is my excuse that your lordship had not his commission sooner …[41]

Three days later, on 17 December, Sir George had more negative news:

> Your commission for generalate of the forces in North Wales and 3 adjacent counties, I cannot get dispatched … About a week hence I hope it will be done; the reason of this last stay was because the Prince of Wales had a commission to be captain general of all Wales and the marches (which I knew not until now) and your lordship must be his lieutenant general in North Wales, Cheshire, Shropshire and Worcestershire I have got the prince his warrant for it, which he signed yesterday. My Lord Capel's commission must be superseded, ad then your lordship's will pass under the prince's seal, and afterwards be confirmed under the great seal.

---

40 *Ibid.*, p. 530.
41 Ryder, p. 32.

However, more realistically Radcliffe added 'as things stand in Ireland, we had rather have you stay there a while, as conceiving the peace and security of that kingdom depends much upon your person and presence.'[42]

Capel had already been recalled to Oxford, and arrived back there on 19 December, henceforward to serve as a civilian member of the Royalist administration. On 23 December Digby confirmed that Ormonde, now made Lord Lieutenant, should remain in Ireland:

> My lord, in two former letters I wrote unto your lordship several arguments for and against your lordship's coming over hither; but now that the army come out of Ireland appear so steady and so well settled in their affections to his majesty's service, the chief argument for your coming over ceases, and his majesty conceives that your person will be more necessary there, and that your name of general here will suffice.[43]

So Byron would for the moment remain in operational command of the army from Ireland, with Ormonde theoretically general, though plans were already underway for Prince Rupert to take control in Wales and the Marches. It is arguable that the delay and confusion in sorting out the Royalist command structure had a negative effect on the events which followed. This is doubtful, especially as Ormonde never displayed any great ability as a field commander. More serious was the inability to transport all of the Irish army at once, and its division between Chester and the west of England.

In any event, the Leinster contingent was about to take the field.

---

42 Carte, *Life of Ormonde*, vol. V, p. 529.
43 *Ibid.*

3

Nantwich: the Campaign

For the 7,000 or so citizens of Chester, the arrival of over 3,000 troops from Ireland had the impact of a minor earthquake. Whilst Chester had experienced the passage of many soldiers to and from Ireland over the centuries, the latest arrivals proved a sore trial. In itself, billeting them on citizens was a major disruption, and from the moment of their arrival the soldiers evidently behaved badly. A petition of the citizens to Lord Byron later in the spring enumerated some of the grievances.[1]

The soldiers on reaching Chester quickly spent the pay they had been given and the Irish money which had been proclaimed to be legal tender in England in the taverns and brothels of the city. Drunkenness was inevitable, followed by brawling in the streets. Their own money exhausted, the soldiers sold the cattle and other goods they had seized on the march to Chester, and in some cases the clothing they had just been issued with. The wives, leaguer ladies and assorted camp followers who had accompanied the troops, their presence probably tacitly accepted by the officers from fear of mutiny, proved equally troublesome.

Much of this, of course, was a natural reaction of troops returning from active service, and Ormonde had warned that such behaviour was inevitable, whilst some citizens were quick to profit from the situation. The Assembly issued a proclamation against the 'lawless and criminal pillaging' by his Majesty's soldiers, and also against 'divers evil disposed persons inhabiting within this city and elsewhere who have received such plundered goods and cattle, and buy or otherwise obtain the same at under values'. Equally condemned were 'divers persons of the city of Chester, who buy of the King's poorer and more improvident soldiers the stockings shoes and other apparel delivered to the same soldiers for their equipment'.[2]

On Friday 1 December the Assembly agreed that £100 of the Chester civic plate should be delivered to Lord Capel (still nominally in command in the area), on condition 'that the soldiers be removed forth of this City to quarters elsewhere by Monday next'.[3]

---

1   See Chapter 5.
2   Chester Assembly Book, quoted in Morris and Lawson, p. 55.
3   *Ibid.*, p. 56.

This was certainly an optimistic plea, though on 7 December Capel issued a receipt to '[The] Mayor and Aldermen of the City of Chester four hundred ounces of gilt plate by way of advance or contribution to pay and provision of and for the forces from Ireland now in his Majesty's service in these parts.'[4] This was of course not quite what the worthies of Chester had hoped for, but they would have to entertain their unwelcome guests a little longer.

Lord Byron arrived in Chester a day later than the troops, and consultations began on their next move. It is sometimes claimed that, thirsty for glory, Byron took the field prematurely. But Ormonde had recommended that the troops from Ireland should not be left idle, and as Byron's theoretical superior, his wishes carried great weight, as well as being clearly well-founded. The same strategy had been advocated by Orlando Bridgeman, no doubt reflecting the opinion of the Lancashire Royalists of the Royalist high command who had taken refuge in Chester. Byron quickly came to the same conclusion.

So, on 12 December, the Royalist army, apparently with morale high, and in some cases perhaps encouraged by a message of thanks from the King, marched out of Chester on the opening of their campaign. Sir Nicholas Byron, uncle to Lord John Byron, and Governor of Chester, wrote confidently to Prince Rupert:

> Hawarden castle, being as poorly surrendered by composition as it was basely betrayed at first, gives us assurance of our good success against the rebels, who are in very great distraction. This day appointed we march out of Chester, into those parts that have been most useful to the rebels, and where we come upon the place, shall dispose ourselves according to the best opportunity we shall meet withall. This being my Lord of Ormonde's army, I am only a volunteer for the present, till his Lordship's pleasure is further known upon all occasions …[5]

Captain Birch, in what may have been his final letter, told Ormonde's secretary: 'This day we march out 4,000 foot at least, and 1,000 horse. We may go where we will for our enemies, if we have God's blessing, which I hope we shall not want, if not for our own, for our enemies' sakes.'[6]

Clearly some local troops had reinforced the Anglo-Irish units, which did not total more than 3,000 foot. Byron had brought 300 men of Lord Molyneux and Sir Thomas Tyldesley's Lancashire Regiments with him. The other 700 included some new recruits and men of Francis Gamull's Chester City Regiment, some of whom, despite undertakings that they should serve only in Chester and its environs, evidently were with Byron in the initial stages of his campaign. Byron had brought 1,000 horse with him, his own, Tyldesley and Molyneux's Regiments. One of the Lancashire regiments may have been detached to patrol the outskirts of Chester on its Wirral side, and replaced by John Marrow's Regiment.[7]

---

4   British Library, Harleian MS 2135.
5   Warburton, vol. II, p. 333.
6   Carte, *Original Letters*, vol. I, p. 33.
7   Details from Stuart Reid, *Officers and Regiments Of the Royalist Army* (Southend-on-Sea: Patizan Press, n.d.)

Byron's objective was to clear the enemy out of central Cheshire, above all by the capture of their main stronghold of Nantwich. This was a departure from the original plan, reported by Bridgeman to Ormonde of making the recovery of Lancashire and the capture of Liverpool the main task of the Anglo-Irish army. Although winter campaigns were by no means uncommon, Byron has been criticised for his decision. On the other hand, Ormonde, who at this stage Byron still expected to be his overall commander, had emphasised the need to keep the troops from Ireland fully occupied and their behaviour in Chester had confirmed his view. Furthermore, the capture of Nantwich and central Cheshire would greatly increase the security of Chester itself, which would otherwise depend on rather uncertain protection from local forces in North Wales. With Nantwich taken and hopefully reinforced by further troops from Ireland, Byron would move into Lancashire.[8]

The immediate Royalist target was Parliamentarian-held Beeston Castle. Towering 160 metres above sea level on its sandstone crag, with precipitous drops on two sides to the Cheshire Plain, thirteenth-century Beeston Castle dominates the surrounding countryside. It controlled the route from Chester through the Peckforton Gap to the Midlands and its panoramic view made it a superb observation post.

The defences of Beeston consisted of a large outer ward on the lower slopes of the crag, with a fortified gatehouse and a curtain wall with towers set at intervals around it. Occupying the summit of the crag, and separated from the outer ward by a deep dry ditch cut into the rock, was the inner ward with gatehouse and towers and protected on three sides by precipitous cliffs. By 1642 the castle had fallen into disrepair, described by Parliamentarian writer Nathaniel Lancaster, as 'no more than the Skeleton or bare Anatomy of a Castle'. In January 1643, Sir William Brereton, who 'prized it by its situation', lost no time in garrisoning Beeston before the Royalists could pre-empt him.[9]

Efforts were made to repair the defences, with gaps in the walls of the outer ward 'made up with mud walls' and huts built to house the garrison. The governor's quarters were in the towers of the outer ward gatehouse. Not much else was done to strengthen the defences, and as the Parliamentarians gained the upper hand in the war in Cheshire, Beeston seems to have been regarded as a quiet backwater. Precautions were relaxed and the size of the garrison reduced. 'A captain or two being wearied out of the charge of such a prison, it was committed to Captain [Thomas] Steele, (a rough-hewn man, no soldier) whose care was more to see it repaired, than the safe custody of it.'[10] By the autumn of 1643 Beeston was being used as a supply depot, storing arms, ammunition and the valuables of a number of the leading Parliamentarian gentry of the Nantwich area. It was garrisoned by about 60 men of the local trained band, all second-line troops.

The capture of Beeston appeared a formidable task for Byron's men. On the night of 12/13 December, a Royalist force consisting of some companies

---

8   Significantly, no contemporary Royalist account criticises Byron's decision.
9   Nathaniel Lancaster, *Chester's Enlargement* (London, 1647), p. 21.
10 *Ibid.*

of Francis Gamull's Chester Regiment of Foot and Captain Thomas Sandford's company of firelocks arrived before Beeston.

The exact course of events is the subject of some dispute. Gamull's men staged a demonstration before the outer gate. Steele reacted by ordering virtually all of his men down to the outer bailey to counter this threat. This left the way open for Sandford and eight of his firelocks to gain entry to the castle and occupy its dominating inner ward. It is often stated that they achieved this feat by scaling, 'between moonset and dawn' the virtually sheer northern face of the crag, which was generally regarded as impregnable, with the result that the curtain wall here was very low, and so gaining entry into the inner ward.

However no contemporary account explicitly claims that this was how Sandford gained entry, and although local boys, until recent times at least, used to make the climb, there have to be serious doubts whether a party of troops, albeit including some local men, encumbered as they were with firelocks and other equipment, could actually have undertaken such a climb in pitch darkness.

A Chester Royalist, Randle Holme, wrote: 'Colonel Gamull with the assistance of Captain Sandford and his firelocks, in the midst of a dark night, surprised the innermost ward of Beeston Castle and garrisoned it for the King.'[11] A Parliamentarian account simply says that Sandford and his men gained entry to the castle 'by a byway, through treachery, as is supposed.'[12] The fullest Royalist account, in their propaganda news sheet *Mercurius Aulicus*, which might have been expected to have made great play of such a climbing feat, if it had actually occurred, also makes no such suggestion, reporting that on the night of 12 December:

> Lord Byron sent out the firelocks and about 200 commanded musketeers to Beeston Castle ... and having two men to be their guide that had formerly been very conversant in the Castle, assaulted the Outer Ward, and presently forced the entrance, after that they fell on the river [*sic* Inner] Ward (where the greater part of their provision and all their ammunition was stored up), and very courageously soon made themselves masters of it, we caused the Rebels to betake themselves to the several Towers of the Castle, where having little provision and no Ammunition, they desired a treaty, which was presently granted, wherein it was concluded that they should march away with such baggage as did properly belong to soldiers, leaving all the ordnance and ammunition behind them with all plate and other goods laid up in the Castle, which was the place wherein the rebels of that county chiefly confided.[13]

A possible reconstruction of events is that Sandford and his firelocks stealthily approached the outer ward on its northern side, where the slope of the hill, though steep enough to have resulted in the perimeter wall being less formidable than elsewhere, was relatively easy to climb. Encountering

---

11   British Library, Harleian MS 2135.

12   Thomas Malbon, *Memorials of the Civil War in Cheshire* (The Record Society, 1889), p. 91.

13   *Mercurius Aulicus*, (ed. Thomas, 1971), p.731.

few if any defenders, they were perhaps led by their guides to the sally port which is known to have existed in the outer ward defences, slipped inside, and made their way undetected to the entrance to the inner ward. They may have stormed its gatehouse, although examination of the present-day dry ditch shows several potential points at which the inner side could have been scaled. In fact the inner ward may have been undefended, for Lancaster says that 'there was nothing there but stones and a good prospect.'[14]

Possibly threatened by an attack from Gamull's men at the outer gateway, with the terrifying Sandford loose in his rear, Steele – understandably, given his inexperience and the poor quality of his troops – lost his nerve and surrendered. He might, just, have been forgiven this, but now made the fatal error of entertaining Sandford to dinner in his quarters and sent a supply of beer up to the firelocks guarding the inner ward. For the Cheshire Parliamentarian leadership, alarmed by the speedy fall of such a supposedly impregnable stronghold, and doubtless even more infuriated by the loss of their possessions, Steele's fraternisation with the enemy was the final insult. On reaching Nantwich at the head of his surrendered men, Steele was imprisoned, and shortly afterwards court-martialled and shot.

It seems that Captain Sandford was appointed Royalist governor of Beeston, judging by a letter (misdated by Warburton) which he sent to Prince Rupert:

Sir,

My hopes to be drawn near to your Highness's commands, emboldens me to present unto you this rude testimony of my ambition. As I have been happy in your smiles, so I beg the honour of your service. I am, with my firelocks, zealous in desire to wait on your pleasure: It is not advance of title I covet, but your commission to reduce me to my old duty, which shall really testify that I am, sir

Your Highness's faithful servant,

Thomas Sandford

From my garrison in Briston [sic Beeston] Castle.

10 (December) 1643[15]

With Beeston in their hands, the Royalists spread out across the central Cheshire Plain, gradually closing in on Nantwich. The local Parliamentarian chronicler, Thomas Malbon, wrote, '... so that from the time the Castle was lost ... the town was never in quiet, neither did they go to bed either day or night.'[16] On 17 December Major James Lothian, a Scottish professional soldier who was one of Brereton's most capable commanders, sortied out of Nantwich with a party of horse towards Burford: 'Where Colonel Marrow's Regiment of Horse (consisting of many gallant young Cheshire Gentlemen) gave Major Lothian the meeting, and after a short bickering took Lothian prisoner, and about 12 more, sixteen were slain in the place, and the whole

---

14 Lancaster, op. cit.
15 Warburton, vol. II. p. 337.
16 Malbon, p. 92.

party driven back with a shameful rout into Nantwich.'[17] The writer boasted that, 'The Rebellion in Cheshire hath had its full Reign, and is now (thanks be to God) at the last gasp.'[18]

Malbon, in Nantwich, wrote that:

> The King's forces advanced towards the Town of Nantwich, into Stoke, Hurleston, Brynley, Wrenbury and all the country thereabouts, Robbing, Plundering and taking every man's goods all the next week after, until Friday the 22 December 1843, upon which day they passed over the River of Weaver, to Audlem, Hankelow, Buerton, Hatherton Blakenhill, Wybunbury and all the rest of the Towns thereabouts. And upon Saturday they marched to Bartholmley, giving an alarm upon the Hall of Crewe.[19]

There now occurred one of the most notorious incidents of the war. Some armed villagers apparently commanded by their minister, had barricaded themselves in Bartholmley Church. Malbon describes what happened from the Parliamentarian viewpoint:

> The King's party coming to Bartholmley Church, did set upon the same; where about twenty neighbours had gone for their safeguard. But Major Connaught (Major to Colonel Sneyd, whom they in the church did take for Lord Brereton) [a local Royalist, unrelated to Sir William Brereton] with his forces by welcome entered the church. The people within got up into the Steeple, but the Enemy, burning forms, pews, rushes and the like, did smother them in the Steeple that they were enforced to call for quarter, and yield themselves. But when this was granted by the said Connaught. But when he had them in his power, he caused them to be stripped stark naked, and most barbarously and contrary to the Laws of Arms, murdered, stabbed and cut the throats of them, viz. Mr John Fowler, Henry Fowler, Mr Thomas Elcock, James Boughey, Randell Hassell, Richard Steele, William Steele, George Burrowes, Thomas Hall James Butler and Richard Cowell, and wounded all the rest, leaving many of them for dead.'[20]

Royalist accounts confirm that a number of the defenders of the church were killed. Robert Byron, writing to Ormonde, said, 'Having made our quarters at Betley, at a convenient distance from Nantwich, the first business we undertook was the taking in of a church, which after summons they refusing to surrender, we took and put all the men to the sword; which hath made the rest love churches the worse since.'[21]

Byron's description was backed in a letter to the Earl of Newcastle, intercepted by the Parliamentarians, in which Lord Byron said, 'The rebels had possessed themselves of a church at Bartholmley, but we presently beat them forth out. I put them all to the sword: which I find to be the best way to

---

17 *Mercurius Aulicus*, (ed. Thomas, 1971), p.731.
18 *Ibid.*
19 Malbon, p. 93
20 *Ibid.*
21 Carte, *Original Letters*, vol. I, p. 34.

7 Bartholmley Church. Scene of the notorious 'massacre' on 23 December 1643. ©Alexander P Kapp, reproduced under Creative Commons licence. Grayscaled. <https://creativecommons.org/licenses/by-sa/2.0/>

proceed with this kind of people, for mercy to them is cruelty.'[22] This seems clear enough, and earned Byron the epithet thereafter in Parliamentarian newssheets of 'Bloody braggadocio Byron'.

But Malbon's account suggests that the course of events was less clear cut. There was clearly confusion among the defenders of the church as to the identity of the attackers. They misheard the name of the enemy commander as Major John Connock, who indeed was major to Colonel Ralph Snead, of Staffordshire, and likely to spare them. In fact, it appears to have been Major John Connaught, of Robert Byron's Regiment of Foot. Realising their mistake after surrendering, some of the villagers barricaded themselves in the tower, and at least one opened fire on the Royalists. Connaught duly smoked them out, and following long established practice in the Irish war, killed at least some of them.

His action was long remembered in Cheshire, and in October 1654, John Connaught was tried at Chester Assizes, charged with the murder of 'several persons' in Bartholmley Church. The trial concentrated on the death of John Fowler, the schoolmaster. Connaught with a battleaxe (worth 6d) had struck Fowler on the left side of his head inflicting a fatal wound. He was

---

22 *Mercurius Civicus, London's Intelligencer*, no. 35, 18–24 January, 1643[4], ed. S.F. Jones (Reading: Tyger's Head Books, 2014), vol. II, p. 26.

found guilty and sentenced to death, and was executed at Boughton on 17 October 1654:

> The matters he died for were clearly proved, and yet he seemed to take great glory in his innocency, and would freely tell of his other sins, as gaming, drinking, nay conjuring [stealing] which were some of them not known, and yet would stand in denial of a thing that was proved.[23]

The Royalist operations continued. As Malbon reported:

> On Christmas Day and St Stephen's Day [26 December] they continued plundering and destroying all Bartholmey, Crewe, Haslington and all the places adjacent, taking all their goods, victuals, clothes and stripped many, both men and women, almost naked. And on Christmas Day, 1643, towards night, another party of the King's forces marched to Sandbach, most cruelly plundering and spoiling everyone.[24]

Even allowing for propaganda, there is no doubt that plundering by the Anglo-Irish troops was both systematic and widespread. The same activities had occurred even in supposedly friendly locations in North Wales and Chester. It may be that their commanders would have been unable to restrain their men anyway, but there is no evidence that they tried.

Any hope that the victims may have had that Brereton would be able to check the onslaught were speedily dashed. The growing threat had caused the Lancashire Parliamentarians to decide to reinforce Brereton with 1,300 men under Alexander Rigby. A rendezvous was arranged at Middlewich.

Colonel Robert Byron initially encountered some of the enemy at Sandbach. As he told Ormonde:

> I doubt not, but before this comes to your Excellency's hands, you will have heard of the carriage of our business with Sir William Brereton at Middlewich on St Stephen's Day; but lest it should suffer any mistake (as it may well do) by such as take it but by report, I think it my duty to give your excellency this following relation … On Christmas Day we rose with the army upon intelligence that Sir William was drawing to a head at Sandbach, a place famous for strong ale. When we came within a mile and a half of the place, we discovered about 200 horse of theirs seeming to make a pass good against us. We drew up in order, and as soon as we were ready, advanced towards them; they instead of making the pass good, drew themselves off and away, and left us their quarter, but not a drop of ale.
>
> This night we lodged at Sandbach, and having sent parties of horse abroad to know what was become of the zealous crew, in the morning notice was brought us they were all at Middlewich, whither we marched directly. We were but three regiments there, Warren's not being yet come up, and Sir Fulke Hunckes's with a

---

23 R. Parkinson (ed.), *Autobiography of Henry Newcombe* (Manchester: Chetham Society, Old Series 26, 1852), p. 51; Peter Gaunt, *Cheshire History No 5*, 1995–5, pp. 18–21.

24 Malbon, p. 96.

regiment of horse remained behind, for the safety of our quarters and baggage. So Col. Gibson had the van, I the battle, and Sir Michael Earnley the rear.

When we came near the town, the enemy were drawn out, twice musket-shot from the town, and had placed themselves in hedges and ditches to as much advantage us as could be. Col. Gibson drew upon my left-hand whither I know not; I fell on right before me, where I saw the enemy most busy. I disputed with them an hour and something more, and could not make them budge. All this while I had never a second; at last I discerned some few of Gibson's men coming, at the same instant I was shot: the enemy (it seems) seeing relief coming, quit, and began to run; but gave fire as they went, till they came to the town, There almost 300 of them took sanctuary in the church; the rest ran through the town, where our horse overtook them, and did pretty good execution upon them; and because we would not be hindered in our pursuit of them, we were glad to give quarter to them in the church. There were slain about 300 and upwards, prisoners 274. We got good store of excellent good arms, and good store of munition: there was hurt of my regiment myself, three captains, and, and 41 soldiers, whereof 15 killed outright. Captain Farrell and his Lieutenant died the next day. The whole service of that day fell upon my regiment: I pray god they never do worse than they did then.[25]

Mercurius Aulicus added further details, based partly on a despatch from Lord Byron:

On Monday last December 25 his Lordship marched from Betley in Cheshire to Sandbach, and though the Rebels were there, and had many Passes, yet durst not dispute any of them, but suffered his Lordship to quarter there that night, next morning he followed them to Middlewich, where a new force of Rebels out of Lancashire were added to them, in all making up two thousand foot and 500 horse. This double strength out of Lancashire and Cheshire gave them encouragement to withstand his Lordship's march for about an hour and a half at the end of Middlewich, my Lord had but part of two Regiments drawn up to make way through their great body, who notwithstanding before any field pieces were drawn up, shamefully fled into Middlewich. His Majesty's forces entered with them, and presently approached the Church, which was possessed by a company of Lancashire men, who seeing their own forces routed, and their great General Sir William Brereton (according to his custom) running away, begged for quarter, which was granted unto them. In the meantime his Lordship's horse pursued the fugitive Rebels, and did extraordinary great execution upon them; for above 500 Rebels were slain outright (I speak with the least) betwixt 3 and 400 taken prisoners, 5 foot colours, 23 barrels of powder and above 600 arms. Divers of their Army were drawn out of Lancashire, Colonel Ashton and other Commanders of note amongst them, whereof some are taken Prisoners, His Majesty's forces lost only 8 Common Soldiers. Captain Farrell and his Lieutenant are dangerously wounded, and Colonel Robert Byron is shot in the leg, but without danger.[26]

---

25 Carte, *Original Letters*, vol. I, pp. 35–36.
26 *Mercurius Aulicus*, (ed. Thomas, 1971), pp. 749–50.

Thomas Malbon said that the encounter took place in Booth Lane (the modern A road on the outskirts of the town), and that the Parliamentarians withdrew with the loss of 200 dead and prisoners. Other Parliamentarian sources admitted to 30 dead and 100 prisoners.[27]

The Royalists had had a substantial success. Robert Byron may have been magnifying his own role in the fighting, but his account does give the impression of some reluctance by some of the Anglo-Irish troops.

Brereton evidently retreated with the Lancashire troops, and the garrison at Northwich was abandoned. Byron could now steadily tighten his pressure on Nantwich. His next target was Crewe Hall, which had been garrisoned by the Parliamentarians.

> The King's forces laid great Siege against the same house, and on St James' Day [other sources say St John's Day] 1643, in Christmas, they in the house slew from the house about three score of the King's party and wounded many; but the King's party increasing to a very great number, and Nantwich not being able to relieve them, and they in the House wanting both victuals and ammunition upon Innocent's Day at night, not able to hold out any longer perceiving no aid coming to them (although as valiant Soldiers as any were) were enforced to yield up the house, and themselves prisoners to the King's party, having quarter given them, and being in their custody (to the number of one hundred or more) were all put prisoners into the stable and afterwards put into Betley church.[28]

Lord Byron wrote confidently that day to the Earl of Newcastle:

> I have already despatched two messengers to your Excellency to give you an account of my proceedings in these parts. I am now at Sandbach. I have thought fit to acquaint your Excellency, immediately marched towards them, but no that Brereton for the relief of Nantwich had prevailed with the Lancashiremen to draw thence 1500 Foot, which I having notice of immediately marched towards them, but no sooner came in sight of him but immediately, according to his custom he ran away in great confusion; so that now those forces are so dispersed that they are not like to meet together again, and I doubt not by God's assistance in a short time to clear this County (if your Excellency's forces advance towards Stockport) to be able to set footing in Lancashire...[29]

The Royalists continued to close in on Nantwich. Malbon reported:

> On Saturday night the 30th December 1643, about four hundred of the King's forces came back over the water to Wrenbury, and the places thereabouts and in short time besieged the Town round on that side, and another party of them were at Wistaston, Willaston, and the rest of the town on that side.[30]

---

27 Malbon, p. 96.
28 *Ibid.*
29 *Ibid.*, p. 94; *Mercurius Civicus*, no. 35, 18–24 January, 1643[4] (ed. Jones, vol. II), p. 26.
30 Malbon, op. cit.

Byron established his headquarters at Wistaston and prepared to reduce the remaining two outposts of the Nantwich garrison at Acton Church and Dorfold Hall.

On 2 January the Royalists occupied Dorfold Hall without resistance:

> … so that those in the town were enforced to tend the walls both day and night. But Acton Church was kept with a reasonable force by Captain Sadler, sent forth of the town, who did defend it very manfully against many assaults and cannon shots made by the King's party. From the Church the Parliament party killed the cannonier, and two more of them. And also the Widow Paum dwelling near the church and five of them in her house also slain with shot were slain from the church.[31]

At about this time, Sir Nicholas Byron wrote confidently to Prince Rupert:

> I am pleased to send here enclosed a relation of our proceedings since my last to your Highness, since these parts are in a manner cleared, for Nantwich is in much pain and frets underhand. So the settling of the business is the greatest work to be done in Cheshire, Shropshire and North Wales, upon which my Lord Byron intends to march for Lancashire, this last blow [Middlewich] having made a fair way for his design there. At his departure I hope it will not be thought fit that I should be left at Chester, under the command of the Mayor and his regiment of citizens, and if at last I be thought capable of a regiment of foot of my own, I must humbly acknowledge the favour from your Highness, though it would seem

8 Crewe Hall, home to the Parliamentarian Crewe family. Captured by the Royalists during their approach to Nantwich. ('Crewe Hall at the time of Sir Randulph Crewe' (1558–1646), in *Bartholmley: In Letters From a Former Rector to his Eldest Son*. London: (Longman et al., 1856), facing p.324).

---

31 *Ibid.*

strange a place of that consequence, and castles depending on it, should be left, guarded by citizens, which would invite incursions to be made into the county by parties of the rebels, if not otherwise protected. I humbly crave your highness … that I may have a commission to raise 1,000 or 1,200 foot for the defence of that government I am entrusted withall …[32]

In theory Ormonde was still regarded as the intended general of the army from Ireland, though on 6 January command in Wales and the Marches was instead given to Prince Rupert. Byron may have known that this was likely when on 5 January he wrote to Ormonde:

At the first landing of these forces your Excellency sent out of Ireland, there was so much difficulty to provide them with necessaries, that I thought fit to acquaint your Excellency with it, lest the sending over of more too suddenly might cause some great inconvenience, but now that it hath pleased God to bless this army with so good success, that instead of being confined to a little nook, we are now masters of almost all the County, have beaten Brereton in the field, taken all the castles and towns, excepting Nantwich, before which we now lie, and hope in a short time to gain. I suppose Your Excellency, if you please send over the rest of the forces that allotted for this part of the kingdom, and doubt not but there will be sufficient contribution for their maintenance, or the rather because an invasion from Scotland daily expected here, as the only means to support the decaying rebellion, and which is likely to receive the greatest opposition from this Army of your Excellency…[33]

Ormonde replied on 16 January:

My Lord,

His majesty's choice of your lordship to command in those parts, and over the men I had the good fortune to send so seasonably to his service, I find generally approved, and that approbation confirmed by the happy success of your conduct in the defeat of those rebellious forces, that before your coming, and the arrival of these men, had upon the matter possessed these counties, and strucken fear into others. In all this I conceive infinite satisfaction, and next to the prosperity of his majesty's just aims, in nothing than in that it hath pleased him to direct my endeavours into a hand that is so like to improve them in his service, and to whom I desire so much to be known by all the particular services and offices of friendship I shall be able to do.

There are some reasons that, notwithstanding the difficulty of providing for more men in those parts, induces me to send you two regiments more of foot and four troops of horse. The foot will not be much above 1,000, and the horse not many more than 160.

First I hope that by the happy overthrow you gave the rebels since the date of your letter, you have extended your quarters, and consequently your ability to give subsistence to these men now to be sent; and if you had not, yet I suppose

---

32 Warburton, vol. II, p. 342.
33 Carte, *Life of Ormonde*, vol. VI, p. 4.

this addition of strength will enable you to advance with more security into, and live upon the charge of, the enemy's country.

Secondly, I very much fear, if the sending of these men (for whom I cannot possibly gain a support in this kingdom) should be delayed, there might arrive here some of the rebels' ships, whereby his majesty would not only lose the service they will do him there, but they will be such an overcharge to our little means, that they will endanger the starving of themselves and the rest of the army; or (which is as bad) be seduced to join with a party here as ill-affected as the worse there. The same inconveniences will follow, if I send them not whilst his majesty's fleet is upon that coast to countenance their landing; for when they are gone, it is too probable the Liverpool ships will look out again, if that town be not in the meantime reduced; which I most earnestly recommend your lordship to think of, and attempt as soon as you possibly can, there being no service that to my apprehension can at once so much advantage this place and Chester, and make them so useful to each other.

A third reason is a fresh report of the Scots advancing to the aid of the rebels, in which case I was certified there was an intention to draw those forces to encounter them. If this should fall out to be so, I suppose it may be done with better effect to their interruption, and with more security to what you have so lately reduced, by this access of strength.

Upon these grounds, I shall, with all the speed I can, embark the aforesaid two regiments of foot, and four troops of horse. The foot under the command of Col Broughton and Col. Tillier, the horse under the charge of Sir William Vaughan, for all which your lordship will be pleased to provide, as for men in want of all things, and so used to that want, that I doubt not any reasonable provision will satisfy them …[34]

On 17 January, a letter from Sir George Radcliffe to Ormonde at last resolved the command of the army from Ireland:

After long attendance, and sundry stops removed, about your commission for North Wales and 3 adjacent counties, when I had it ready to be sealed, I was just then countermanded, and forbidden to proceed, for Prince Rupert must have it in all points (so far as I understand) as your lordship should have had it. It was an accommodation for his highness, and no disrespect to your lordship, that caused this change …

The Irish soldiers in Cheshire, who served so cheerfully under your lordship's name and authority, will still, I hope, quit themselves like men under the command of so eminent a person as the prince …[35]

Ormonde was continuing to urge support for the troops from Ireland. On 19 January, still unaware that Rupert would now be in command, he wrote to Sir Orlando Bridgeman (knighted in recognition of his efforts):

---

34 *Ibid.*, pp. 10–11.
35 *Ibid.*, p. 13.

In the first place I shall earnestly recommend it to you to continue your care of that little army that went hence, who have already given such good proof their constancy to the King and courage in his service. Next, I am to inform you that I find it absolutely necessary in relation to our wants here, and perhaps not ill for the King's service there, to send hence with all possible speed two regiments of foot and some troops of horse; for which you will be pleased to make the best provision you can, as for the former, these being nothing inferior to them. If I cannot get shipping for them all at once, I must send them as I can: at this time there cannot go above 1300 foot and 140 horse at the most. How many more the regiments and horse troop will consist of, I cannot certainly tell, but I think not of many; but these will be with you by the next fair wind after this. I shall hasten them, for fear the King's fleet should remove, the Liverpool men get out, or some parliament ships arrive in this harbour, all of which is probable enough, and either sufficient to hinder the sending of any aids hence, when it may fall out to be great use of them; as doubtless there will be, if the Scots come to England.[36]

On 20 January Lord Digby sent Ormonde a rather tortured explanation of the decision to give the command to Rupert instead of to him:

The truth of it is, his majesty finding daily the necessity of your constance residency in Ireland during these distractions, and the impossibility to admit of your absence from thence, without infinite hazard of that kingdom: and on the other side that army requiring some extraordinary person to command it, that might in some measure repair the miss of your lordship, his majesty thought nobody capable of doing that but his nephew Prince Rupert. And therefore at once to remove from your lordship the temptation to come over, and to place somebody in the head of that army, who might correspond to your lordship in quality and reputation, he hath made his nephew general of that army, and of all those countries, and commanded me to acquaint your lordship thus freely with this affairs both there and here seem to oblige him to it … no ways doubting but your lordship will approve of that …

The army hath hitherto been successful and victorious in all its enterprises, as if it had been still animated by my lord of Ormonde's spirit. God continue it the same vigour and good fortune still; for I believe it will fall to its share to be the principal bulwark of this kingdom against the Scots. And your lordship is desired by his majesty to procure and hasten over to it all the additions of strength which that kingdom can furnish, either upon new levies, or out of what you can further spare of the old army: and that you will be pleased to send word speedily what numbers may be expected, and in what time, that we may send back the ships for the transportation of these …[37]

A major factor in the decision to place Rupert in command was his desire to distance himself from the intrigues of the court at Oxford, but some days would pass before he arrived in the Marches, and until then Byron would continue to exercise sole command.

---

36 *Ibid.*, pp. 16–17.
37 *Ibid.*, pp. 21–22.

Meanwhile military operations were continuing. The Nantwich garrison managed to strike back on 6 January, when a raiding party captured a convoy of seven wagons of supplies and ammunition on its way to Byron from Chester. But this was not enough to deter the Royalist attack. During the next few days Byron completed his investment of Nantwich. The Royalists lacked the strength to completely encircle the town, and probably established roadblocks on the routes into Nantwich at Beam Bridge, Wistanston, Dorfold Hall, Acton, and Wrenbury. As Beam Bridge had been demolished by the Parliamentarians, a pontoon bridge was constructed over the Weaver to link the two parts of the Royalist army.

Byron was determined to capture Nantwich before he began the intended advance into Lancashire. By now the weather was probably deteriorating with snow, and Byron has been criticised by later writers for commencing a siege in these conditions. However even Clarendon, who was rarely supportive of actions by the military, grudgingly admitted the importance of taking Nantwich:

> It cannot be denied that the reducing of the place at that time would have been of unspeakable importance to the King's affairs, there being between this and Carlisle no town of moment (Manchester only excepted) which declared against the King, and these two populous counties of Chester and Lancaster, if they had been united against the Parliament, would have been a strong bulwark against the Scots.[38]

Nantwich, with a population of about 2,000, now swollen by refugees, was sited on both banks of the River Weaver. Much of the larger area on the eastern bank of the river had been destroyed in the great fire of 1583, but was mostly rebuilt within two years. Nantwich was the second-largest town of Cheshire, its pre-war economic prosperity based on a livestock market, salt production and tanning.

Nantwich had no pre-war defences. In December 1642 the short-lived Cheshire neutralist movement constructed three small redoubts, each mounting a small gun, at the entrances to the principal streets. Contemporary accounts of the First Battle of Nantwich, in January 1643, make no mention of any defences, but in February 1643 the Cheshire Parliamentarians established their headquarters in the town and began fortifying it, 'and continued … until they had fortified all the Town round about with strong Trenches and mud walls of clods and earth.'[39]

In May 1643 Nantwich's defences had proved able to withstand a rather half-hearted assault by Lord Capel. This was followed during the summer by the clearing of some of the suburbs particularly on the western side of the town towards Acton. In December more of the suburbs were demolished. By now the mud walls and ditches had been strengthened by at least three forts or sconces, covering the entrances of the town at Hospital Street ('Mainwaring's Sconce'), Beam Street ('Lady Norton's Sconce'), and on

---

38 Clarendon, vol. V, p. 231.
39 Malbon, p. 41.

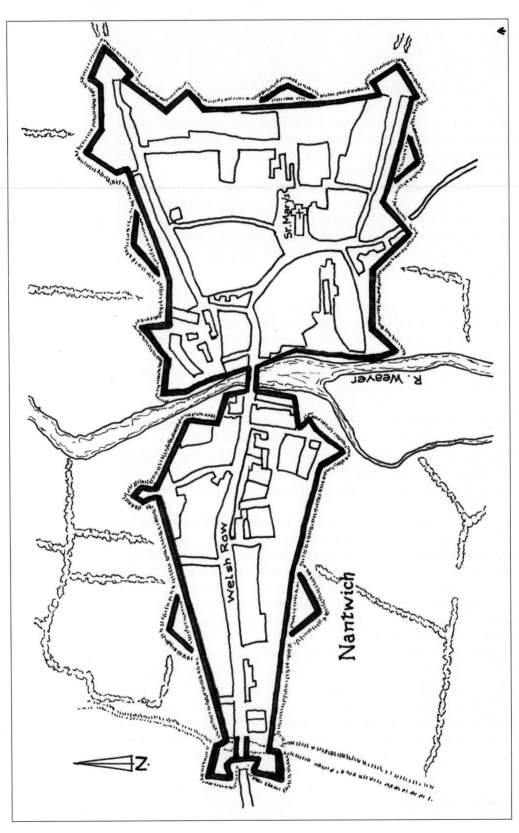

Map 2 The defences of Nantwich.

the north side of Welsh Row ('Wickstead's Sconce'). Other entrances were defended by bulwarks and barricades linked with the mud walls.

On 10 January, believing the morale of the defenders of Nantwich to be low, Byron issued a summons to surrender:

To the Commanders, Soldiers and habitants of the Town of Nantwich

That it may appear to all the world that neither I nor the Army under my conduct, desire the blood and ruin of any (as we have been most falsely and maliciously scandalised in that behalf) but that our chief aims and endeavours are to reduce the people to their obedience to his Majesty, and settle the country in peace without the shedding of blood, I have thought good, before I engage myself upon the town, to let you know:

That I do in his Majesty's name charge and command you, to deliver up the said town of Nantwich, with all Arms, Artillery, Ammunition, and other things therein into my hands, for his Majesty's use; and that all Commanders, Soldiers and others immediately lay down their Arms, and submit to his Majesty's grace and mercy.

I promise pardon to such that shall readily lay down their Arms and submit, and shall give safe conduct to those that shall desire to go to their houses in the Country and will protect both them and the Inhabitants of the Town, their persons and estates, except such as his Majesty hath excepted.

If you refuse such conditions, I shall by God's help use other means for the recovery of his Majesty's rights and vindicating of his and the Country's wrongs. If you, and those many good people, who are forced to be among you shall perish, both your own blood and theirs shall rest on your own heads.

I am content to allow two hours for return of an answer, and admit a cessation of arms on both sides, till that time be expired,

If you will send two men of quality, the one a Soldier, the other a Townsman, to treat with me, or such as I shall appoint upon the time and manner of the render of the Town, I will give safe conduct and caution for their safe return.[40]

The summons was rejected verbally at the entrance to the town, amidst cheers from the garrison.

Byron had meanwhile been preparing his artillery – notably a battery probably including a culverin, which was positioned at Dorfold Hall – and now ordered his guns to open fire.

Malbon recounted:

They, having planted a great piece of Ordnance near Dorfold House, did about 11 o clock in the night, shoot and discharge many gleed [glowing] red bullets into the Town; whereof one of them did light in a hovel of Kidds [logs] of Mr Thomas Wilbraham's, at the upper end of Welsh Row towards Dorfold, and set the same on fire; but through God's mercy and help of many women carrying water and taking great pains (for the men durst not move from the walls) did quench the same; little harm being done. But they [the Royalists] seeing the fire, shot very

---

40 *Magnalia Deo*, in J.A. Atkinson (ed.), *Tracts Relating to the Civil War in Cheshire* (Manchester: Chetham Society, 1844), p. 102.

fast with their cannons at the fire, intending to kill those which came to quench the same, and did kill a daughter of one John Davenport with a Cannon bullet, which was the first that was either slain or wounded in the Town, from the first beginning of the siege.[41]

Spasmodic bombardment continued during the next week, the defenders striking back with a number of sallies. In one of them, the Parliamentarians captured a woman, presumably one of the Royalist camp-followers or traders, who had twenty half crowns in her pocket. On 16 January another raid killed several of the besiegers and captured some arms and ammunition.

Byron meanwhile was facing other problems. An ammunition convoy had been despatched for him from Shrewsbury and as protection from the enemy garrison at Wem, was to be escorted in the later stages of its journey by Sir Richard Willys and his regiment of horse, and that of Marcus Trevor, accompanied by Sir Nicholas Byron.

On the night of 12 January, the convoy reached Ellesmere in Shropshire, and possibly relaxed its vigilance. An officer of Trevor's Regiment described what happened next:

> At Ellesmere Sir Richard Willys and our Regiment quartered. In a very dark and tempestuous night we had our usual guards and a patrol with a Lieutenant and 30 horse abroad. Mytton [Colonel Thomas Mytton, commanding the Shropshire Parliamentarian forces based at Wem] slipped by that party, and fell into the quarters and carried away divers horses and men. Among the rest Sir Nicholas Byron, and I think Sir Richard Willys with two or three of his captains were taken prisoners. Mark Trevor and Sir Thomas Corbet [lieutenant-colonel to Trevor] very narrowly escaped. This lessened our Regiment near 80 horse, but most of the men preserved.[42]

A Parliamentarian account gives further details:

> The rebels [sic] … sent a strong convoy to Shrewsbury for arms and ammunition, both to supply themselves and Chester. The most vigilant and valiant commander, Colonel Mytton, had by his spial secret knowledge thereof, but prudently and providentially made neither motion, nor took any seeming notice of it until they had been at Shrewsbury, where the rebels furnished themselves with eight large barrels of powder, seven hundredweight of match and other ammunition. In their return they quartered the first night at Ellesmere, eight miles from the garrison at Wem, and within fourteen miles of that garrison four thousand more of the rebels were quartered, which I conceive made the convoy over-confident that the noble colonel durst not peep beyond his works, but he that very night, being the 12th of this instant, with a party of horse and foot, in much silence, marched to Ellesmere, and undescried fell upon the enemy in his quarters, where besides what were slain, took prisoners Sir Nicholas Byron, Governor of Chester, Sir Richard Willys, Sergeant Major General of the Horse, with his brother, Major Willys, Captain

---

41 Malbon, p. 103.
42 HMC 12th Report, p. 142.

Ottley, Captain Hatton, Captain Dixon and one other captain, besides a hundred inferior officers and troops, and two hundred and fifty horse and arms, 30 of the horse being the primest in these parts. He took also all the powder, match and arms that the said convoy had furnished themselves withall at Shrewsbury, which renders the exploit more famous and of greater consequence, for in all probability the enemy is in want of powder …[43]

In another blow to the Royalists, a ship carrying munitions from Bristol to Chester was lost when its crew mutinied and took it into Liverpool.

It is unclear how short of ammunition Byron was as a result of these losses, but it may have led to a decision three days later to make an immediate assault on Nantwich, though there were other reasons for haste.

Brereton's defeat at Middlewich had emphasised to the Parliamentarian leadership that local forces alone were unable to meet the Anglo-Irish in battle without reinforcements from elsewhere. Their choice fell on Sir Thomas Fairfax and his 1,800 Yorkshire horse, who had been expelled from their home territory by Newcastle's victory at Adwalton Moor in July, and after assisting the East Association forces at Winceby and the recovery of Gainsborough, were wintering in Lincolnshire. Fairfax was to pick up reinforcements from the Midlands and then join Brereton and the Lancashire forces in the neighbourhood of Manchester.

Fairfax was far from enthusiastic about his mission. 'I was the most unfit of all their forces, being the worst paid, my men sickly and almost naked.'[44] Nevertheless he began his march, hoping to collect en route reinforcements from Derbyshire and Staffordshire.

Unfortunately for the Parliamentarians, Byron had had intelligence of their movements, as he related in a letter of 14 January to Prince Rupert, which acted as a situation report to his new commander:

I received your Highness' letters, which brought me the happy news of the settlement of the command of this army upon your Highness, and the great honour your Highness hath done me in thinking me worthy of the employment immediately under you. The supplies your Highness sends of arms and ammunition will be extremely welcome here, but this I shall humbly recommend to your Highness, that I hold it much safer and fitter for your Highness to make your magazine at Chester, rather than at Shrewsbury, which is a disaffected town, and hath only a garrison of burgesses, who will be ready enough to betray it to

9 Sir Thomas Fairfax, the future Lord General of the New Model Army, was in early 1644 one of the rising stars of the Parliamentary cause. (Frontispiece, C.R. Markham, *A Life of the Great Lord Fairfax* (London: Macmillan, 1870). Engraved by C.H. Jeens, after portrait by Robert Walker and studio).

43 *The Weekly Intelligencer*, 29 Feb 1644, p. 363.
44 Fairfax, *Short Memorials of Thomas Lord Fairfax. Written by Himself* (London, 1699; reprint London: Pallas Armata, 1985), p. 37.

the Rebels, and an old doting fool there as governor, who hath no command at all over them, which I have not had time yet to reform; but I hope your Highness will, when you come.

Our business of Nantwich hath been somewhat retarded by Fairfax his approach to relieve it. So that I was enforced to draw forth almost all the horse I had and 1,000 commanded foot, with them marched towards Newcastle [under Lyme], where I heard they had a Rendezvous, and the same night, sent Marrow with a strong party, who fell into their quarters, took divers of their inferior officers, and above 100 horse and arms, and killed at least as many men, amongst the rest [Denbigh's lieutenant-colonel] who commanded those troops, is thought to be slain; we took Lord Denbigh's lieutenant-colonel's Cornet, and Colonel Graves his trumpet.

But they have requited that loss lately by a strange accident, for upon the report of Fairfax coming with so great a strength of horse, I desired Sir Richard Willys to advance with all his regiment and to convey some ammunition which was coming from Shrewsbury to me, which he accordingly did, and quartered at Ellesmere within 4 miles of Wem, a strong garrison of the rebels, and there lay, it seems, so carelessly, that the enemy at midnight fell into their quarters and surprised most of the officers, amongst the rest my uncle Byron and Sir Richard Willys himself with 8 barrels of powder, which was coming to this army, what other loss they had, I know not, for the news came to me but this morning.

I have not delivered Colonel Gibson his commission [as Major General of Foot] yet, but defer it till your Highness coming have received intimation so to do from my Lord Digby in regard if your Highness thinks fit to make offer of it to Sir Michael Earnley. I hope very shortly to give your Highness a good account of Nantwich, without which all we have done in this county is nothing.[45]

It seems that Fairfax and his Yorkshire horse were not involved in this action. A report in *Mercurius Aulicus* gives some further details:

The Lord Byron, having intelligence of several bodies of Rebels (to make a confluence of forces) marching against him, thought fit to fall on part of them before they came together, and therefore upon notice that 400 horse, belonging to the Earl of Denbigh and Sir Thomas Fairfax were quartered at Newcastle under Lyme, he took what horse could be spared from the siege of Nantwich, and 1000 commanded foot, with which he marched towards them, and on Saturday night last sent a strong party to Newcastle, where the party fell into their quarters, and killed above 120 men, and took above as many horses and arms, having routed all the rest, among the slain the Earl of Denbigh's Lieutenant-colonel is conceived to be one, among the colours that were taken one was Captain Samuel Roper's, whose motto was 'Rubris sanguine ut sanguinem sistas'. This Roper is a Lawyer, steward of the Lord Byron's Courts, whose Lieutenant was here taken prisoner and his Cornet slain. The Carbines and Pistols which were taken were most of them new, and provided on purpose for this design, whereunto they intend to

---

45 British Library Add. MS 18981, f.326.

join all their strength that can be made by the forces of the Earl of Denbigh, the Lord Gray, Brereton, Gell and Fairfax, for the relief of Nantwich.[46]

Writing later to Ormonde, Byron criticised the Earl of Newcastle for lack of support:

Some letters were intercepted from Sir Thomas Fairfax (who was then in Lincolnshire with 30 troops of horse) to Brereton, wherein he assured him to assist him with all that force, and to bring the foot of Staffordshire along with him to join those of Lancashire. Whereupon I acquainted my Lord of Newcastle with the design, and desired him (his army then lying that way) to prevent Fairfax's march; which if he had done, the town had within a few days been delivered up to me. But his occasions drawing him back into Yorkshire, Fairfax immediately advanced into Staffordshire, and being come as far as Newcastle with a good part of his horse, lest he would draw the foot together of that county, I immediately rose with almost all the horse I had, and a party of commanded musketeers, and fell into his quarter, not being above 8 miles from me, took above a hundred of his horse together with their colours and officers, killed and hurt as many more, and drove away the rest in such confusion, that they rested not till they came into Lancashire.[47]

Although Byron appears to have overestimated the damage he had done to Fairfax, both the increased enemy activity, and possibly a shortage of powder for his artillery, may have been key factors in his decision to attempt to storm Nantwich. He was also no doubt concerned by a steady trickle of casualties, and the effects of the by now harsh winter on his men out in the open.

He also had reason to believe that morale in Nantwich was falling. Malbon admitted later that:

The siege thus continuing and the town never in quiet since the loss of Beeston castle, being wholly surrounded by the King's party. So that the Market was lost, and none durst come to Town to bring either any provision or fuel, nor fetch any Salt; nor any issue forth or come in; yet (blessed be to God) there was not for the present any want of any needful thing, although the officers and Soldiers in town, besides townsfolk, were many.[48]

On 16 January Byron sent a second summons:

Whereas I am certainly informed as well by divers of the soldiers who are now my prisoners, as by several other creditable persons, that you are not only in a desperate condition, but that the late summons I sent to the town hath been suppressed and concealed from the inhabitants thereof; and they most grossly abused, by being told that no mercy was intended to be shown by this army to the town, but that both man, woman and child should be put to the sword, I have

---

46 *Mercurius Aulicus*, (ed. Thomas, 1971), pp. 798–9.
47 Carte, *Original Letters*, p. 37.
48 Malbon, p. 98.

therefore thought fit once more to send unto you, that the minds of the people with you may be dispossessed of that false and wicked slander which hath been cast upon this army; and I do charge you (as you will answer Almighty God for the lives of those persons who shall perish by your perfidious dealings with them) that you impart and publish the said summons I sent to the people with you, and that you yield up the town of Nantwich into my hands for his Majesty's use and submit yourselves to his Majesty's mercy which I am willing to offer unto you. Though I am confident that neither of yourselves, nor by any aid that can come to you, there is any possibility for you to escape the hands of this army. If you please to send two gentlemen of quality to me, the one a commander, the other a townsman whereby you may receive better satisfaction, I shall give safe conduct and hostage for their return. I do expect a present answer from you.[49]

This time Sir George Booth, governor of Nantwich, sent a written response:

We have received your late summons and do return this answer; that we never reported or caused to be reported that your Lordship or the army intended any such cruelty, we thinking it impossible for Gentlemen and Soldiers so much to forget humanity: and if any have informed you otherwise, it is their own conceit, and no reality. Concerning the publishing of your former summons, it was publically read among the Soldiers and Townsmen as your Trumpeter can inform you, and since that time multitudes of copies have been dispersed amongst the Townsmen and others, and from none hath it been concealed or detained. For the delivery of this Town, we may not with our consciences, credits or reputations, betray that trust reposed in us for the maintaining and defending this town as long as the enemy shall appear to offend it. Though we be termed traitors and hypocrites, yet we hope and are confident, God will evidence and make known to the world in his due time (though for the present we should suffer) our zeal for his glory our unfeigned and unspotted loyalty to his Majesty and sincerity in all our professions.[50]

The defenders might well have been strengthened in their determination to resist if they had seen two unsent missives from Captain Thomas Sandford, which may have represented the attitude of many of the more zealous soldiers from Ireland.

To the officers, soldiers and Gentlemen of Nantwich these:

Gent, let these resolve your Jealousies. Concerning our religion, I vow by the faith of a Christian, I know not one Papist in our army. Also, so I am a gent, we are not Irish, but true born English, and real Protestants

10 Sir George Booth, of Dunham Massey. Active for the Parliamentarian cause during the Civil Wars, he was to part of the leadership of the uprising of 1659, known as 'Booth's Rebellion'. ('Sir George Booth, of Dunham Massey. Active for the Parliamentarian cause during the Civil Wars, he was to part of the leadership of the uprising of 1659, known as 'Booth's Rebellion'. ('Sir George Booth First Lord Delamer', 1816, engraved and published by Thomas Rodd)

---

49 *Ibid.*, pp. 106–7.
50 *Ibid.*

Born and Bred And know you we intend loyalty towards His Majesty, and will be no other than faithful to his service.

Thus gent, believe from yours

Thomas Sandford.[51]

A second message was written on 15 January:

Gent, your Drum can inform you Acton Church is no more a prison, but now free for honest men to do their devotion therein. Therefore be persuaded from your Incredulity, and Resolve God will not forsake his Anointed. Let not your zeal in a bad cause dazzle your Eyes any longer, but wipe away your vain conceits that have too long led you into Blind error. Loath I am to undertake the trouble of persuading you into obedience, because your erroneous opinions do violently oppose reason among you. But ever (if you love your Town) accept of quarter, and if you regard your lives, work your safety by yielding your Town to the Lord Byron for his Majesty's use; you now see my battery is fixed, from whence fire shall eternally visit you, day and night, to the terror of your old and females and confusion of your thatched houses. Believe me gent. I have laid by my former delays, and am now resolved to batter, burn and storm you. Do not wonder that I write unto you (having officers in chief above me); tis only to advise (because I have some friends amongst you whose safety I wish) that you accept of my Lord Byron's conditions. He is gracious and will charitably consider of you. Accept of these, as a summons, that you forthwith surrender your town, and by that testimony of your Fidelity and Fealty to his Majesty you may obtain favour. My firelocks (you know) have done strange feats both by Night and by Day; and hourly we will not fail in our private visits to you. You have not received my alarums wherefore expect suddenly to hear from Thomas Sandford, Captain of firelocks, from my battery and approaches before your Welsh Row the 15 Jan.[52]

However the first action after the rejection of Byron's summons on 16 January was another sortie by the garrison from the scone at the back of Mainwaring's house towards Bramhall's Barn. Here the Royalists 'had made some walls and works for their preservation. But the Townsmen quietly entered the same, and drove them away, and found some of their clothes; there killed some of them and brought in some Arms and Ammunition, with loss only of one Blackshaw (a good soldier) who ventured too far.'[53]

Next day Byron's guns opened in an intensive bombardment, firing, Malbon claimed, 'four score and sixteen times, but did neither execution nor harm at all.' Byron launched his assault early on 18 January. A copy of the orders issued by Richard Gibson, who was acting as Major General of Foot in place of Sir Michael Earnley, who was sick, gave details of the Royalist plan for the attack on the western side of Nantwich:

---

51 Malbon, p. 107.
52 *Ibid.*, pp. 107–9.
53 *Ibid.*, p. 103.

Major [Hammond], the regiment under his command [Hunckes' Regiment] and the firelocks, with the scaling ladders, they and all the Dragooners, armed with firelocks or snaphaunces, to, fall on first, so near unto the fall of the river, on this side of the Water as may be; on the left hand of the Bulwarks. Then to be seconded with a hundred musketeers. Then a strong body of Pikes, then a reserve of musketeers, and let the Soldiers carry as many faggots as they can. This to be at five o'Clock in the morning. Upon the discharge of a piece of Ordnance. Word God and a Good Cause.[54]

The Royalists aimed to launch simultaneous assaults at three points. The firelocks and dragoons were to move swiftly, mount the defences with their scaling ladders and take the enemy by surprise. But they were spotted, traditionally by a young boy on the walls. The warning gave the garrison and townspeople just enough time to man their defences.

Robert Byron, in his report to Ormonde, infers that not all of the attackers displayed great enthusiasm:

In the neck of this [the loss of the ammunition convoy] we received another great loss by storming the town; which being generally agreed upon by a council of war, was accordingly put into execution. Some of the regiments did very gallantly, and not only entered their works, but my Lieutenant-colonel with some of my regiment got within the town; but for want of seconds, the enemy being very strong within, were forced to retreat to our great loss.[55]

Robert Byron's men probably broke through at the Pillory Street entrance, but the Parliamentarians closed the gap before the Royalists could be reinforced and they had to fight their way out.

A Parliamentarian version of the assault relates that the attack began an hour before dawn, signalled by a cannon shot. It was:

A costly assault; for they left dead at the wall line Lieutenant-Colonel Boulton, one Captain, many Officers, the prime of their Soldiers of the Red Regiment [Warren's Regiment?]; many they cast there into the river, and carried many off dead and wounded. At Wickstead's Sconce was slain Captain Sandford (the threatening man that talked of eternal fire) and his Lieutenant, and some few soldiers besides left, and many carried off slain and wounded. At Pillory Street end, left behind, one Captain, two Lieutenants, two Ensigns, seventeen soldiers of the green regiment, and carried off 60 slain and wounded thence. At the back of Mr Mainwaring's house were left slain two lieutenants, and thirteen soldiers, and many dead and wounded carried off. At the sconce near the Lady Norton's was left slain one Captain and 15 soldiers, besides what were carried off. There are with us of them deadly wounded officers and soldiers 18. One of their own party reports they lost in the assault 300 men, but we understand they lost and had wounded 500.[56]

---

54   *Ibid.*, p. 106.
55   *Ibid.*, p. 106.
56   *Magnalia Deo*, pp. 105–6.

Thomas Malbon, who must have witnessed events, reported:

> Upon Thursday morning directly at Break of day, the King's forces did very fiercely assault the town on every side. But the Town defended themselves, being then ready at the Walls, very valiantly and resolutely to Die, rather than lose the Town, where there was for the space of an hour and something more, very good service performed on both sides. But the King's forces fled when it was fair daylight, no faster than their legs could carry them. Leaving behind them their scaling ladders and many wood kidds (logs), which they had brought with them, and some of their Arms, And about one hundred bodies which they could not take with them (for haste) and many wounded.[57]

The Parliamentarians claimed that a 15-year-old boy shot Sandford (possibly the same one who allegedly raised the alarm), and with his loss his men were discouraged and fell back. One mortally wounded firelock was taken into the town, where he died. It seems that the women of the town played a role in the defence, emptying buckets of hot brine on the attackers.

The Parliamentarians admitted to only three dead and three wounded. Royalist casualties were heavy. Robert Byron's estimate is probably the most accurate: 'Upon this service we lost Lieutenant-colonel Bouton [*sic* Boughton, Warren's Regiment] and Sandford, with four Captains more. Many Lieutenants and Ensigns slain, and divers Captains and other Officers wounded: of soldiers hurt and slain 400.'[58]

The army from Ireland had suffered its first serious defeat.

---

57 Malbon, p. 104.
58 Carte, *Original Letters*, vol. I, p. 41.

4

The Battle of Nantwich

The repulse of their attempted storming of Nantwich on 17 January, did not, publicly at least discourage the Royalist commanders. Robert Byron told Ormonde: 'These were great losses, yet such as we were in hope in a short time to recover again. For all this misfortune our soldiers retained their courage still, which gave encouragement to the continuance of the siege.'[1]

John Byron assured Ormonde that, 'we still block it [Nantwich] up and if it be not speedily relieved doubt not but by God's help to take it, which being got Cheshire is wholly gained and Lancashire not likely to hold out long...'[2]

Clarendon, however, writing after the event, felt the decision was a mistake:

> The seventeenth of January they made a general assault upon five several quarters of the town, somewhat before daybreak, but were with equal courage opposed from within, and near three hundred men lost, and spoiled in the service; which should have prevailed with them to have quitted their design. But these repulses sharpen rather than abate the edge and appetite to danger; and the assailants, no less than the besieged, desiring an army would come for their relief, both with equal impatience longed for the same thing; the Irish (for under that name, for distinction's sake, we call that body of foot, though there was not an Irishman amongst them) supposing themselves superior to any that would encounter them in the field, and the horse being such as might reasonably undervalue those here to oppose them.[3]

It may be true that over-confidence played a part in Byron's decision, but he may equally have felt that continuing the siege was the least worst option. He could expect the foot regiments of Tillier and Broughton, and Vaughan's horse, to join him within days, more than replacing his losses. A retreat to Chester, admitting defeat, would damage further the already shaky morale of his men, and recreate the problem of how to maintain them. Fresh supplies of munitions, including 50 barrels of powder and 50 hundredweight of match,

---

1   *Ibid.*
2   Bodleian Library, Carte MSS, XI, f.9.
3   Clarendon, vol. VII, p. 402.

had been despatched from Oxford on 22 January, and might be expected within a short time.[4]

Furthermore there was reason to believe that the defenders of Nantwich could not hold out much longer. Malbon later admitted as much: 'No market was kept, nor any provision or fuel brought to the own, and many Cattle kept within the walls for fear of plundering, and neither hay nor straw could be had for them, in regard of the great store of horse, for service kept in the Town. So that things began to be scarce both for man and horse.'[5]

Byron also seems to have been confident that the reverses inflicted on the enemy at Middlewich and Newcastle under Lyme had been sufficiently severe to deter, the Lancashire Parliamentarian forces at least from a speedy relief attempt. He had some grounds for this. Fairfax had been unenthusiastic when first receiving orders to go to the aid of Nantwich:

> In the coldest season of it, I was ordered by the Parliament to go and raise the siege of Nantwich; which the Lord Byron, with the Irish Army, had reduced to great extremity.
>
> I was the most unfit of all the forces; being ever the worst paid, my men sickly, and almost naked for want of clothes. I desired the Parliament that they would be pleased to supply these wants: not to excuse myself, as [one] who had no will to stir, though well enough accommodated with all these; and a business of such importance. But their answer was a positive direction to march; for it would admit of no delay: which indeed was as grievous to me as that injunction to the Israelites, to make bricks without straw.
>
> But foreseeing I should have such a return to my desires, I had, seeing the necessity of the business, upon my own credit got so much cloth as clothed 1,500 men, and all ready to march when these orders came to me.
>
> So on the 29 December we got forwards from Falkingham in Lincolnshire to Nantwich with 1,800 Horse and 500 Dragoons; and a Power to call the Regiments of Lancashire and Cheshire to make up the body of the Army.[6]

Thomas Fairfax is often less than reliable in his versions of events and makes no mention of the reverse at Newcastle under Lyme, but he certainly was correct in his depiction of the Lancashire commanders as being reluctant to support him. The leaders of the Lancashire Parliamentarians were divided among themselves and their forces scattered. Brereton was more willing, but his confidence had been shaken by the defeat at Middlewich. However, news of the Scots advance into Northumberland removed any serious danger of a thrust into Lancashire by Newcastle's forces, and undermined the Lancashire Parliamentarians' main excuse for not co-operating with Fairfax.

---

4   *The Royalist Ordnance Papers*, ed. Ian Roy (Oxfordshire Record Society, 1963 and 1975), part II, item 247, p. 327.

5   Malbon, p. 102.

6   Fairfax, *Brief Memorials*, p. 40

Sir Thomas claimed that in any case he found 'more readiness in the inferior officers and common soldiers [and] I got up, in a few days, near 3,000 foot.'[7]

This would have given Fairfax a total of rather more than 2,000 horse if his own force had been intact, and Brereton had had his regiment of horse at full strength. However Robert Byron, who had no reason to minimise enemy strength, gave Fairfax only 1,200 horse. He also had elements of at least six Lancashire and Cheshire foot regiments, which may have totalled 3,000 men. Byron however describes many of them as a 'rabble of cudgelers'. Such hastily levied contingents of miscellaneously armed 'clubmen' had been a feature of the forces of both King and Parliament in the war in Lancashire, and they had also been used by the Fairfaxes in Yorkshire. So Fairfax's strength in effective foot may have been nearer to 2,000, which is the estimate Lord Byron gives in his report to Ormonde.[8]

With some considerable misgivings, Fairfax and his relief force set out from Manchester on 21 January to march through the snow for the relief of Nantwich, believed to be at its last gasp. He noted of his opponents:

> They were Men of Great Experience, who had run through all sorts of services, and were not new to the Policies of War … acquainted with the greatest hardship, habituated to cold and want, and whatever ever suffering a winter siege could require … They were put in heart by their former successes, and that would make them the more desperate, and they were valiant before, being used to nothing but conquests.[9]

It is unclear how well-informed Byron was at this stage regarding Fairfax's movements.

He would later complain that the general hostility of the local population made it impossible to obtain any information other than that gained by sending out patrols of horse, and certainly the behaviour of the Royalists had done nothing to endear them to the civilians. He also evidently considered that the harsh winter conditions would delay any relief march.

There were two principal alternative routes which Fairfax could take. He rejected the eastern, and theoretically more direct way via Middlewich, for reasons which he did not explain. It is very likely that the bulk of the Royalist forces were deployed on eastern side of Nantwich, towards which this route would have taken the Parliamentarians, and by which Byron might have expected Fairfax to march.

Whatever his reasons, Fairfax decided to march via Northwich and Delamere, approaching Nantwich from the north-west, and making slow progress in the difficult weather conditions.

On 24 January Fairfax entered Delamere Forest, then an area of mixed woodland, pasture and bogs. He clashed with a party of Byron's horse, capturing a major and 30 troopers. If he had not already been aware, this

---

7   *Ibid.*
8   Carte, *Original Letters*, vol. I, p. 38.
9   Fairfax, *Brief Memorials*, p. 25.

must have alerted Byron to the enemy approach. Clarendon would claim later that Byron underestimated the threat:

> The Irish, being so over confident that he would not presume to attack them, that though they had advertisement of his motion, they still believed that his utmost deign was by alarms to force them to rise from the town, and then to retire without fighting with them. This made them keep their posts too long...[10]

Byron, not unnaturally, made no such admission. He would, however, have been anxious to give the garrison of Nantwich as little time as possible to forage in the absence of the bulk of the Royalist army, so he had to decide when and where best to engage Fairfax. He told Ormonde:

> So soon as I had intelligence of their approach (which in this ill-affected country could never procure but by parties of horse, which I sent forth) it was resolved we should rise and fight with them, being equal with them in horse, and not far inferior in foot, as having 1,500 to meet their 2,000; withal our men being much impaired by sickness and hurt, and not a few ran away.[11]

This estimate needs some examination. Byron had begun the campaign with 4,000 foot. Since then he had lost perhaps 100 at Middlewich, up to 400 in the unsuccessful assault on Nantwich. A small number, perhaps 200 will have been detached to garrison Crewe Hall, Beeston and any other strongpoints. This would have left him with around 3,300. Clearly some will have been sick, and by now, suffering from the rigours of winter campaigning, there had obviously been desertions. It may well have been that the effects on the soldiers' morale of these hardships and the failure of the 17 January assault had been greater than Robert Byron for one had admitted. But allowing for as many as a thousand losses from various causes, it seems likely that Byron still had 2,000–2,500 foot available.

The Royalist army was of course divided in two by the River Weaver. There were normally three crossing points in the vicinity of Nantwich: one via the stone bridge into the town itself was held by the garrison. The second, about two miles to the north-east, at Barbridge, had been broken down by the Parliamentarians during the course of the campaign, and replaced by the Royalists with a temporary structure. There has been some debate about the nature of this, but most probably it was a wooden bridge of boats. The third crossing, at Shrewbridge, on paper was about two miles to the south of the town, a distance which in practice was considerably lengthened if the water meadows on either side of the Weaver were to be flooded.

It is unclear what proportion of the Royalist army was on either bank. It has been suggested that all of the horse were on the eastern bank, which is unlikely, as we know that patrols had been operating across a wide area. However Byron may have assumed that a relief attempt was most likely to be made on the eastern side. Most of his guns were positioned on the western

---

10 Clarendon, op. cit.
11 Carte, op. cit.

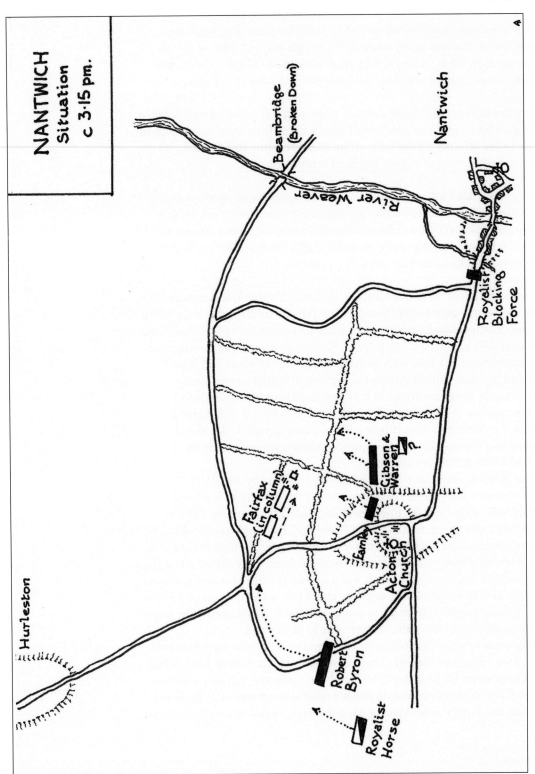

Map 3 The Battle of Nantwich, at roughly 3:15 p.m. on 25 January 1644.

bank of the river, initially with the heavier pieces in a battery at Dorfold Hall, though some lighter pieces were later apparently shifted to the 'works' near Acton Church.

The initial positions of the Royalist foot are also uncertain. Considering that the greater part of Nantwich was situated on the eastern bank of the Weaver, it would have been logical for Byron to have positioned the bulk of his foot there. Robert Byron's Regiment was certainly among them, and most probably Warren and Earnley's Regiments also, leaving Gibson, Hunckes and probably the firelocks on the western side. The weak foot regiments of Tyldesley and Molyneux are not specifically referred to in any accounts, and most likely had been divided up by companies and attached to the weaker of the Irish units.

Byron's own whereabouts are unclear, though he had previously had his headquarters at Wistanton on the eastern side of Nantwich, and may well still have been there. Command on the western bank of the Weaver seems to have been exercised by Richard Gibson, who, with Sir Michael Earnley currently sick, was acting as Major General of Foot.

Byron was aware of Fairfax's approach by the afternoon of 24 January, and probably soon afterwards began moving troops back to the western bank by way of his temporary bridge. It is unclear how many had got across by nightfall. Malbon suggests that the transfer was already in progress:

> Upon thawing of a great Snow … the River Weaver began to Rise. And the King's party, being afraid that the water would take down a platt they had made for their passage over the River, a little below Beambridge, for their passage to relieve the one the other (for Beambridge being a fair stone Bridge, almost but newly made, was a great part of it beaten down).
>
> On the 24 Jan 1644 they conveyed over the River all their Ordnance and Carriages and most part of their horse and foot towards Acton Church.
>
> On the 24 January the river was raised so high that their platt was carried down, and they by no means could cross the River, the one to the other.[12]

Malbon infers that the bulk of the Royalist troops had crossed to the western bank before the bridge broke during the night. Byron however gives the impression that many troops were still on the eastern side, and faced a long detour in the morning to reach the west bank. Certainly some did, including, though he is a little evasive, Byron himself. It would not, however, have quite the effect on the course of events as is sometimes suggested.

It seems most likely that Robert Byron's Regiment of Foot, and possibly Warren's and Earnley's as well, perhaps 1500 men, were initially on the east bank of the Weaver, very likely with at least Byron's Regiment of horse. It also seems most probable that it was some of Warren and Earnley's men, probably leaving small detachments to hold the siegeworks on that side, who crossed back to the West before the plank broke.

---

12 Malbon, pp. 110–111.

The remainder, because of the flooded water meadows, would have to make a detour of six miles before they could cross the Weaver at Shrewbridge. Fairfax halted for the night on Tilstone Heath, eight miles from Nantwich.

Richard Gibson, according to Byron, was 'confident we had advantage enough over them'. It seems that his, or Byron's, original plan was to meet Fairfax about three and a half miles west of Nantwich, at Barbridge, where the Chester road crossed a stream. This would have been far enough away from Nantwich to make an effective sortie by the garrison in his rear unlikely. A blocking force, consisting of the 400 musketeers of Sir Fulke Hunckes' Regiment would be stationed east of Acton Church, covering the crossing of the Weaver from Nantwich itself.

Robert Byron claimed that his brother had intended to place 400 musketeers at Barbridge, planning to stand on the defensive in this reasonably strong defensive location. But in the event only about half that number were in position at dawn on the 25th, and only 100 musketeers blocked the Welsh Row exit from Nantwich. About 1,000 others were initially taking up position across the Nantwich–Chester road in the vicinity of Acton Church. Gibson had placed some of his lighter guns here, possibly, as often suggested, in the churchyard, but more probably in what Fairfax described as the Royalist 'works'. Aerial photographs show traces of a redoubt on the forward slope north-west of the church, which seems a more likely location. Here Gibson would be joined in the course of the morning by the remainder of the Royalist foot as they arrived from Shrewbridge to the south.

Fairfax may be assumed to have broken camp at Tilstone Heath at about dawn (around 7:00 a.m.) and resumed his march. It was about seven miles to Barbridge, where the Parliamentarians must have arrived by mid morning. Finding the way blocked by Byron's outpost, Fairfax 'caused some foot and dragoons to be drawn out to force it, which by god's assistance, they did in half an hour's space, and they took a major and some prisoners.'[13] The assault was spearheaded by the dragoons of Thomas Morgan, whose brother, a lieutenant, was killed in the fighting.

Fairfax's advance guard pushed on to the higher ground at Hurleston, which they reached at about 1:00 p.m. Here, whilst they waited for the rest of their column to catch up, Fairfax and his senior commanders, probably including his brother, Sir William Fairfax, Sir William Brereton, and possibly Assheton or Rigby of the Lancashire forces, held a council of war.

The terrain in 1644 had fewer trees than is the case today, and the Parliamentarians could make out the Royalist position in the vicinity of Acton Church, about a mile away. Some of the Parliamentarian advanced to within cannon shot of the Royalists, (a variable distance, but perhaps about 700 yards). The Royalist guns opened fire, but without effect.

Looking at the enemy position, it appeared to Fairfax and his officers that only about half of the enemy, mainly foot, about 1,000 in number, were as yet in place. Fairfax had now obtained information, probably in a message from Nantwich, of the events of the previous night, and that 'Lord Byron, was

---

13 Fairfax, *Brief Memorials*, p. 46.

prevented by overflowing of the water, from joining with that party at Acton Church; but heard that he was taking a compass to get over the river to join with it.' But the remainder of the Parliamentarian force seems to have been rather slow in joining Fairfax, and as a result 'we gave him [Byron] time to obtain what he fought for.'[14]

This probably means that all of the Royalist foot were now taking up position around Acton Church. The Royalist horse from the eastern bank seem to have arrived last, and as a result could only deploy on the left flank of their foot. Although Byron does not say as much, it clearly would be most likely that he himself had joined Gibson. Whatever he may have thought of Gibson's deployment, it was too late to change it.

It was now about 2:00 p.m., and Fairfax was in a difficult and potentially deteriorating situation. The course of action he now followed has sometimes been misunderstood, and indeed described by one writer as 'attempted military suicide.'[15]

Sir Thomas had always been doubtful of his ability to defeat the Anglo-Irish with only the forces presently under his command, and the idea of attacking the now reinforced Royalist position around Acton Church and thus forcing his way through to the Welsh Row entrance to Nantwich no longer seemed viable.

The alternatives were not greatly more attractive. Fairfax could not stay where he was, and if he retreated, his uneasy composite army might well disintegrate, and Nantwich be doomed. If Sir Thomas attempted to detour either north to the crossing of the Weaver at Church Minshull, or south to Shrewbridge, he might face a contested crossing of the river, he would be moving further away from any possible assistance from the Nantwich garrison, and Byron might take him in the rear.

So Fairfax and his officers decided on the apparently high-risk course of bypassing Acton Church by cutting across the fields to the north east of it, and aiming for the track named Welshman's Lane, and so linking up with the Nantwich garrison at the Welsh Row entrance to the town and possibly offer battle next day if the Royalists chose to remain in the area.

This approach meant exposing the right flank of the Parliamentarian army to possible attack from the Acton Church position as it crossed the fields. It must even then have appeared a high-risk choice. Fairfax was indeed at times a rash commander, whose actions not always met with success, but he must have had grounds for supposing the gamble to be an acceptable one. One reason was that from information he had received, the area between Acton church and the western edge of Nantwich was only lightly held by the enemy, and so a sortie by the garrison might cause the Royalists serious problems. The defenders had been alerted by Royalist troop movements and the sound of their cannonade. So Fairfax could hope for assistance fairly quickly when he began his one and a half mile approach march across the fields.

---

14 *Ibid.*, p. 44.
15 John Lowe, 'The Campaign of the Irish Royalist Army in Cheshire, November 1643–January 1644', in *Transactions of the Historic Society of Lancashire and Cheshire for the year 1959* (Liverpool : printed for the society, 1959), vol. 111.

It was also fairly obvious that although Gibson's men at Acton Church were being reinforced all the Royalist forces had not yet arrived, and would take some time to deploy properly. Fairfax's move might take them by surprise and be completed before the Royalists had time to react effectively. All in all, Sir Thomas must have felt that he had no option but to take a calculated risk.

If Fairfax's plan was to succeed, speed was essential, but once again there was delay. It was necessary to deploy the troops into column again, led by pioneers to cut gaps where necessary in the hedgerows. They were supported by a 'forlorn hope' of Captain John Hodgeson's West Riding of Yorkshire musketeers. The nature and number of enclosures at the time of the battle is unclear. Probably they were fewer than is the case now. There was limited room for manoeuvre between the right flank of the Royalists and the flooded water meadows of the River Weaver, but, as Fairfax reported, 'We resolved to make our way with pioneers through the hedges, and so to march to the town to relieve it, and by it to add some forces to ourselves, to enable us better to fight with them.'[16]

No surviving account states exactly where Fairfax branched off the Chester–Nantwich road and headed across country. He would presumably have wanted to make as short a detour as possible, and we know that his advance forces were already within cannon shot of the Royalist position near Acton Church. It is most likely that the Parliamentarian column struck off across the fields in an easterly direction at the modern junction between the A51 and A534 at Burford, intending to swing south-east and strike Welshman's Lane around the spot known as Welshman's Green and then move towards Welsh Row to link up the Nantwich garrison.

Royalist sources, consisting mainly of the accounts by the Byron brothers, are silent as to how much disarray Fairfax's move may have thrown them into. Lord Byron, without explicitly saying so, implies that he did not arrive on the scene until after Gibson had already deployed the bulk of the Royalist troops. Gibson, he says:

> … was confident that we had advantage enough over them … The place of battle was in an enclosed field, where horse could do little service, and not above a mile from Nantwich; which I fore-warned the Major-General of, and desired special care might be taken lest we should receive prejudice by any sally out of the town, which he assured me he had done, His own regiment had the right wing; my brother's the left; Warren's and Sir Michael Earnley's the battle. Hunckes' Regiment was to wait upon them that should attempt to sally out of the town.[17]

Warren's men had supposedly been encouraged by the recent arrival of George Monck, who had been reassured by a recent audience with the King, and given a commission to raise his own regiment of foot. For the moment he was serving as a volunteer with his old regiment.

Byron's version of events is misleading in a number of respects. He was clearly anxious to push as much responsibility as possible onto Gibson (who,

---

16 Fairfax, *Brief Memorials*, p. 39.
17 Carte, *Original Letters*, vol. I, p. 38.

conveniently being a prisoner at the time, was unable to make his own case), and Byron also gives the impression that the Royalist army was much more formally deployed than actually seems to have been the case. Robert Byron is somewhat more forthcoming: 'Our army was drawn into several enclosures, there our horse (which we were superior in) could do no good, nor we help one another, by reason of the great distance from one another.'[18]

Clearly then, the Royalists were not well deployed. This was probably due to their being forced to form up as units arrived off their line of march. Gibson (or Byron) could have hoped to take advantage of the enclosed nature of the ground to fight a defensive action, but it was not at all what they would have chosen if they had any choice. The horse, judging by lack of mention by any participants of their use elsewhere in the battle, rather surprisingly all seem to have taken up position, as they arrived from the eastern bank of the Weaver, on the Royalist left flank, where the terrain made them somewhat ineffective. This suggests that virtually all of Byron's horse must have been on the eastern side of Nantwich prior to the platt bridge being broken, any on the western bank being too few to have any significant role.

Unsurprisingly, neither of the Byron brothers admits that, despite the still disorganised state of their deployment, their troops took the offensive. In fact, of course, Byron had little option if he were to avoid either abandoning operations against Nantwich, or fighting still more unfavourably, next day after Fairfax had linked up with the Nantwich garrison. It has been suggested that what followed was a spoiling attack which got out of hand, but there is no reason to believe that the Royalists intended anything less than a general attack, which in the event was delivered in a somewhat piecemeal fashion.

At about 3:00 p.m., Fairfax's men had just begun their detour across the fields, moving slowly because of the need to keep together and to clear a path through the hedges. Details of their order of march are sketchy, but it seems that their baggage, and whatever light guns they may have had with them, were in the centre of their column, with in the van, Lambert's horse and Brereton and Assheton Cheshire and Lancashire foot, together with Captain Hodgeson's forlorn hope, The foot commanded by Lancashire Colonel Richard Holland John Booth's Cheshire troops were certainly in the rear, probably with Sir William Fairfax's Yorkshire horse and Sir Thomas Fairfax's own regiment commanded by Major Rousby. The 'rabble of cudgellers' are not referred to in any account of the action. Probably they were in the centre of the column with the baggage and guns.

It is clear that Fairfax's timetable was falling seriously behind schedule, and he received reports of a Royalist force approaching to attack his rear. This was Robert Byron's Regiment of Foot, possibly the last of the Royalist foot to deploy, on their left wing, but not a separate force as Fairfax evidently believed. Robert Byron wheeled right to attack the rear of the Parliamentarian column. At the same time Gibson, with Warren (and perhaps Earnley's, though this regiment may have initially formed a reserve body near Acton

---

18 *Ibid.*, p. 41.

Church) and possibly supported by some of Hunckes' men, extended to their right and advanced towards the head and right flank of Fairfax's column.

There has been much debate in an attempt to fit what we know of the action into the pattern of a conventional battle, with armies drawn up in orthodox formation, or to have Fairfax somehow switching from column, facing right and deploying into line in order to meet a general attack on his flank. Battles are seldom so tidy, and Nantwich was probably significantly confused. What actually seems to have happened were two initially separate engagements about a quarter of a mile apart, between (approximately) the two halves of each army, which it is hoped the following account will clarify.

Seeing Robert Byron's men approaching his rear. Fairfax faced about Holland Booth's troops, and supporting them with his regiment of horse, led them back to engage the attackers. Fairfax left two very brief accounts of what was now happening, which, read together, make the onset of the battle reasonably clear, and also emphasise how the nature of the terrain limited observation of events unfolding. In his despatch of 29 January to the Earl of Essex, Fairfax wrote:

> … but being a little advanced in our march, they [presumably messengers from the rear] told me the enemy was close upon the rear. So facing about two regiments, being Colonel Holland's and Colonel Booth's, I marched not far before I came to be engaged with the greatest part of their army. The other part presently assaulted our front.[19]

In his *Short Memorials* written many years later, Fairfax is slightly more explicit:

> But after we had gone a little way, word came that the Enemy wee in the Rer. So facing about two Regiments and my own Regiment of Horse, commanded by Major Rousby, we relieving those who were already engaged. And so the fight began on all sides. Those that fell on our Rear were those that lay on the other side of the town; which had passed the river. Those that were drawn up under their Works fell on our Van, which was marching towards the Town, Thus was the battle divided; there being a quarter of a mile betwixt us.[20]

It seems that Gibson's men, possibly because they had to align themselves first, and also bearing in mind their alleged performance at the battle of Middlewich in December, attacked somewhat later than Robert Byron, although the two engagements must have begun within moments of each other.

Fairfax, with the two parts of his army now back to back, though separated by a quarter of a mile, and with the baggage and guns, and possibly the cudgellers, forming the 'meat in the sandwich', was under severe pressure.

---

19 Fairfax, *Brief Memorials*, p. 46.
20 Despatch to the Earl of Essex, reprinted in John Dixon, *The Business at Acton* (Nottingham: Caliver Books, 2012), p. 137.

Battle was joined just after 3:30 p.m., and continued for about two hours, until soon after dusk. The initial Royalist attacks seem to have met with some success. Captain Hodgeson, with the Parliamentarian van, admitted that 'much ado we had to get our party into order' for the troops had to hastily deploy into line to meet the advancing Royalists. The Parliamentarian van was evidently still somewhat disordered when Gibson's force came into contact with them. Fairfax said of the encounter between the Parliamentarian van and Gibson: 'they [the Parliamentarians] were once in great danger.'[21] whilst Byron claimed that Gibson's assault 'had much the better of them' forcing the Parliamentarians back, probably towards Fairfax's detachment, and taking a number of guns.

Robert Byron also seems to have had some initial success in his attack on Fairfax's rear though he was rather more moderate in his claims than his brother was, saying that 'Gibson's regiment and mine held them in very good play, and lost nothing by them.'[22] Fairfax, however, suggests that the Parliamentarians were initially in serious trouble: '... we in the other wing were in as great distress, but that the horse, commanded by Sir William Fairfax, did expose themselves to great danger to encourage the foot, though capable of little service in the narrow lanes.'[23]

In his *Short Memorials* Fairfax once again gives a little more detail: 'In the division first engaged, our foot at the beginning, gave some ground, but our Horse recovered this, by beating the Enemy's horse out of the lanes that flanked our foot).'[24] The location of these 'lanes' is unclear, but probably refers to the Chester–Nantwich road and the one leading north eastwards from it towards Beambridge, which were unsuitable for cavalry movements, but in which the Parliamentarians evidently fared better than their opponents.

The whereabouts and actions of the Royalist horse during the battle are obscure. Lord Byron, who may at some stage have been with them, is dismissive of their role: 'The ground was so enclosed the horse could be of little service, and some of them, who were struck with a panic fear, so disordered the rest, that though they did not run away, yet it was impossible to make them charge.'[25]

Clearly, for whatever reason, possibly lack of time to reorganise after their morning march, the Royalist horse performed badly. Although the terrain might indeed have been unsuitable for large-scale cavalry actions, Byron's own regiment had performed well in a similar situation at the First Battle of Newbury. It may be that after their long period of service in the open field during the winter, the Royalist horses were in poor condition.

As it was, the Royalist horse seem to have made some half-hearted probes along the 'lanes' in support of Robert Byron, whose men were fighting in the angle between the two roads, but were quickly deterred, with little actual contact, by Sir William Fairfax and the Parliamentarian horse.

---

21 *Ibid.*
22 Carte, *Original Letters*, vol. I, p. 41.
23 Fairfax, *Brief Memorials*, p. 46.
24 *Ibid.*
25 Carte, *Original Letters*, vol. I, p. 39.

11 Sir William Brereton, Parliamentarian commander in Cheshire. His army was defeated at Middlewich. (From Edward Daniell's *Portraits of the Parliamentary Officers of the Great Civil War*, London, 1873)

In the action between Gibson and the Parliamentarian van division, the foot commanded by Sir William Brereton and Ralph Assheton (the latter apparently supporting Hodgeson's 'forlorn hope' in the hedges) are singled out by Fairfax as performing 'very good service', as did Lambert and Major Copley with the horse. There are no references to any Royalist horse being in action in this part of the field. It may be rather that the threat of attack by the Parliamentarian horse caused the Royalist foot to 'bunch up' defensively, and their attack in consequence to lose its impetus. Certainly this was evidently happening, and both of the Byrons place the main blame for this on Henry Warren's Regiment, and to a lesser degree on Earnley's men. Warren seems to have been on Gibson's left, though possibly in a different enclosure. Earnley's Regiment's position is more uncertain. It may nothave advanced to the attack with the rest (whether on orders or from some other reason), and may still have been in the vicinity of Acton Church. If ordered up in support, it seems to have moved slowly.

Lord Byron wrote that: 'Colonel Warren's men, and Sir Michael Earnley's at the same time (notwithstanding all the endeavours of their officers) retreated almost without fighting a stroke.'[26]

Robert Byron modifies this accusation:

> Warren's Regiment, though they had their beloved Colonel [George] Monck in the head of them, was no sooner charged but they broke, and being rallied again, the next charge ran quite away. Some say they played foul-play and ran over to the enemy, at least 60 of them, and fired upon us.[27]

It is possible that these suggestions were unproven accusations by the Byrons to explain their defeat, but, as we shall see, they seem to have been accepted by the Royalist leadership including George Digby as being the main cause of the Royalist defeat. To some extent the problem may have been foreshadowed by the possibly hesitant performance of some of the Anglo-Irish foot at Middlewich in December, and sagging morale may have been intensified by the losses suffered in the unsuccessful assault on Nantwich on 17 January, and the general hardships of the campaign.

The number of actual defections to the enemy is also unclear, but it is apparent that the two firelock companies of Sandford and Langley took service in their entirety with the Parliamentarians after the battle, and if they were attached to Warren and possibly Earnley, may have chosen this moment to change sides.

---

26 *Ibid.*, p. 40.
27 *Ibid.*, p. 41.

Certainly something of the sort described by the Byrons does seem to have taken place on Gibson's left. A Parliamentarian account, suggested by Dore to have been based upon a lost despatch by Sir William Brereton, said that the action was 'bravely performed on both sides, and the day doubtful for a good space, but at last upon an instance unexpected the enemy gave ground.'[28] This does suggest that Warren and Earnley's men did at least for a time perform better than the Byrons claimed, but does confirm that a sudden collapse took place.

It has been suggested that George Monck was in some way involved in a defection to the enemy, but the fact that he was imprisoned in the Tower of London until December 1646 following the battle makes this highly unlikely. It may simply have been the result of confusion caused by wrong or mistaken orders.

Another possible explanation may have been a shortage of ammunition following the loss of the munitions convoy captured at Ellesmere. On the other hand the Parliamentarians claimed to have captured a considerable quantity of powder after the battle, and match and shot could be manufactured in the field. On the other hand, it is possible that Warren's men at least were employing the tactic recommended by Monck in his *Observations upon Military and Political Affairs* written in 1644. In brief, this recommended deploying the musketeers in three ranks in front of the pikes and loading and firing in situ, without wheeling to the rear. Such a tactic of 'salvee' firing, whilst potentially resulting in a devastating volley, could rebound disastrously if ammunition ran short, or if the enemy stood firm.

With Warren's men in serious disarray at least, some of the Parliamentarian van units were able to advance and begin to put pressure on Gibson's left flank, as well as engage Earnley's already shaky unit. But there was no general Royalist collapse: Robert Byron claimed that 'Gibson's regiment and mine held entire,'[29] though Robert Byron's men were probably anyway under less severe pressure.

So the issue was still in doubt when probably around 4:15 p.m., the Nantwich garrison took a hand. Alerted by the sound, and to some extent the sight, of battle, a force of 7–800 musketeers, probably Sir George Booth's own regiment, made a sortie from the western suburb of Nantwich, drove off the 100 or so musketeers whom Hunckes had placed to guard the bridge over a small stream to the west of the town, and came to the support of Fairfax's embattled men.

Though, based upon Fairfax's rather uninformative wording, it has sometimes been suggested that the Nantwich troops merely reinforced the van of the Parliamentarian army, they actually fell upon the rear of Gibson's foot. This is confirmed by a letter from Sir William Brereton, written in October 1645, when urging that Vaughan's force then marching to the relief of Chester should be engaged at some distance from the town so that the garrison should not attack the Parliamentarians in the rear. He went on:

---

28 Lowe, p. 103.
29 Carte, *Original Letters*, vol. I, p. 42.

> We learnt this by experience upon our enemy, the Irish army, at Nantwich. For our soldiers (when the battle was in hot dispute, the success being very doubtful) issued out of the town and put a period to the debate, fell upon the rear; routed that part of the army and made way for a glorious victory.[30]

Advancing along the Chester road, the garrison musketeers overran any guns in Acton churchyard, and then swung slightly to the right to take Earnley's men in the rear. This regiment collapsed, and Gibson's men found themselves under attack from flank and front. They do not however seem to have been completely surrounded: some at least, including a number officers, held together, and conducted a fighting retreat into Acton Church, the churchyard having presumably been vacated by most of the troops from the Nantwich garrison.

Robert Byron's foot were now alone, and with additional troops coming up to support Fairfax and his rear division, it was time for Byron to attempt to extricate his men from a tight spot. Byron's all musketeer unit effected this with considerable skill, as their commander related: 'It was now high time for my men to think of a retreat, which they did against two regiments of the enemy that pursued them, keeping them off with fire in the rear till they recovered the horse which secured them.'[31]

Robert Byron's force escaped with the loss of only 10 men, though Sir Francis Butler, its lieutenant-colonel, was captured when he rode into an enemy foot unit, having mistaken its colours for his own.

Lord Byron claimed to have remained in the field for another two hours, attempting to recover his baggage and guns, which suggests that they were not in Acton churchyard, but nearer the edge of the battle zone. But as darkness fell, he began his retreat to Chester, with most of his horse intact, but with only about 1,300 of his foot remaining.

On the battlefield Fairfax was completing 'mopping up' operations. Those of the Royalist foot led by Gibson who had fallen back into Acton Church stuck it out through a bitterly cold night, and surrendered at dawn to besiegers who had kept themselves warm by lighting bonfires.

The besieged Nantwich garrison had taken advantage of the transfer of most of the Royalist troops to the western bank of the Weaver to dispose of those, perhaps more disposable local troops rather than his veterans, whom Byron had left to hold the siegeworks on the eastern side of the town. Malbon gives an account of the closing stages of the battle:

> … and the townsmen perceiving [the withdrawal] took advantage of the same, issuing forth into their works, round about that side of the river, towards Beamheath, driving all there away and did level and throw down all their works, and brought in much Hay and fuel. And for fear lest they upon the fall of the water, should have returned again, they fired a very fair new house of Mr Jefrey Minshull's. The Barn, Stable and all buildings belonging to the same; and also

---

30 *The Letter Books of Sir William Brereton,* ed. R.N. Dore (Record Society of Lancashire and Cheshire, 1990), vol. II, item 471.

31 Carte, *Original Letters,* vol. I, p. 42.

another great house of his on the Heath side near Milston lane. [Had] Daylight not failed, there had but few of them escaped: the Night being very dark, the King's party could not be pursued; (as was intended); But the fight being ended, many of the parliament forces be [laid] good fires and continued in the Lady field at Acton Church all night. That part of the King's side which had taken [refuge in] Acton Church and Dorfold House, called for Quarter, which was granted.

There was slain of them about forty; and on the other side but three; nor but few wounded. And thus (through God's mercy and assistance) the Siege was raised, and the Town was preserved from a most bloody and malicious Enemy. All the common sort of the prisoners, to the number of fifteen hundred and more, were put into the Church at Nantwich; where they continued Friday, Saturday and Sunday, maintained by the Town. And the many of them took up Arms for the Parliament, and were listed under Several Captains, and all the wounded were put forth of Town, which were able to go, and some of them died. There were amongst them about 120 women taken also, which were put forth of Town, only some poor women in the Town took the best of their cloths from them which they had gotten by plunder.[32]

Fairfax claimed that the Royalist right wing had lost about 200 dead, which if accurate, was probably near enough the total number of Royalist fatalities. Lieutenant-colonel George Vane (Gibson's Regiment) was incorrectly numbered among them. Prisoners numbered around 1,500, who were imprisoned initially in Nantwich church. About a third of them, including apparently in their entirety, Sandford's and Langley's firelocks, enlisted with their captors. This in most cases, other then it seems that of the firelocks, was a matter of expediency rather than conviction.

Particularly serious were the losses among the officers. *Magnalia Dei* gives a list of their names.

Those who can be identified by regiment are:

Richard Gibson's Regiment
Colonel Richard Gibson
Captain John Atkins
Captain Nicholas Deane
Captain William Sydenham
Captain Arthur Ward

Sir Michael Earnley's Regiment
Colonel Sir Michael Earnley
Lieutenant-colonel William Gibbs
Captain William Long
Lieutenant Thomas Ady

Henry Warren's Regiment
Colonel Henry Warren

---

32 Malbon, p. 114.

Colonel George Monck
Captain John Disney
Captain Fisher
Captain Cooke

Sir Fulke Hunckes' Regiment
Lieutenant-Colonel Edmund Hammond
Captain Robert Bainbridge
Captain George Betts
Captain Litcole [Lydcot, Nicholas]
Captain William Spotswood
Captain William Willier
Lieutenant Hugh Poulden
Lieutenant Rewes
Ensigns Busby, Lewis Humphrey [Capt Greene], John[?] Godsclue
    [Captain Bainbridge]

Robert Byron's Regiment
Lieutenant-Colonel Sir Francis Butler

Firelocks
Captain Syon Finch [probable successor to Sandford]

Lord Byron's Regiment (Horse)
Major Gilbert Byron

Also captured, their regiments uncertain:

Captain Lucas

Lieutenant[?] [Captain William?] Long
Lieutenants Norton, Roe, Paulett, Goodwin, Liverson, Duddleston,
    Pate, Morgell [Morgan], Lestrange, Shipworth, Ankers, Billingsley,
    Castilion, Milner, Bradshaw, Walden, Lyons, Smith

Ensigns Brown, Brereton, Bach, Fines, Arkwright, Davis, Southwood,
    Addiss, Smith, Mahoone, Rise, Dodsworth, Musgrave, Pemicock,
    Dunsterfield, Elliar, Eiclash, Philips, Heard, Thomas, Morgan,
    Budby, Terringham, Wither

Cornets Lee, Carpenter

Quartermasters Lee, Petty

Sir Ralph Done and Colonel Sir Richard Sherlock
Master Shurlock, Chaplain to a Regiment
Twenty 'gentlemen of companies' [reformadoes?]
41 sergeants

40 drummers
63 corporals
4 canoniers
22 colours
Common soldiers 1,500
6 guns, 5 of them brass
20 carriages
Divers of the Wagons
Rich Plunder

Also captured and arousing some horrified interest in Parliamentarian newssheets were:

'120 women, many whereof had long knives'; the implication, which was probably correct, was that many of these women were Irish. Fairfax was evidently rather at a loss as to what to do with them, and they were eventually sent to Wales, their fate thereafter unrecorded.

5

'Mightily in Love with the Irish': Prince Rupert and the Soldiers from Ireland, February–May 1644

After the battle of Nantwich, the inquest.

Byron and the remains of his army withdrew to Chester, unmolested by the enemy. Their return clearly dismayed the townspeople. The Byron brothers meanwhile were informing Ormonde, and presumably the King, of the disaster. Lord Byron told Ormonde that he had:

> … gathered together of several regiments, which were betwixt 1,000 and 1,200, where now we are in a sad condition, the enemy braving us to gates of the city, though with our horse we have hitherto beaten them back with loss to themselves.
>
> All the comfort we can have is the recruit that your Excellency is sending; but truly, my lord, the enemy is grown so strong upon their late success that without a larger supply we shall be able to do little good, and I could wish they were rather Irish than English, for the English we already have are very mutinous, and being for the most part these countrymen, are so poisoned by the ill-affected people here that they grow very cold in this service. And since the rebels here called in the Scots I know no reason why the King should make any scruple of calling in the Irish, or the Turks, if they would serve him…[1]

Robert Byron wrote in similarly pessimistic terms on 31 January:

> We lost all our artillery, munition, and baggage, all our colonels taken prisoners, [Sir Fulke Hunckes seems to have avoided capture] and most of the rest of the officers. We have rallied again of the soldiers about 1,300, and I believe many are yet straggling in the country.

---

1   Carte, *Original Letters*, vol. I, p. 39.

We hear many of the soldiers taken prisoners especially of Warren's, have taken conditions with them. Thus your excellency see what a desperate condition this country is in; which wholly relies upon such supplies as your Excellency shall think fit for our relief.[2]

Byron's explanations for his defeat seem to have been generally accepted among senior Royalists. Ormonde, of course, had always feared desertion or mutiny among the troops sent from Ireland.

On 1 February Lord Digby wrote to Ormonde from Oxford:

This bearer is hastily despatched only to let your excellency know the unfortunate defeat which the Irish army under my lord Byron hath lately received in Cheshire, by Sir Thomas Fairfax coming to relieve Nantwich; wherein, though the numbers lost have not been great, yet the loss of so many gallant officers, as Earnley, Warren, Gibson, Butler and Monck taken prisoners, convert it into a great overthrow, and occasions this sudden despatch to your excellency, earnestly to desire you to dispose all the forces that can be spared in that kingdom to a readiness to come over hither with all speed to supply and recreate that army under my lord Byron.

Colonel Wake's squadron of ships that lies still at Beaumaris, shall have directions to transport them with all possible diligence.[3]

On 8 February Digby assured Ormonde:

I am very glad to hear of the two regiments of foot, and four troops of horse more, which your excellency is sending over; whereof my lord Byron's late defeat makes the necessity more pressing. Though I must needs tell you that the Irish will be much more welcome supplies, in regard that the English there in Leinster being most Welsh and Cheshiremen, are very subject to be corrupted in their own countries, and the treacherous revolt of some of them, was the occasion of my Lord Byron's late misfortune, I must therefore entreat, and press it to your lordship to hasten by all means possible the levies and transportation of Irish, to whom no temptation or corruptives here can be applied.[4]

Digby urged Ormonde to support a previously mooted scheme to raise troops in Ireland: 'I was in good hopes that by this time my Lord Taffe, colonel Barry, Dick Power and Milo Power, would have been in good forwardness with their regiments; towards which the King hath granted them a good proportion of London debts there in Ireland…'[5]

The 27 January edition of *Mercurius Aulicus* also did its best to minimise the consequences of defeat:

… the joint forces of the Earl of Denbigh, the Lord Gray, Fairfax, Brereton, Gell, and others fell upon the Lord Byron, who beat them all back twice with good

---

2 *Ibid.*, p. 44.
3 Carte, *Life of Ormonde*, vol. VI, pp. 28–9.
4 *Ibid.*, p. 33
5 *Ibid.*

execution, till the garrison out of the Town made their way over a Pass and fell on his rear (some others failing in expectation) which disordered his foot so as the horse were forced to preserve themselves (being hindered by the enclosed ground from charging the Rebels) which indeed they did, for of 1,700 horse, the Lord Byron lost not above ten; and the foot made far better shift than could easily have been hoped for in such a Disorder, some betaking themselves to Beeston Castle, some to Holt Castle, others to Crewe House, Doddington House, and other Garrisons near Nantwich, and above 1500 came together in Chester; all which places are still entire to His Majesty; who hath not lost one garrison by the coming of this great rebellious body into Cheshire, who were no sooner there, but as soon went out again; for most of them are since gone back into Lancashire. The hedges which hindered the lord Byron's horse, made amends in his foot, for by means of those enclosures, the foot saved themselves, where the rebels' horse could not follow them. The truth is, there were divers brave Commanders taken prisoners, though none killed or wounded, but Colonel Gibson, who had a light cut on his Arm. Of common soldiers betwixt 5 and 600 (I speak with the most) and about 50 killed, 5 pieces of Cannon and 15 carriages.[6]

As for the captured women, *Mercurius Aulicus* claimed: 'these women with long knives, [were] poor women that have no livelihood but what their husbands fight for against Papists.'[7] As mentioned at the end of the previous chapter, apparently Fairfax quietly released them.

The same writer claimed that as the Nantwich prisoners were being taken to Wem, with the intention of enlisting them in the garrison, 200 of them overpowered their guards, and fled to the Royalist garrisons at Crewe House, Doddington House and Chester.[8]

On 3 February *Mercurius Aulicus* quoted a despatch just received from Byron saying that:

> Since the late fight near Nantwich, he hath very much recruited his Army, forces from all quarters coming daily in unto him, which were scattered to several Garrisons upon the late disorder; insomuch that he was above 1,500 foot and 1700 horse together in a body the very next day after the fight…[9]

This was certainly an over-optimistic view. Writing on 2 February to Prince Rupert, who though Captain General in the Marches was still in Oxford, Sir John Mennes, former General of Artillery to Lord Capel and currently holding a watching brief in Shrewsbury, said that:

> … above 500 of our Irish prisoners [from those captured at Nantwich] have taken up arms for the rebels besides above 200 who came to them before … I have not heard from my Lord Byron since his loss but by a letter writ to the high sheriff and governor [Sir Francis Ottley] which in effect bids us be careful of ourselves, as

---

6   *Mercurius Aulicus*, (ed. Thomas, 1971), pp. 812–3.
7   *Ibid.*
8   *Ibid.*, p. 823.
9   *Ibid.*, p. 815.

he will be for those parts, as that the gentlemen are somewhat troubled they can expect no help from him.[10]

Byron on 6 February was bitter in his complaints to Ormonde:

I must make my humble suit unto your excellency which I hope is sent from court concerning the sending over of a considerable number of Irish natives with as much speed as may be, the English (excepting such as are gentlemen) not being to be trusted in this war, whereof I have daily some sad experience or other for this day Major Lisle and Captain Fisher [Warren's Regiment] to whose care I had [given] the keeping of a house [Crewe Hall] strong enough to have resisted any army, at the least a month, were forced to desist … through the treachery of their soldiers, who upon the first appearance of the enemy before it with a cannon, threatened to kill their officers, unless they would deliver it up, the greatest part of them running over to the rebels, with one Sergeant Hannow, a Scotchman, and the rest running away without any offer of resistance. So that your Excellency may see they will not employ that courage for the King against the Rebels in England, which they did so freely upon all occasions in Ireland, and therefore how requisite it is that a speedy supply be sent of such as we may be confident will not be corrupted. This bearer, Major Verney, is henceforward in this service, and desirous to bring over some men to make up a regiment for myself, for which I shall happily desire your Excellency's allowance in it. The rebels are retreated with most of their forces into Lancashire upon apprehension of my Lord of Newcastle's falling upon them on that side, which if it had been sooner done, had prevented all this mischief. Prince Rupert, I hear is upon his march towards these countries.[11]

The capture of Crewe Hall was part of the mopping up by Fairfax of the isolated small garrisons which had been set up by Byron during the Nantwich campaign. Malbon gives the Parliamentarian version of events:

On Monday the fifth of February, Nantwich forces having besieged Crewe Hall [kept by the King's party] from Thursday before, though at a fair distance, began to assault the House, which when Captain Fisher perceived, who kept it for the King's use, desired a parley, which was agreed unto. That he and them therein should all presently depart, away and yield up the house, leaving their Arms behind them, which they did, being in number (with those which were wounded) one hundred and twenty, and many of them came the same day to Nantwich, where they were entertained. But the Captain had carried himself so basely towards the Neighbourhood thereabout that the Country people would have killed him when he was come forth, had he not been preserved by those to whom he had yielded up the house.[12]

The question arises as to whether the alleged mutiny was directly the result of the garrison being all or largely from Warren's Regiment. There does seem to

---

10 John Lewis (ed.), *May it Please Your Highness*. (Newtown: Jacobus, 1995).
11 Carte, *Life of Ormonde*, vol. VI, pp. 46–47.
12 Malbon, p. 120.

have been a greater degree of disaffection in this unit than some of the others. But the Royalists would also find, when they retook some garrisons which had been manned by deserters or prisoners from the Irish forces, that those same men were ready enough to re-enlist with the King. It is perhaps most likely that their attitude was that of professional soldiers, with no marked allegiance to either side, who acted largely out of self-interest.

There was a similar outcome next day, 7 February, when the Parliamentarians appeared before another of Byron's minor garrisons:

> Dodington Hall, being also kept by the King's party was also assaulted by Nantwich forces, and upon some shot with their great ordnance [very possibly the guns captured in the battle of Nantwich] which they had brought with them, the Captain in the House perceiving, and knowing there was no hope of any Aid, likewise desired a Parley, which was condescended unto. The Agreement was that the house should be delivered up, and the Soldiers and wounded should depart away with forty of their Arm. Whereof the greatest part of them with their Arms came to Nantwich, where they were entertained … the number in all being about [blank]. They left behind them almost two hundred Arms, and good store of victuals, powder, matches and Bullets.[13]

On 16 February it was the turn of Adlington Hall, which after a fortnight's siege surrendered. The garrison of 140 men was given free quarter, and allowed to march away, leaving behind 700 arms and 15 barrels of powder.[14]

However early in February, the Anglo-Irish presence in the Welsh Marches received a strong boost with the arrival of the foot regiments of Henry Tillier and Robert Broughton, about 1,700 men in all, Ormonde, prior to their departure, had said 'not more then 1,700'. Other estimates varied between 1,000 and 1,800, and the four weak troops of horse (160 men) under Sir William Vaughan.

Henry Tillier is a slightly enigmatic figure, sometimes claimed to be a French Huguenot, although in fact the name Tillier had been known in the London area since the fourteenth century. He was evidently a professional soldier with European experience, serving first as a lieutenant in the Cadiz expedition of 1625, and as a captain in 1627 in the ill-fated La Rochelle campaign. After this he was appointed firstly as captain-leader of the Artillery Company of Westminster, and in the same role with the Society of the Artillery Bishops' Wars Tiller was comptroller of the ordnance at Berwick. He went to Ireland in 1642 as lieutenant-colonel to Sir Fulke Hunckes; his regiment was drawn from a number of units in the Leinster forces and may have been an all-musketeer unit. Certainly later in 1644 they were greencoats, and may have worn this colour on arrival in England or been issued with them soon afterwards. Richard Symonds, writing in 1645, confirmed this.[15]

Robert Broughton, of Marchwiel, near Wrexham, was another experienced professional soldier with European experience, who had seen service in the

---

13   *Ibid.*, pp. 120–21.
14   *Ibid.*, pp. 121–22.
15   Richard Symonds, *Military Diary*, ed. Stuart Peachy (Southend-on-Sea: Partizan Press, 1989)

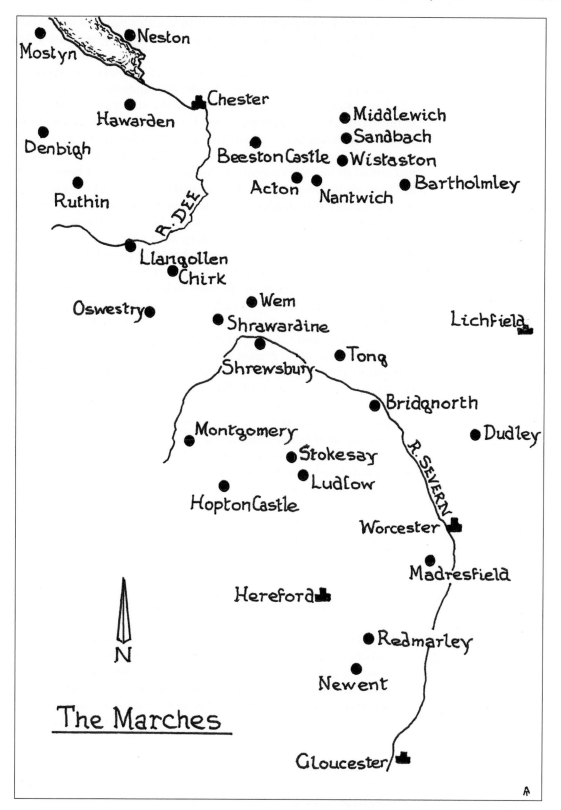

Map 4 The Welsh Marches, 1643–1646. The Marches were to be the principle area of operations for many of the Anglo-Irish regiments.

Bishops' Wars before going to Ireland in 1642 with a regiment largely raised in North Wales. His men may also possibly have been greencoats, at least after refitting at Shrewsbury.

Sir William Vaughan, despite the efforts of a number of researchers, remains a rather enigmatic figure. He attended Shrewsbury School in 1584 which may suggest he was from a branch of the numerous Vaughan family of the Welsh Marches, perhaps, as has been suggested, the Herefordshire/Radnorshire border but no proof this has yet been found. It is also possible, though less likely, that he was connected with the various Vaughans who had settled in Ireland. Vaughan, a professional soldier, had been knighted by Ormonde for his role in the battle of Rathconnell in 1643. A capable and ruthless cavalry commander, Vaughan brought with him to England four weak troops of Sir Thomas Lucas's Regiment of horse, which he would quickly expand. Initially however on 21 February, Byron had to issue an order to the Deputy Lieutenants of Flintshire 'that horses be provided for a regiment arrive from Ireland, many of their horses having been lost on the passage.'[16]

This latest contingent of troops from Ireland landed at Beaumaris and Neston at the end of January or early in February. Byron, partly because of the problems he faced in maintaining the remains of his original army in the depleted area around Chester still under his control, and possibly because he feared the discontent evident among his own men would spread to the newcomers, initially quartered them in the Ruthin area, but Sir John Mennes explained to Prince Rupert on 10 February:

> I have just received a letter from my Lord Byron, which tells me that 1700 foot are landed out of Ireland, under the command of Tillier and Broughton. These his lordship intends to send hither, because they cannot make provision there. I shall endeavour here to make what shift I can to assist them, which must be in providing victuals – for money is a thing we hear not of – if your Highness be pleased to write to the high sheriff, to command him to bespeak hose and shoes for them. I know that may be readily done, or any other thing that is not ready money. We have here about five hundred suits of clothes, which I have stayed for your Highness. They should have been sent to Chester; but their own clothes were good enough to run to the enemy … The foot will be here within five days …[17]

Byron also wrote to the Prince:

> I thought it my duty to advertise you, that the two regiments of foot under the conduct of Colonel Broughton and Colonel Tillier, which landed out of Ireland, are now upon their march towards Shrewsbury, there being no possibility to provide for them here. I gave Sir John Mennes notice of my intention before your Highness came from Oxford, and it will be yet 4 or 5 days before they can be at Shrewsbury. I have given order to some horse to convey them to Oswestry, where

---

16 National Library of Wales, Puleston MSS, p. 308.
17 Warburton, vol. II, pp. 373–4.

your Highness may be pleased to command another convoy to meet them and to bring them to such quarters as you shall please to appoint them.[18]

Next day Byron added:

The Irish foot are now at Ruthin, and from thence will march by the way of Oswestry to Shrewsbury, where your highness may please to command a convoy to meet them, by reason of the garrison at Wem. They will expect the same conditions as the first Irish had, that landed here, which was for all the officers a monthly entertainment, for every common soldier half a crown, a suit of clothes and shoes and stockings. Since their first landing, the officers of the first regiments have received nothing but their month's pay, but the common soldiers have had free quarter, and twelve pence in money, duly paid them every week, which is more than ever they had in Ireland, to which pay I humbly desire your Highness would be pleased to keep both them and all the other foot you have with you, else it will cause a mutiny amongst them that are here, to which they are as inclinable as any soldiers in the world.[19]

Some of the soldiers who had enlisted with the enemy before or after Nantwich were now switching sides again. It was reported at Shrewsbury on 23 February that:

On Saturday three musketeers of the late Irish defeated at Nantwich and gone into Wem, came hither with their arms [whilst] this afternoon 1,500 of the Irish which lst landed in Wales are come into this town. Lord Byron this afternoon came hither whose army as himself affirms is in a very good condition in Cheshire, so that this month we hope to be 7,000 or 8,000 in the field.[20]

There is some evidence that Sir Fulke Hunckes' Regiment had escaped from Nantwich with lighter casualties than might have been expected. In February it apparently had virtually as many men as when it arrived from Ireland:

To the High Constables of the Hundred of Chirk and to either of them For as much as 400 foote souldiers of Colonell Hunckes his Regiment by special order of the Lord Byron be in garrison at the Towne of Wrexham for the defence of this county and are to have free quarter and twelve pence apiece every week the charge whereof amounted to above one hundred and twenty pounds and for payment to be maintained by the Hundred of Bromfield Yale and Chirk in pursuance whereof we have granted warrants to levy and your proportion being forty pounds is to be levied by you. These are therefore in his Majesties name to charge and command you.
    this 24th day of February 1643/4.[21]

---

18 Bodleian Library Firth MS, C.6, f.11.
19 British Library, Add MS 1891, f.51.
20 HMC Portland MS, I, pp. 170–71.
21 BCW Project regimental wiki for Hunckes' regiment < http://wiki.bcw-project.org/protestant/foot-regiments/sir-fulk-hunck?s[]=hunckes>.

But overall, Byron was possibly being rather optimistic. During the Nantwich campaign and following the failed assault on the town 'many cartloads [were] brought to Chester that were wounded and maimed.'[22] The return of the defeated and no doubt embittered soldiers to Chester sparked a fresh round of complaints from the townspeople concerning brawling, theft and general disorder by the soldiers, and again by their womenfolk, including disapproval of their failure to attend church on Sundays.[23] Byron, a strict disciplinarian, cracked down.

> 1643[4]
>
> An Irish soldier was hanged on the gibbet for killing his fellow soldier desperately, in Ram Ashbrooks house Taylor, in Eastgate Street.

> March 17
>
> Another soldier was hanged for making a mutiny on Sabbath day; about the same time another soldier was hanged at two mills on the heath for the like offence.[24]

Byron meanwhile was building up his own regiment of foot, for which he had requested soldiers be provided by Ormonde. On 8 March Ormonde told Digby: '… there went yesterday hence five good companies of foot, consisting of both Irish and English, that are utter strangers to the place they go to.'[25]

These were evidently intended for Byron's Regiment, and may have been collected in Ireland by a recruiting agent, Colonel Thomas Napier. Byron wrote to Ormonde:

> Lieutenant-Colonel Mayne is safely arrived here with the five companies of my Regiment which I must reckon amongst the many other obligations I have to your Excellency. Upon your Excellency's permission to make choice of the field officers of my regiment, some officers of this army recommended unto me, one Captain Till to be major of the regiment, which I unadvisedly, I must confess, assented to being delivered to me, both for a man of worth and experience and well esteemed by your Excellency. But now upon the coming of my Lieutenant-colonel, I was told he is a person so distasteful to the soldiers and of so mean quality that none will serve under him, and therefore shall humbly desire your excellency to approve some other who is fitter for that command may be more acceptable to the soldiers …[26]

If the man concerned was James Till, Byron's doubts were well-founded, as this man later defected to the Parliamentarians. Thomas or Francis Manley, of Erbistock near Denbigh, seems to have been appointed Major. Most of the junior officers apparently were recruited locally, in Flintshire, Denbighshire, Cheshire and Shropshire, where more rank and file may also have been

---

22 Quoted in Morris and Lawson, p. 57.
23 Cheshire Archives, DCC 26 Thomas Cowper, Account of the Siege of Chester, f.32.
24 British Library Harleian MS. 2135, quoted in Morris and Lawson, p. 56.
25 Carte, *Life of Ormonde*, vol. VI, p. 64.
26 Bodleian Library, Carte MS 10, f.544.

obtained.[27] Royalist hopes of more Irish regiments were dashed when the Irish Confederacy denied permission to recruit.[28]

At Shrewsbury, unsurprisingly, Rupert had little trouble from the 'Irish'. One reason probably was that he involved them in action almost immediately. On 4 March he took a force of 800 horse and 600 musketeers from the Irish regiments to surprise a Parliamentarian force at Market Drayton, which included the Earl of Denbigh's horse, and allegedly those of Thomas Mytton and Sir Thomas and Sir William Fairfax. The Parliamentarians were surprised and suffered a number of casualties, although the action was over before the Royalist foot came up.[29]

On 21 March Tillier's men saw more serious action. The key Royalist garrison of Newark on Trent was under siege by Parliamentarian forces under Sir John Meldrum, and Rupert was requested by the King to go to its relief. Speed was essential, and as well as horse, the relief force consisted of 1,000 musketeers drawn from Broughton's and Tillier's regiments, and 120 of Sir Fulke Hunckes', probably under Tillier's overall command. Hunckes had accompanied Tillier and Broughton from Ireland, and it seems that his regiment was now stationed at Shrewsbury.

The foot were transported along the Severn by boat, probably the local Severn 'flats', from Shrewsbury to Bridgnorth where they joined Rupert and the horse. During the successful Royalist action at Newark, Tillier's men attempted to seize a bridge of boats over the River Trent, but were repulsed.[30]

Meanwhile, back in Shropshire, Colonel Robert Ellice, whose Welsh regiment of foot had been routed in November by Brereton and Middleton at Holt Bridge, was joined on 24 March by Sir William Vaughan and his horse

12 Severn flats. The vessel on the right is one of the 'flats' of the type used to carry the Anglo-Irish foot along the Severn to Bridgnorth at the start of operation to relieve Newark in March 1644. (Engraving: 'The Itinerant', engraved by J. Walker, 1798, from an original drawing by C. Catton)

27 Reid, vol. 1, p. 28; BCW regimental wiki.
28 Carte, *Life of Ormonde*, vol. VI, p. 64.
29 *Mercurius Aulicus*, (ed. Thomas, 1971), p. 871.
30 *Ibid.*

in an attempt to regain Apsley House, recently taken by the enemy. After a two-hour bombardment, the garrison surrendered. Ten of the garrison were to be hostages until a number of Royalist prisoners equal to the strength of the garrison were released. However it was stipulated in the Articles of Surrender that, 'It is agreed by both sides that no soldiers that have served in Ireland shall be taken for any of the ten that are to remain prisoners, but may without breach of articles remain in Sir William Vaughan his Regiment, if they will not return to Wem.'[31]

The Royalists were taking the offensive again in the northern Marches, albeit on a small scale. In February Byron had asked Rupert for muskets: 'In a former letter, Your Highness signified your intention to bring 2,000 muskets along with you, if 500 of them could be spared for this place, it would presently put us in a condition to be able to wait upon your Highness in the field.'[32]

On 2 March he told the Prince, ' ... we can make here full 2,000 foot. I want nothing but arms for them.'[33]

Most of these will have been the troops who had escaped from the defeat at Nantwich, together with stragglers who had come in since then. Although Rupert concentrated on filling out the depleted regiments rather than raising new ones, it seems that up until this point Byron had obtained few new recruits. Nevertheless, he was now able to undertake limited operations, and on March 30 told Rupert:

> Since your Highness went hence (Rupert had visited Chester to confer with Byron), I drew forth 500 foot and 600 horse, with a piece of battery, unto that part of Flintshire which lieth betwixt Bangor and Wem [Maelor], from where no contribution will be had, in regard of the many petty garrisons possessed there by the Rebels, but upon the sight of our great gun two of them yielded upon quarter, and the other two were quitted before I could come to them, yet not so, but that a party I sent overtook them before they could get into Wem, and killed them. In these houses we took 200 muskets and 4 barrels of powder and a good proportion of other arms. I am now going to quarter near Wem, which I hear is in great distraction, by which means we shall spare our own and eat up their provisions ...
> I have a humble suit to your Highness that of the arms your Highness hath taken [in the relief of Newark] a proportion may be reserved for the unarmed men at Chester, conceiving it much better for your Highness's service that such as know the use of their arms, have them, rather than new-raised men.[34]

Some of these men were prisoners taken at Nantwich who had been put into the minor garrisons of the northern Marches. These included Cemmeshal[?],

31 *The Ottley Papers*, ed. William Phillips, in *Transactions of the Shropshire Archaelogical and Natural History Society*, 2nd Series (Shrewsbury: Adnitt and Naunton, 1894–1896), vol. V, p. 231.
32 British Library, Add MS 18981, f.95.
33 *Ibid.*
34 *Ibid.*, f.106.

Plate 1: Musketeer, Irish Confederate Army. (Illustration by Seán Ó Brógain © Helion & Company 2019)
See Colour Plate Commentaries for further information.

Plate 2: Ensign, Tiller's Regiment. (Illustration by Seán Ó Brógain © Helion & Company 2019)
See Colour Plate Commentaries for further information.

Plate 3: Pikeman. (Illustration by Seán Ó Brógain © Helion & Company 2019)
See Colour Plate Commentaries for further information.

Plate 4: Cavalry Trooper. (Illustration by Seán Ó Brógain © Helion & Company 2019)
See Colour Plate Commentaries for further information.

Plate 5: Senior Officer. (Illustration by Seán Ó Brógain © Helion & Company 2019)
See Colour Plate Commentaries for further information.

Plate 6: Musketeer. (Illustration by Seán Ó Brógain © Helion & Company 2019)
See Colour Plate Commentaries for further information.

Plate 7: Colours carried by Lord Inchiquin's regiments. (Illustration by Dr. Les Prince © Helion & Company 2019) See Colour Plate Commentaries for further information.

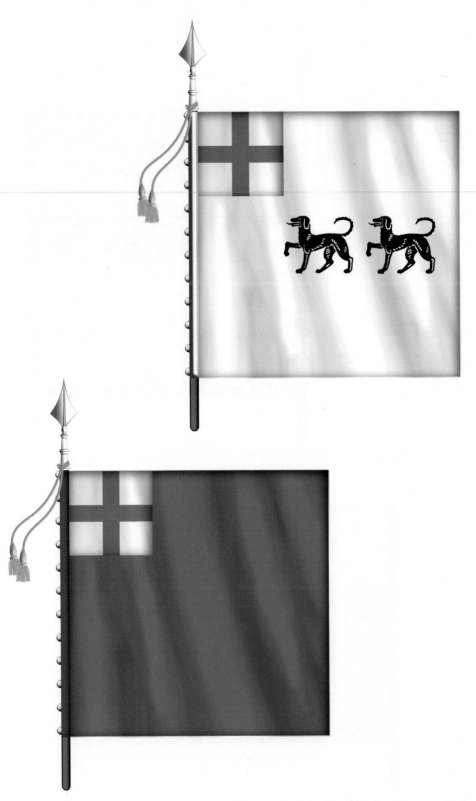

Plate 8: Colours carried by Tillier's and Talbot's regiments. (Illustration by Dr. Les Prince © Helion & Company 2019)
See Colour Plate Commentaries for further information.

Bettisfield and Hanmer. 'They are of those men that came over from Ireland that turned when they were taken prisoners at the Wich.'[35]

According to *Mercurius Aulicus:*

As for the remnant in Flintshire and Denbighshire, the noble Lord Byron hath this week taken both their Garrisons at Hamner. Emerall House was given up upon condition, that they might march away with their lives; but as soon as they came forth all the whole Garrison (except four Common Soldiers and the Captain) voluntarily offered themselves to his Lordship, desiring to be listed, that they might make amends … These two Garrisons had been blamed ten days since for coming to plunder at farne [Farndon] which made them more pliable for submission to the Lord Byron.[36]

It is clear that the Parliamentarians had had mixed success in trying to persuade the Nantwich prisoners to serve them. Fairfax and Brereton had offered some of them to Robert Monroe, commanding the Scots army in Ulster which had not been included in the Cessation, though it is unclear whether this offer was taken up.

The most reliable of the former Anglo-Irish Royalist troops were undoubtedly the firelocks and dragoons, who would become a vital part of Brereton's Cheshire Army (see Appendices II and III).

The Royalists were still hoping to raise more Irish troops. On 21 March Lord Digby wrote to Ormonde:

This bearer, Major Dillon, is desirous that he may have leave from your excellency to raise a troop of horse in Ireland, and transport them hither into England; and entreating my recommendation to your excellency. I could not deny it to him, being a person who, besides his particular relation of near kindred to me by marriage, hath behaved himself very well in these wars. So whatever favour your excellency shall afford him shall go on [my] score of obligation …[37]

There is no evidence that Dillon succeeded in raising his troop, still less transporting it to England, but the King was still hoping for the regiments which he had commissioned Lord Taaffe and others to raise in Ireland.

On 29 March Digby told Ormonde:

Your excellency is desired to express to my lord Taafe and to Jack Barry the particular notice which the King takes of both their affections and industry in his service; as some testimony whereof for the present, his Majesty is pleased to confer upon them and Dick Power … one third part of such Londoners or other rebels debts of this kingdom, as they shall discover for the raising of three regiments of foot for his service over and above another third part due of course to the discoverer, which they have. And … the third part whereof they have made

35   Brereton, Letter Books, vol. II, Appendix XI, p. 596.
36   *Mercurius Aulicus*, (ed. Thomas, 1971), p. 889.
37   Carte, *Life of Ormonde*, vol. VI, p. 65.

discovery, be employed for the arming, maintaining and transporting of these regiments.[38]

The refusal of the Irish Confederates to allow this recruitment made these units stillborn, and indeed transport was an increasing problem. Ships which the Royalists had attempted to send Ormonde with supplies had twice been chased back by Parliamentarian ships. This does not however, indicate that no Irish soldiers joined the King after this point.

There were concerns, expressed a month previously by Byron to Prince Rupert, that the Parliamentarians might make a landing to seize Beaumaris in Anglesey, sometimes used to land men and munitions from Ireland. As a defence against this, Digby told Ormonde:

> This bearer, lieutenant-colonel Trafford, will acquaint your excellency more at large with the resolutions here for the securing of Beaumaris and the adjacent straits of Wales, so necessary for our communications with Ireland, which, in short, concludes in this: in case Prince Rupert approve of it whereof Trafford will certify you, that your excellency will be pleased to send over to Beaumaris three hundred men well-armed, and such a commander with them, as may be a discreet and active man, fit to take the whole charge, as colonel or major-general of Anglesey, Caernarvon and Merioneth.
>
> I believe the bearer hath inclination enough to the thing, but upon very small acquaintance I cannot judge of his fitness.[39]

Ormonde replied on 1 April listing the various difficulties he faced in meeting the King's and Digby's requests:

> I need not tell your lordship how ready I shall be to give all possible assistance to this gentleman [Major Dillon]; the recommendations your lordship hath given him, my lord, may assure you sufficiently of so much. Howbeit, either for the charges in furnishing, or the safety in transporting his troop here to be raised, I cannot, I dare not, be accountable; both in regard of the great difficulties we are here put to for want of monies (the Irish pay in the monies due from them to his Majesty very slowly, and are in great arrears), wherewith fittingly and sufficiently to provide and furnish such forces as otherwise we might supply his majesty hence withall; as also the great hazard they will run in their transportation, whilst the ships employed by the parliament, as it were, block up these coasts some now riding (as I hear) upon the point of Air near Mostyn, betwixt Beaumaris and Chester. The same lately took away some barques, with much scandal and insolency, out of the very port of Holyhead, they being bound hither with provisions for the relief of this place, so as if some reasonable course be not taken from that side of the clearing of these coasts, his majesty's subjects here shall neither have traffic or livelihood from that side, nor his ministers the means to send but there very despatches safely from hence. And these are the two main difficulties why the arms and ammunition, mentioned by myself and Sir George Hamilton, cannot at

---

38 *Ibid.*, pp. 76–7.
39 *Ibid.*, p. 78.

present be speeded hence … For we not only want money to fetch them from the merchants, owners thereof, but safety of transportation for them … until those common spoilers be removed from these coasts …[40]

Meanwhile the troops from Ireland were playing an active role in continued operations in the Welsh Marches. On 30 March. Prince Rupert's Secretary, William Bellenden, reported to him from Shrewsbury:

> By Sir John Mennes' letter, your Highness will understand the success of my Lord Byron's proceedings and ours, and how much our condition is bettered. Monday last we discharged free quarters not without some growling amongst the soldiers, and whereas your Highness did appoint 3s worth of provisions to be given each soldier a week, I have only raised issue so much as comes to 1s 10d, which I did by the advice of some of the officers, it being sufficient with the shilling in money appointed for them; more would have caused a waste. Neither could we, without danger of mutiny, hereafter have lessened the proportion once given them; this I hope your Highness will approve of. There comes in great store of provision, so that we promise your Highness a full magazine of corn at your return …[41]

Rupert was currently in Oxford in meetings agreeing Royalist strategy for the coming campaigning season. On 4 April Byron wrote to the Prince congratulating him on his victory at Newark, and reporting on Colonel Trafford's mission to Ormonde in virtually the same terms that Digby had. He went on to describe his own activities:

> After the Rebels were deprived of their small garrisons in Flintshire I was persuaded to look upon Wem, upon assurance that the greatest part of the garrison had deserted it, but found that only Mytton and his horse was gone out of it, and had left a sufficient strength of foot in the town, which is so fortified and advantageously sited, that I did not think it fit to attempt anything upon it, until I had been provided of materials for it, which may be easily done, the houses being all thatched, and standing very near the works.[42]

Mytton had drawn off his horse, along with troops from Stafford, Longford House and Tong Castle, planning an attack on the Royalist outpost at Lilleshall; he was intercepted by Sir William Vaughan and suffered losses claimed by the Royalists to include 200 dead, and a large number of prisoners.[43]

Exaggerated though this claim probably was, the Royalists felt that the garrisons of Longford House and Tong, with Wem, Parliament's only garrisons in Shropshire, had been sufficiently weakened to be vulnerable. The Parliamentarians felt Tong in particular to be threatened, but Longford House fell first, when it was summoned on 3 April by Prince Rupert, returning from his victory at Newark, 'and instantly it was delivered to his Highness.'

---

40 *Ibid.*, pp. 83–4.
41 Warburton, vol. II, pp. 402–3.
42 British Library Add MS 18981, f. 206.
43 *Mercurius Aulicus*, (ed. Thomas, 1971), p. 915.

Henry Tillier and his regiment were tasked with dealing with Tong. Tillier related the result to Rupert:

> Your highness being absent from these parts, I send this letter at hazard. Upon Thursday last [25 April] I came before Tong, and have taken the Church, the College and the Castle. I began with the Church first, and drove the Rebels from thence into the College the next morning after I came, and finding that they were in a fright I sent a drum to the college to summon them, whereupon they yielded presently, and that day marched away with their Arms: upon which I sent to the Castle to see if they would take quarter which at first they denied. And shortly after there came one running away from the Castle that persuaded me to send once more. And having sent I found that they were wavering, and having parleyed with them the next Morning they marched away. I have put a garrison in the Castle which is a strong place and worth the keeping, but for the College it were better to demolish it, than to be at the charge of a Garrison, for they are do far asunder that they cannot relieve one another. I am now quartered at Shifnal, and the villages thereabouts, till I know your Highness pleasure …[44]

With only Wem still unreduced in Shropshire, Prince Rupert had cause for satisfaction at the performance of the troops from Ireland, and as Arthur Trevor told Ormonde, 'Prince Rupert is mightily in love with the Irish, and counts the loss of the army that came thence into England a maim.'[45]

Samuel Moore, the Parliamentarian governor, may have been unclear what to surrender 'on mercy' actually meant. By the unwritten laws of war, the fate of the prisoners was entirely at the discretion of their captors. They might be spared, or even released, but equally they might be killed. The latter was the fate of all of the prisoners other than Moore himself: they were taken into a cellar and killed by Woodhouse's men. What is less clear are the circumstances in which this was done. Woodhouse and his officers absented themselves, and Moore was told by one of them that the killings had been done on orders 'from Oxford'. In the circumstances, if correct, this almost certainly meant Rupert himself. There were other examples, notably at Birmingham in 1643 and Bolton in 1644, of Rupert's ruthlessness when away from the moderating influence of his uncle, the King, and he may well have wanted an example making of the garrison at Hopton as a warning to others.

It may also be an indication of the unease of Woodhouse and some of his fellow commanders that when the Royalists laid siege to Brampton Bryan Castle, the defenders were allowed to surrender on terms, with Woodhouse expressing his regrets to the Prince that terms had been agreed before Rupert's orders (unstated) had reached him.[46]

Much of April was spent finalising plans for the summer. Byron and Rupert had been under pressure from the Earl of Derby – the unsuccessful Royalist commander in Lancashire, now in 'exile' at Chester – and from

---

44 Lewis, *May It Please Your Highness*, p. 24.
45 Carte, *Life of Ormonde*, vol. VI, p. 87.
46 John Barratt, *Civil War Stronghold: Beeston Castle at War* (Birkenhead: Caracole Press, 1995), p. 132.

13 An antiquarian print of Hopton Castle. Broughton, Tillier and Vaughan had played a major role in regaining the initiative in the Marches for the Royalists, but Prince Rupert's enthusiasm was not shared by many of the inhabitants. Ever since the incident at Bartholmley in December, the war in the Welsh borders had entered a grimmer phase. Another, and most notorious, example of this had occurred at Hopton Castle in March. After withstanding several attacks, the garrison had surrendered 'on mercy' to Royalist troops under Colonel Sir Michael Woodhouse; what followed is unclear, but allegedly all those surrendered were massacred by their captors. Until the winter of 1642/43, when he had returned to England to serve as Lord Capel's major general of foot Woodhouse – a professional soldier – had served in the garrison of Trim, which had been notorious for its ruthless actions. He had raised a regiment in Denbighshire and Shropshire which was known officially for a time as the Prince of Wales' Regiment of Foot. Woodhouse and his men had distinguished themselves, though suffering heavy casualties, at the First Battle of Newbury in September, and Woodhouse had been knighted. Returning to Shropshire, Woodhouse and his Regiment, with other local troops, had been entrusted by Rupert with the capture of Hopton Castle. (Engraved by Samuel and Nathan Buck, 1731. From *Views of Ruins of Castles & Abbeys in England*, 1726–1739, part 2)

14 Hopton Castle, restored and open to the public. (Photo: Charles Singleton)

15 A gun platform forming a possible Ravelin position at Hopton Castle. (Photo: Charles Singleton)

16 One of many cannonball impacts on the walls of Hopton Castle. (Photo: Charles Singleton)

the Lancashire colonels with Byron, to advance into Lancashire to relieve the Countess of Derby, besieged in Lathom House. The Lancashire Royalist leaders promised large numbers of recruits there, and the easy capture of Liverpool.

This, of course, would be a revival of the strategy proposed when the Irish troops first arrived in England, but Byron at least was initially unenthusiastic, as apparently was the Royalist command in Oxford. They (correctly) felt that Lathom House was not in imminent danger, and Byron as late as 4 April was opposing any advance into Lancashire before Rupert's army was fully prepared:

The importunate lord [Derby] is gone to trouble your highness notwithstanding all my endeavours to stay him here, assuring him that your Highness would move towards Lancashire so soon as with convenience you could and sooner no importunity could make you. If it be he will urge your Highness to send me before you, I doubt not, but your Highness will thoroughly consider of the business before you decide.

Besides Colonel Hunckes his regiment, I believe there are here 2,000 foot effective if there were arms for them, which almost half of them want, which I humbly desire your Highness to take into your consideration and to give order for the speedy sending of some arms, whereby we will spare our country and infest theirs …[47]

Byron's reluctance towards what he evidently regarded as a premature move into Lancashire is apparent, but, three days later, his views were changing.

Upon the importunity of the Lancashire gentlemen, I am forced to renew their humble suit to Your Highness that you would be pleased, as soon as you are in a condition to march, to look that way with your army before Lathom be lost; which they conceive may run some hazard, if not speedily relived upon the access of our forces to it from other parts of Lancashire. The constant intelligence from that County every is, that if Your Highness once appear there, the greatest part of the Rebel forces will desert them and join with you and that country being once reduced, all this part of England will presently be clear; the rebellion in these parts being wholly supported from thence.

Yesterday I sent my own regiment of foot to Frodsham, with an intention to have kept that bridge [across the Weaver] but the enemy appeared there so strong that after a little skirmish wherein some men were lost on both sides, we were forced to quit that Town, and to quarter two mile on this side of it, the Rebels having cast up a Work on the other side of the bridge, which we were not strong enough to beat them out of: at the same time I sent a party of horse to Audlem, a town betwixt Nantwich and Wem, where we took 14 of their horse with the men and arms and missed very narrowly some ammunition that was convoying to Wem.

Whensoever your Highness shall intend to march towards Lancashire, your best way from Shrewsbury will be to Whitchurch and [Market] Drayton, and

---

47 British Library Add MS 18981, f.245.

thence to Knutsford which will be a convenient place for me to wait upon your Highness, with those forces I have here, but I shall humbly desire your Highness I may have 800 muskets, which with 200 pikes I have caused to be made here will completely arm these men.

Upon the relief of Lathom, Your Highness will be sure to have Liverpool, whereby the intercourse between these parts and Ireland will be secured, and the Rebel ships, for want of a harbour, not be able to continue upon this coast, and nothing will more daunt the Scots and hinder their designs than to take the support of that country from them.

I have (according to your Highness's command) sent a trumpet to Manchester concerning the exchange of Colonel Monck, who is not yet returned; and this day the commander at Nantwich sent me word, that they would be contented to ransom such of our prisoners for a month's pay as we have no exchanges for, upon promise that they may do the like hereafter for such of theirs as shall be taken; wherein I humbly desire to know your Highness resolution, that accordingly I may return them an answer …[48]

Partly because of a lack of suitable officers of similar rank for the Royalists to offer to exchange, the colonels taken at Nantwich were still prisoners. Monck would remain a prisoner until the end of the war; Gibson, possibly because his sympathies were switching to Parliament, also remained unexchanged, as did Warren. Earnley was exchanged in July.

Rupert evidently shared Byron's thoughts on the importance of Lancashire, and Byron was shortly afterwards sent as Rupert's emissary to Oxford, to press the case for this. One possible reason for this change of heart may have been the unlikelihood of further substantial reinforcements from Ireland.

On 15 April Ormonde wrote to Rupert, telling him that considered Colonel Trafford to be the most suitable commander for the 'three companies, well-armed and commanded', he was preparing to send to North Wales. But much more pessimistically, he told the Prince: 'I hope I shall be able to send 800 or 1,000 good men reasonably well-armed; but without shipping and provision be sent, our wants are such, that I shall be able to do little towards the recruiting the army under your Highness's command.'[49] In a postscript, he added: 'I most humbly and earnestly beseech your highness to make use of your power towards the release of those gallant men that were sent hence, and are now prisoners. Your Highness' favours to me gives me boldness to let you know I cannot be more obliged in the person of any man than that of Col. Warren.'[50]

At the end of April Ormonde told Digby that Captain Bartlett was about to transport Trafford and his men to Beaumaris.[51] But as late as 17 May Parliamentarian naval activity in the Irish Sea was still preventing them from

---

48   John Lewis (ed.), *Your Highness's Most Obedient Servant* (Newtown, Jacobus, 1996), pp. 8–10.
49   Carte, *Life of Ormonde*, vol. VI, pp. 90–1.
50   *Ibid.*, p. 103.
51   *Ibid.*, p. 123.

sailing, especially bearing in mind the recent fate of Colonel Willoughby's men.[52]

By now, Rupert's decision had been made: on 17 May the Archbishop of York told Ormonde: 'Prince Rupert (the only hope for this miserable kingdom) is going to York to fight one battle for the kingdom of England; the consequence is no less.'[53] On the 20th this was confirmed by Secretary of State Edward Nicholas:

> Very great and important occasions have kept Prince Rupert out of Lancashire, and until the Scots shall be repelled he will not possibly have any time to fall into Lancashire, though his Highness says he intends to visit some part of that county in his march towards York, which he began the 16th of this month. God prosper him with good success.[54]

---

52 *Ibid.*, p. 124.
53 *Ibid.*
54 *Ibid.*

6

Marston Moor

With plans for the summer theoretically finalised, Prince Rupert left Oxford on 5 May, and returned to Shrewsbury. On 16 May he set off on the first stage of his northern campaign. Skirting Parliamentarian-held Nantwich, reached Knutsford on the 23rd, after a not particularly rapid march. It is possible, as has been suggested that no final decision had been made whether it would be necessary to march directly to the relief of York via Sheffield,[1] or whether the original plan to move via Lancashire could still be followed.

At Knutsford Rupert was joined by Byron and the Chester contingent, and Byron would later claim that it was on his advice that Rupert decided to move first into Lancashire.

The Anglo-Irish foot were the backbone of Rupert's infantry. Different accounts give slight variations on numbers, but what could be called the Royalist 'Marches Army' totalled in round figures around 2,000 horse and 5–6,000 foot.[2] With the qualified aid of De Gomme's plan of the Royalist deployment at Marston Moor, it is possible to reach some reasonable estimate of numbers.

Rupert had not apparently raised any new regiments since his arrival on the Welsh border, The only efforts had been made to fill out some existing units with new recruits. We have seen that Byron favoured rearming existing troops rather than arming raw levies, and it does seem that this may have been the method used for the Anglo-Irish, resulting in no great increase in their numbers.

The only additional units with the Royalist foot seem to have been Rupert's own Regiment, and Robert Ellice's Welsh Regiment, which apparently returned to the Marches at some point during the Lancashire campaign.

If we estimate this and Rupert's Regiment to have mustered between them up to around 1,200 men, this leaves around 4,800 foot to be accounted for; these must be assumed to have consisted of the Anglo-Irish foot, Tillier's and Broughton's Regiment. Each formed two divisions at Marston Moor, so allowing for losses of a couple of hundred men in the fighting in Lancashire, they evidently began their march with around 800 men each. Sir Fulke Hunckes' Regiment, which had been with Byron at Chester, but not included

---

1   Malcolm Wanklyn, *Decisive Battles of the English Civil War* (Barnsley: Pen & Sword Military, 2006), pp. 107–8.
2   Carte MS 15, f.465.

in his estimate of 2,000 men, had been left at Shrewsbury to strengthen its garrison and act if necessary, with Marrow's Regiment of Horse, as a small field force. To Byron's force should be added the approximately 500 men of his own regiment of foot.

At Marston Moor this formed one division, as did Henry Warren's Regiment, whilst Gibson's and Earnley's were combined in one body presumably of around 500 men. Robert Byron's Regiment of Foot, which probably still mustered around 700 men, had rather surprisingly been left to garrison Liverpool. Allowing for the possibility that one or two companies had been left to stiffen the garrison of Chester, this total of 1,700 men equates reasonably well with Byron's estimate of 2,000 men from the original force sent from Ireland, and suggests that comparatively few new recruits had been added to them, although a number of junior officers and some of the men captured at Nantwich had been exchanged.

So in all, the Anglo-Irish foot with 3,800–4,000 men made up at least two thirds of Rupert's infantry when the campaign began. Without them no attempt to regain Lancashire or relieve York would have been possible.

Byron was uneasy about the way in which the Royalist Marches had been stripped of so many veterans. He told Ormonde: 'This falls out unluckily for the King's affairs in these parts, in [that] the army is drawn hence, before these countries can be reduced, but if it please God to make us successful against the Northern Rebels, I doubt not but we shall easily prevail against all the rest ...'[3] The need to begin the campaign earlier than possibly Rupert and Byron had intended made the advance into Lancashire more important in order to obtain the recruits promised there.

The squabbling Lancashire and Cheshire Parliamentarian leadership failed to unite to meet the threat. Instead of attempting to hold in strength the various crossings of the Mersey, the Lancashire Parliamentarians persisted in their ineffectual siege of Lathom House, so that when Rupert appeared outside Stockport on 25 May he encountered only 3,000 fairly raw troops under Colonel Robert Duckenfield. These were cleared from the hedgerows outside the town by Colonel Henry Washington's Regiment of Dragoons, and the Parliamentarians fled, leaving the bridge over the Mersey free for the Royalists to cross into Lancashire.

Skirting around strongly defended Manchester, Rupert gained large numbers of ill-armed if enthusiastic recruits who were enlisted under the Earl of Derby, Lord Molyneux and Sir Thomas Tyldesley, and swung west, hoping to gain more recruits as he headed for Liverpool.

Henry Tillier, now Rupert's major general of foot, was ordered to take his regiment, with a troop of horse, to secure quarters for the army in Bolton. The town, strongly Puritan, was known as 'the Geneva of the north', and the townspeople had been joined by the 2,000 troops under Colonel Alexander Rigby who had been besieging Lathom, and had been attempting to reach Manchester until their way was blocked by Rupert's advance. Tillier reported their presence to the Prince, and Rupert decided upon an immediate attack.

---

3   *Ibid.*

The defences of Bolton were fairly weak, consisting of little more than stone and earth 'sconces' at the main entrances to the town, and perhaps wooden gates or barricades. The defenders consisted of Rigby's 2,000 men, mainly musketeers, a few horse and about 500 ill-armed 'clubmen'. These were reinforced by around 500 townsmen, armed with whatever was available.

At about 2:00 p.m. on 28 May the Royalists 'appeared at first like a wood or cloud, and presently were cast into several bodies; divers scouts appeared to discover the way for their entrance with most advantage.'

It is unclear whether Rupert summoned the defenders to surrender before ordering an immediate assault. Calling a Council of War he 'rightly judged [Bolton] would make a vigorous resistance.'[4] The attack was mounted at several points by the regiments of Robert Ellice, Sir Thomas Tyldesley, Henry Warren, and Prince Rupert, a mixture of raw levies and veterans. Already hindered by heavy rain, they met desperate resistance. According to a Parliamentarian account:

> Our commanders were very courageous, and our Soldiers very hardy, and both resolved to stand to it, and in the first encounter gave them about half an hour's sharp entertainment, were close in discharge, as the enemies confessed after, and repulsed them bravely to the enemies' great loss and discouragement, and in their retreat cut them down before them in great abundance, and they fell like leaves from the tree on a winter morning.[5]

Though allowance must be made for exaggeration, it does seem that Rupert's Regiment in particular suffered a number of casualties. Warren's and Rupert's men, under heavy fire from muskets and cannon, failed to penetrate the defences. Ellice and Tyldesley did gain a foothold in the town, but were driven back in a counter-attack by a troop of Lancashire horse. Losses were fairly severe, perhaps 200–300 men according to Rupert's *Diary*.

Exactly what happened next has been the subject of some dispute, but it seems that the defenders unwisely chose to execute in full view of the attackers a Royalist officer captured in the assault – perhaps of Rupert's or Warren's Regiment – 'and hung him up as an Irish Papist'. 'Highly provoked', Rupert called a second council of war, and ordered a renewed assault 'forbidding to give quarter to any person then in arms'.[6]

Apparently the only fresh unit available was Robert Broughton's Regiment. The whereabouts of the remaining Royalist foot is unclear. Broughton was supported by two companies of Tyldesley's Regiment, with the Earl of Derby serving as a volunteer. After '[A] Quarter of an Hour's hot dispute, entered the first man himself [Derby allegedly], who being bravely seconded by fresh supplies the town was instantly attacked on every quarter.'[7]

---

4   John Seacome, *The History of the House of Stanley* (Preston, 1793, p. 244).
5   'An Exact Relation of the Bloody and Barbarous Massacre at Bolton', in *Tracts Relating to the Military Proceedings in Lancashire* (Preston: printed for the Chetham Society, 1844), p. 193.
6   *An Exact Relation*, p.197.
7   *Ibid.*

Some Royalist horse found an unguarded entrance to the town, and took the defenders in the rear. The Parliamentarians began to break, many of them fleeing towards the surrounding countryside. Some vicious street fighting followed, as the Royalist horse scoured the streets, driving the defenders back towards the church and market place in the centre of town. The 'Bolton Massacre' would take its place in the forefront of alleged Civil War atrocities. Certainly there was considerable killing of defenders as resistance degenerated into rout. During this there must have been some civilian casualties, though there is only documented evidence of four women, and no children, being killed. The Bolton Parish Church register, which might have been expected to record the burial of any townspeople, lists only these four women, together with the names of 78 men of the town, many of whom were probably actively involved in its defence.

Derby would be tried and executed after the war for killing in cold blood a former servant of his, Captain William Bootle, though he vehemently denied the charge. Most of the verifiable ill-treatment seems to have consisted of rough handling and insults, rather than widespread killing and also considerable looting, which was the inevitable consequence of the storm of any garrison.

About 700 defenders, possibly mainly townsmen, took refuge in the church, and were granted quarter by Rupert. In all Royalist estimates were of 1,000 enemy dead, and 600 prisoners. It can be assumed that the Anglo-Irish played a significant role in the sack of Bolton, though it may be that Lancashire Royalists, partly motivated by religious differences, were guilty of most of the violence.

The Lancashire Parliamentarian forces were widely scattered, and realistically made no attempt to oppose Rupert in the open field. Reinforced by the Northern Horse, and some troops from Derbyshire, the Royalists moved westwards towards Liverpool, their principal Lancashire objective.

Liverpool had not expanded greatly beyond the original limits of the medieval borough. This occupied a peninsula of land which lay between the River Mersey and the great tidal inlet of the Moss Lake Stream which was known as the Pool. To the east Liverpool was overlooked by the sandstone ridge on which stood the village of Everton. To the north were the town fields where the inhabitants grew their crops and grazed their cattle. In all the town probably consisted of about 200 houses, with a total population not exceeding 1,500. The most notable landmark was the castle, with four or five towers and a 30-foot-wide moat. In 1559 it was reported to be semi-ruinous, though not beyond repair.

Liverpool was unfortified on the outbreak of war, and may have changed hands twice before being secured by Parliament in the summer of 1643. Its first governor was a local man, Colonel John Moore, and he began urgent work on establishing defences. The eastern side of the town was largely protected by the Pool, and this was supplemented by other works. They followed the common pattern of earthen ramparts, with mounts or sconces at intervals. In front of the ramparts was a ditch, 36 feet wide and nine feet deep, which ran from north of the Old Hall to the Pool. This would have been strengthened with palisades or storm poles. There were entrances through

PLATE II.

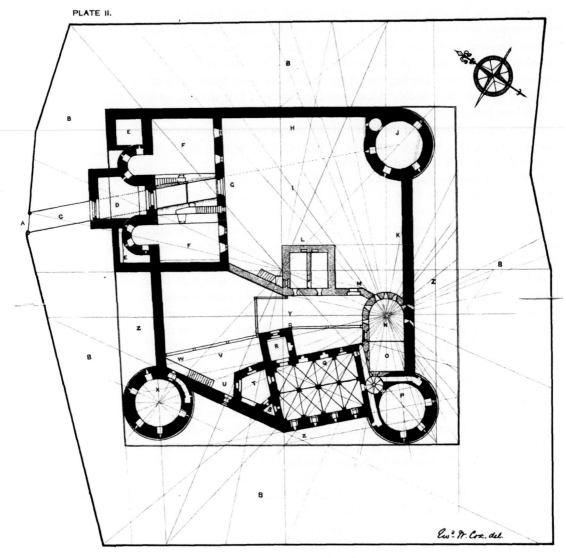

LIVERPOOL CASTLE.

GROUND PLAN.

REFERENCE TO PLAN.

A—Entrance to causeway. Site of long stable.
BBBB—Ditch.
C—Causeway over ditch.
D—Barbican and outer gate.
EE—Square flanking towers to barbican.
FF—Gatehouse.
G—Inner gate. Between the inner and outer gates vaulted passage, with portcullis.
H—East curtain. H marks also probable site of bakehouse and brewhouse.

I—Outer ward.
J—South-east tower, called the "new tower."
K—South curtain.
L—The house covering the well, with two upper rooms used as armoury.
M—Gateway to inner ward.
N—Chapel.
O—Antechapel and screen.
P—South-west tower, called the "prison tower"; and private apartments and main staircase.

Q—The great hall, with vaulted substructure.
R—Porch of hall, with chaplain's room over.
S—Way from butteries below kitchen.
T—Kitchen.
U—West postern, for supplies from river passage.
V—Shed between hall and keep.
W—Stairs (lede) to keep; entrance to cellar below.
X—Keep, called the "great tower."
Y—Covered passage to chapel, called "transsant."
ZZZ—Rock platform.

17 A Victorian architectural drawing of Liverpool Castle prior to its demolition in the late 1890s. No contemporary depictions of the castle seem to have survived. A replica of the castle was to be built by Lord Lever in the 1900s at Rivington, near Bolton. (Plan by Edward Cox, *Transactions of the Historical Society of Lancashire & Cheshire*, 1892, vol. 42)

the defences, covered by cannon, at the ends of Old Hall Street, Tithebarn Street and Dale Street. There were further earthworks and batteries at the approaches to the Pool, and around the castle.

Colonel Moore had made what preparations he could to meet the approaching threat. His foot regiment, and those of the townsmen who were thought fit to be trusted with arms, were reinforced by seamen from the naval flotilla, and by about 400 Scots foot from Meldrum's command at Manchester, who had marched as far as Warrington, and from thence been taken by boat to Liverpool. Large numbers of non-combatants had been sent out of the town, though some still remained, along with the garrison of approximately 1,000 men. Attempts were made to strengthen the earth fortifications with an inner lining of woolpacks to deaden the effects of artillery fire.

Rupert had been joined by a large number of recruits in the course of his march, though he lacked sufficient weapons for them. He and his main force arrived before Liverpool on 7 June, a summons delivered the previous day by a party of horse having been rejected. Looking down on Liverpool from Everton Heights, the Prince reportedly likened it to 'a nest of crows which a parcel of boys might take'. If he actually said anything of the kind, it was probably intended as a morale-raising comment for his troops than as a serious military assessment. A second summons was also rejected, the trumpeter bearing the message having his horse shot under him.

Preparations now began for a full-scale siege, with entrenchments being dug and artillery batteries established on present-day London Road, Copperas Hill and St George's Plateau, and serious operations began with a prolonged artillery bombardment:

> The matter was disputed very hotly until the tenth day of June with musket and great shot without measure out of the town and from the ships, upon which day our line approached within a coit's cast of the gate where our great shot had almost filled the ditch with the ruins of the sod wall, and about noon a furious assault was made by our men where a terrible fight was on both sides above the space of an hour upon the works, the Enemy resolute, ours not seconded retreated with some loss.[8]

It is unclear which troops made the assault, though the Anglo-Irish foot seem the most likely candidates.

It does seem that the artillery bombardment had not been as effective as might have been hoped. Assuming that it began on the 8 or 9 June, it seems to have taken up to 48 hours to create an assaultable breach, whilst in other sieges a few hours sufficed. One reason may have been the deadening effects of the woolpacks, whilst Rupert also lacked the heaviest siege artillery.

Though the site of the assault is not stated, it seems most likely that it was directed against the Tithebarn Street entrance to the town, but was repulsed with some loss. Just how lengthy the Royalist casualty list was is uncertain. The Parliamentarians claimed to have inflicted a total of 1,500 casualties in

---

8   Carte MS.15, f.465.

the course of the siege, but this, comparing for example losses suffered at the siege of Nantwich, is undoubtedly an exaggeration.

What is clear is that Rupert's plans had suffered a setback. Though his losses in men were probably fairly light, and, at least numerically, replaceable, the prolongation of the siege meant that more of his scarce supplies of gunpowder would be consumed.

However all was far from well in the opposing camp. Throughout the next day, as the Royalist artillery bombardment continued, Liverpool's defences crumbled, and the morale of its defenders fell along with them. The degree of commitment of many of the townspeople is open to question, and the terrors of the siege were taking their toll. There must have been many in the town who feared for the fate of themselves, their families and their property if the Royalists stormed Liverpool. They must have felt, and perhaps argued, that it would be better to surrender on terms before this happened.

Up until this point, according to the official Parliamentarian version of events, Colonel John Moore had conducted himself at least creditably in organising the defence. It may be, though few in Liverpool seem to have believed so, that the actions which he now took were motivated as much by a realistic assessment of the hopelessness of the situation as by self-preservation.

At about midnight on 11 June, Moore, together with his officers and some of the men of his regiment, quietly abandoned the positions which they were holding on the north side of the town, and leaving 12 of their colours flying from the ramparts as a feint, quietly withdrew, with as much of their property as they could carry, to the safety of some of the ships in the harbour.

The withdrawal was spotted by Royalist sentries, and reported to Major General Henry Tillier, who commanded the besieging forces on the northern side of the town. He quickly exploited the opportunity, 'which Colonel Tiller perceiving, having the Guard next the Sea [at the northern end of the town] supposing the Enemy to be gone, entered the town with little or no resistance, found about 400 of the meaner sort of men, whereof most were killed, some had quarter.'[9] According to Byron the assault was spearheaded by the 'red regiment', presumably Tillier's, though the colour probably refers to its flags, not its coat colour, which was probably still green.

The attackers were guided by Lieutenant-Colonel Caryl Molyneux, younger brother of Lord Molyneux, who earned a notorious reputation for the supposedly savage part he played in events. It seems unlikely that a systematic cold-blooded slaughter of unarmed civilians was deliberately planned, although feelings were probably running high among Tillier's veterans. In the heat and confusion of the unplanned night attack, coupled with a natural inclination by the Royalists to take no chances, and the desire of the soldiers to have their share of the plunder of the town, which had been promised them by Prince Rupert, increased the number of casualties.

These were undoubtedly heavy, and the episode had a traumatic effect on the townsfolk. After Liverpool had been recovered by the Parliamentarians,

---

9   *Ibid.*

the town council claimed that some 360 died, including 'some that had never borne arms, yea one poor blind man.' Caryl Molyneux, it was claimed, killed seven or eight men with his own hand.

The attacking Royalists pushed swiftly into the centre of the town, seizing the gates and admitting more of their men, including horse. The only serious potential resistance might have been offered by the 400 Scots who had been despatched from Manchester by Meldrum. However they, or at any rate their officers, had no intention of laying down their lives for a lost cause. They drew up in front of the High Cross and also in the castle, and surrendered on the promise of being allowed to return to Manchester.

By dawn on 12 June Liverpool was in Royalist hands.

The expenditure of 100 barrels of gunpowder was one of the reasons for the pause in operations which followed. Rupert also needed time to organise further recruits, who seem for the most part to have been used to fill out Tyldesley's Regiment of Foot or formed into the new regiments of Edward Chisenall and Cuthbert Clifton.

Rupert also began work on strengthening the defences of Lathom House and Liverpool. Part of the garrison of the latter consisted of Clifton's new Regiment, but its strategic importance to the Royalists was highlighted by the addition to the garrison of Robert Byron's Regiment. It may seem surprising that the Prince chose to deny the field army one of its strongest units, but as an all-musketeer regiment, it was well suited for garrison duties. There is a possibility, judging by later evidence of the composition of the Liverpool garrison, that Robert Byron, as governor, was actually given a composite unit formed partly from part of his own regiment and part of Lord Byron's, the other companies of both being given to Lord Byron.

The details of the 'York March' have often been described, and here I will deal mainly with what evidence we have of the role of the Anglo-Irish units at Marston Moor.

There was evidently significant fighting during the afternoon of 2 July, when the Allied cavalry, covering the return of their foot who had begun a withdrawal towards Wetherby, were in position on the forward slopes of the ridge south of the Long Marston–Tockwith road. The Royalist aim was to gain possession of the same ground, as well as the ridgeline beyond, and as the first of their foot, probably the brigade consisting of Prince Rupert's and Lord Byron's Regiments, appeared an attempt was made to push the enemy horse back from their advantageous position: 'The Enemy perceiving that our Cavalry had possessed themselves of a corn hill, an having discovered near unto that hill a place of great advantage, where they might have Sun and Wind of us, advanced thither with a Regiment of Red Coats and a party of Horse,' wrote a Parliamentarian eyewitness.[10]

Given that Rupert's Regiment were bluecoats, the redcoats were probably Byron's foot.

The disputed ground was probably just to the south-east of the village of Tockwith, and consisted of a barely perceptible piece of rising ground

---

10 Captain Stewart's Account, quoted by C.S. Terry in *The Life and Campaigns of Alexander Lesley, Earl of Leven* (London: Longmans, 1899), p. 275.

and a large man-made rabbit warren known as Bilton Bream. Cromwell's Eastern Association cavalry, which formed the left wing of the covering force, 'sent out a party which beat them off, and planted there our left wing of horse.'[11] The failure to secure Bilton Bream was the first significant setback for the Royalists, and Sir Hugh Cholmley was anxious to shift any blame away from Rupert: 'The Prince's Army, ere ever he was aware, was drawn too near the enemy, and into some place of disadvantage, which may be imputed to his commanders that had the marshalling of his forces than to himself.'[12]

By implication both Byron as senior cavalry commander and perhaps Tillier, as major general of foot are indicted, though this remains unconvincing. Preliminary skirmishing had lasted for much of the morning, and it seems unlikely that Rupert was not among the first to arrive on the scene as well as playing a leading part in their deployment. The Royalists problems were caused by the decision of the Allied cavalry commanders to stand firm on their success in denying their opponents, who attacked piecemeal as their troops came up, control of the advantageous ground around Bilton Bream.

As a result the Royalists were forced to deploy on the open moor, about 500 yards north of the ridge. It is clear that for most of the morning Rupert hoped to be able to launch a full-scale attack on the ridge before the Allied foot returned in strength. As a result he naturally occupied a position as close to the enemy as was practicable, but felt unable to take the offensive until the Northern foot arrived.

If we assume that De Gomme's plan gives an accurate picture of how the Royalists actually deployed, which may not of course be entirely the case, the Anglo-Irish foot, supplemented by Tyldesley's Regiment, formed the front line of Rupert's centre. From right to left came Warren's Regiment, commanded by Lieutenant-Colonel Francis Lisle,[13] and possibly numbering no more than 500 men in one division. To its right was Tyldesley's Regiment, about 1,000 men though including many raw recruits. To Tyldesley's right, and together with him forming the centre of the first line was Robert Broughton's strong regiment, again with around 1,000 men, which may suggest that, unlike the Anglo-Irish units with Byron at Chester, it had received some new recruits. Next came Earnley's and Gibson's Regiments, brigaded together, and again probably no more than 500 men. Probably Lieutenant-Colonel George Vane was in command, with Major Palmer as senior officer of Earnley's. On the far right came Tillier's own regiment, possibly under the operational command of Lieutenant-Colonel Hammond, and again around 1,000 men in two divisions.[14]

---

11 *Ibid.*

12 Sir Hugh Cholmley's Account, in *The English Historical Review*, vol. V (1890), p. 348.

13 Lisle – Warren's major at Crewe House in February (see chapter 5) – was killed at Marston Moor, and his obituary ranks him as lieutenant-colonel (Jones, pp. 164–165). Peter Young suggests that a subsequent major, Daniel Moore, led the regiment at Marston after Warren's capture (*Marston Moor 1644*), but presumably Young made this assumption in the absence of any information about Lisle's tenure at the time he wrote.

14 Reproduced in Peter Young, *Marston Moor 1644: The Campaign and the Battle* (Kineton: Roundwood Press, 1970).

Clearly, at least until the Northern foot arrived, Rupert was relying on the Anglo-Irish to bear the brunt of any infantry action, whether offensive or defensive.

Lord Byron's Regiment of Foot, one division of 500 men, was deployed with the two divisions of Prince Rupert's Regiment of Foot, and supported by Marcus Trevor's Regiment of Horse covering what was, at least until the Northern foot could be deployed, a gap between the right of Tillier's line and Byron's horse on the right wing. Even in De Gomme's plan, and possibly more so in reality, it was the weakest part of the Royalist deployment. This brigade was apparently positioned 50 yards or so forward of the main Royalist position. It seems unlikely that Rupert intended these troops to be deployed as firepower support among Byron's horse, who in any case appear from De Gomme to have had musketeer support, perhaps from Washington's dragoons, whose location is unrecorded. It may simply be that Byron and Rupert's foot were deployed where they were after failing to take Bilton Bream in the afternoon.

The battle began with the Allied decision at about 7:00 p.m. to attack all along the line. There has been much discussion of the course of events on the right wing, with commentators divided on whether to accept Rupert's later inference that the Royalist defeat resulted from faulty tactics by Byron, and the more recent view that he was in fact scapegoated by the Prince, and that Cromwell owed his success largely to surprise and superior numbers.

In any event, the Byron/Rupert brigade of foot, which Peter Young suggests was commanded by Colonel Thomas Napier, though this is unclear, was attacked by two brigades of Eastern Association foot who 'In a moment ... passed the ditch into the Moor, our men going in a running march...'[15] The attack was probably assisted by dragoons, and Rupert/Byron's brigade evidently collapsed quite quickly.

Elsewhere, the Anglo-Irish seem to have had mixed fortunes. It is unclear whether Warren's Regiment was quickly in trouble as Cromwell's horse began to roll up the Royalist line. Broughton's Regiment was initially pushed back by Lord Fairfax's foot and some Scots, but supported by Newcastle's foot and Blakiston's Brigade of horse counter-attacked and regained their ground.

Tillier's Regiment, and probably Earnley/Gibson, assisted by the success of Goring's horse against Sir Thomas Fairfax on their left, more than held their ground. They evidently had enough warning of the general collapse as the Eastern Association horse and foot rolled up the Royalist line to their right, to be able to reform and face them, and mount some kind of rearguard action, or were trapped, and made a last stand similar to that of the famous Whitecoats.

Few details are known, apart from a Scots account: 'General Major Lesley charged the earl of Newcastle's brigade of Whitecoats ... and after them charged a brigade of Greencoats whereof they cut off a great number, and put the rest to the rout.'[16]

---

15 Lionel Watson's Account, reproduced in Young, p. 230.
16 *Ibid.*, p. 231.

Richard Symonds wrote later that Tillier's Regiment had been 'destroyed at York', which was an exaggeration. But Henry Tillier himself possibly suffered a head injury and was captured, along with Lieutenant-Colonel Hammond.

There are apparently no complete lists of Royalist officers captured at Marston Moor, so it is difficult to estimate total Anglo-Irish casualties there; clearly they must have been heavy, although no regiment was completely destroyed.

Captain John Disney of Gibson's Regiment was taken prisoner. Known wounded included Colonel Robert Broughton, and of the rank and file Richard Stubbs of Captain Christopher Congreave's Company of Warren's Regiment, who lost an arm. Lieutenant-Colonel Francis Lisle, commanding Warren's Regiment, was killed.

Records of maimed soldiers add a few more names:

William Adderton of Tarvin, then St Botolph's Parish London, served first under Earl Rivers at Edgehill, then in Earnley's at Marston Moor, before ending the war back with Rivers' Regiment in the Donnington Castle garrison.

Roger Ince of Northwich served under Harcourt in Ireland Captain Sydenham's company wounded and a POW at Marston Moor.

Richard Rishton served with Earnley's.[17]

17 Cheshire QSR, reproduced in Young, p. 162.

7

An Army from Munster

It had been hoped rather optimistically that the Anglo-Irish forces being despatched from Munster could arrive in England at the same time and same area as the men from Leinster, but the Earl of Inchiquin quickly explained his difficulties to Ormonde:

> I account it a great addition to my misfortunes, that the state expect such things at my hands as are absolutely impossible; for that I could feed 6,000 foot and 500 horse, from the time of cessation till now, with £500, and that proportion of biscuit and corn cannot be thought; and what help the free access of shipping can afford us to that end, I cannot imagine, except I should pillage them; for to buy their commodities we are not able, and if we were, the country would supply us at far easier rates. Another advantage we have (as it is supposed) in that we had shipping here to transport our men; but that the men must have provisions set aboard for them, and that the officers will not stir without some help of money to keep them from begging as soon as they land, is forgotten; yet I found no way to avoid it, though I endeavoured it with all the industry I could use, and the 2 regiments that are gone had (though sore against my will) no less than £350 between all their officers.
>
> The few ships that are left are of no force, and go all away tomorrow with the remainder of Sir John Paulet's Regiment. By them I do intimate your conditions at Dublin. My direction for landing men is at Bristol, Minehead, or, if we be driven to it, in any part of the west of England; for it was conceived dangerous to carry any of us towards Chester; as well for the danger of interception as the season. As for our horse, it was not held possible to send them that way. I conceive it convenient that the ships you hire be first employed to carry over these here, seeing you are interrupted (at present) in sending from thence ...[1]

Inchiquin felt that unless some troops were sent quickly to England, the funds available to him would not be sufficient to maintain all the forces in Munster.

---

1   Carte, *Life of Ormonde*, vol. V, pp. 498–9.

The first troops to be despatched were the regiments of Sir Charles Vavasour and Sir John Paulet, neither with more than 500 men, which sailed from Cork after 16 October, and reached Bristol before the end of the month.

Vavasour was a professional soldier originally from Lincolnshire, who had served with mixed fortunes in Ireland since 1641. He had previously raised a regiment of foot in Shropshire, Cheshire and Denbighshire for the Second Bishops' War, and in November 1641 was commissioned to raise a new regiment for service in Ireland. For this the Earl of Derby provided 500 men from Cheshire, and after plans to raise additional men in Ireland on its arrival came to nothing, 500 more men were ordered to be recruited in Devon and Cornwall.

The first half of the Regiment arrived in Munster in February 1642, and appears to have reached a maximum strength of 1,092 men.

The Regiment played a leading role at the battle of Liscarroll in September 1642, but in June 1643 it was defeated at the battle of Cloglea, where Vavasour himself was captured and the unit took heavy casualties. Vavasour was quickly exchanged, though one captain and four lieutenants were among the dead. It may be that the regiment was still recovering from this disaster when shipped over to England.

Sir John Paulet (b.1615) was also a professional soldier. He was knighted in 1635, evidently served in Europe until 1639, and was a lieutenant-colonel during the Second Bishops' War. His regiment was raised in the spring of 1642, and shipped to Munster, fighting at Liscarroll.

In August 1642 the Earl of Cork told the speaker of the House of Commons:

> And it is most true that those three Regiments which the King and Parliament sent over for this Province [Munster] under the command of Sir Charles Vavasour, Sir John Paulet and Sir William Ogle, are so lessened, weakened and made unserviceable by fluxes, smallpox, fevers and with long marches and lying upon the cold ground, as we are not able out of these 3 regiments to draw into the field 1200 able and serviceable men: death and sickness having reduced them to this Condition.[2]

It has been suggested that part of Paulet's Regiment remained In Ireland under Lieutenant-Colonel Brockett, but if this was in fact the case, the regiments which Inchiquin sent in this first 'wave' to England were perhaps reinforced from other units.

The arrival of these first troops from Ireland met with a furious reaction from Parliamentarian newsletters. *Mercurius Civicus* claimed that:

> Above a thousand of the Irish Rebels landed lately at Minehead … whereupon many of the garrison soldiers in Bridgewater began to mutiny, declaring, That they would not fight any longer for His Majesty, since he admitted the popish Irish rebels to come over into this Kingdom, which they would not possibly believe

---

2   Ryder, p. 21.

was to establish the Protestant Religion. Insomuch that Captain Wyndham (who is Governor of the said Town) made a large speech to pacify and appease his soldiers the effect whereof was that these Irish, with above 8,000 more, which (as he heard) were shortly to come over hither, wee not Rebels no more than himself or any of them, but they came to establish the Protestant Religion, now almost extinct in this Kingdom, and to set his Majesty again on His Throne (as he pretended). Notwithstanding which Speech and Declaration of the said Captain, many of his Soldiers have deserted the service, refusing to take part with those barbarous Irish rebels, to ruin their own native country and to extirpate the true Protestant Religion. It is also further reported that a thousand Irish rebels more are landed at Bristol, whereupon most of the malignants in the western parts do much lament their former obstinacy and perversness against the Parliament, and are resolved to take part with any Forces which shall be sent from them.[3]

It does seem that the troops from Ireland who were landed in the West (partly probably, because there were 'native Irish' among them), were generally received with more hostility than those landed in the North West. It also seems that preparations at Bristol were not so well organised as those at Chester. On 8 November Secretary Nicholas told Ormonde that, 'there are 3 regiments of the English soldiers landed here at Bristol from Munster and clothes are being prepared for them as fast as may be.'[4]

Clothing for the regiments was to be supplied by Thomas Bushell, the Royalist entrepreneur who in the spring had fitted out the foot of the Oxford Army with suits of red or blue. It seems that Vavasour's Regiment at least was now given yellow coats. It is unclear whether there was any particular significance in this, or whether it was simply the colour of cloth most readily available.

In 1664, Colonel Thomas Pigott petitioned Lord Ashley of the Council of State:

> May it please your Lordship in obedience to your Lordship's letter I do humbly certify your Lordship that in the year 1643 there landed out of Ireland (for his Majesty's service in this Kingdom) the Lord of Inchiquin's Regiment of Foot (to which I was then Major) and Sir Charles Vavasour's, Sir John Paulet's Sir William St Leger's, Colonel Mynne's Regiments of Foot with part of the Lord Kerry's and the Lord Broghill's Regiments of Foot likewise, the soldiers of which Regiments were clothed at and from Bristol by Mr Thomas Bushell to the great content and satisfaction of both Officers and soldiers of each Regiment and for which I never heard that he was paid or satisfied in any part; my cause of knowledge of all this is that I received about 1,000 suits of clothes of him for my own Regiment, and so did most of the other Regiments receive their clothes, and did [afterwards] often

---

3 *Mercurius Civicus, London's Intelligencer*, no. 23, 26 Oct–2 Nov, 1643, ed. S.F. Jones (Reading: Tyger's Head Books, 2013), vol. I, p. 134.
4 Carte, *Life of Ormonde*, vol. V, p. 505.

see them march in them, all which is humbly certified and submitted to your Lordship 7.1.1664. Thomas Pigott.[5]

There were however serious problems with the newcomers. They were placed in the army under Ralph Lord Hopton's command, currently campaigning in Hampshire. Hopton wrote of them:

> There came to Bristol from Ireland two regiments commanded by Sir Charles Vavasour and Sir John Paulet. They both might make between four and five hundred foot; bold, hardy men, and excellently well officered; but the common men were mutinous, and shrewdly infected with the rebellious humour of England, being brought over merely by the virtue and loyalty of their officers, and large promises, which there was then but small means to perform. But the Lord Hopton, struggling through all exigents as he could prepared speedily to draw forth, and designed to have fallen first upon Wardour Castle, being a business (as he supposed) would not have cost him many days (notwithstanding the obstinate courage of Mr [Edmund] Ludlow who defended it). And to that purpose he sent orders to fetch four great iron guns from Weymouth, with pretence for the works at Bristol, and gave those Irish regiments quarters about bath; with private directions to their officers to draw them upon pretence of bettering their quarters on towards Warminster and Hindon. Resolving with them and the rest to have fallen suddenly upon Wardour, and with reasonable success there to have fallen on Lyme and to block up Poole … [Hopton] went himself thither from Winchester and carried £300 with him. Where coming to Fonthill, he was presently entertained by Sir Charles.[6]

However the troops from Ireland failed to arrive at Wardour, and refused to move on from Hendon:

> … and doubting that nothing but money would make them tractable [Hopton] went himself thither from Winchester and carried £300 with him. Where coming to Fonthill, he was presently entertained by Sir Charles Vavasour and Lord Arundell of Wardour, who was then there, with a complaint that the regiment being at Hendon, was in a high mutiny against their officers, insomuch that they durst not adventure to come amongst them. Whereupon the lord Hopton that night appointed a rendezvous of Sir George Vaughan's regiment of horse, and of the two troops of dragoons near Hendon, and with them the next morning early fell into the town upon the mutineers, took some of the principals, and commanded the rest of the regiment to draw out. And upon that terror, and the execution of two or three of the principal offenders he drew the regiment quietly to Winchester.[7]

---

5   BCW Project regimental wiki for Lord President of Munster's Regiment of Foot <http://wiki.bcw-project.org/protestant/foot-regiments/lord-president-of-munster?s[]=pigot>.

6   Hopton, *Bellum Civile*, ed. C.H. Chadwyck Healey (Somerset Record Society XVIII, 1902), p. 43

7   *Ibid.*

The Parliamentarian newsbooks had a different version of events:

> It is reported from the West (although as yet we have not seen letters to confirm it) that many Soldiers who came lately out of Ireland, and had formerly been employed there against the popish rebels, being brought into Bath … with an intent to have joined them with the Cavaliers, and to have fought against the Parliament, yet they (being conscious of the designs of the Cavaliers to introduce Popery into England) denied it (notwithstanding the intreaty of their Commanders) and when they were about to force them to it, they slew and secured divers of them, and are now resolved to keep the City of Bath for the Parliament. Which report should it prove true, (as some are very confident to affirm it) would be a means to have the West suddenly reduced to the command of the Parliament, if some Forces were sent into those parts under sir William Waller, or any other for that purpose.[8]

The Parliamentarian version was incorrect, the mutiny seems to have been about pay and conditions rather than having any political connotations. The immediate result was that Sir Charles Vavasour gave up his command, whether of his own volition or at Hopton's order is unclear, and retired to Oxford, where he died in March 1644.

Vavasour was succeeded by his lieutenant-colonel. Matthew Appleyard (b.1607) was a Lincolnshire man, a professional who later described himself as a 'soldier of fortune'. He had played an active role in the Irish war, and proved himself a highly capable commander.[9] The regiment was marched to Winchester, where it seems to have remained for much of the winter, under Hopton's eye, whilst Appleyard established his control.

The other 'Irish' regiment, that of Sir John Paulet, was evidently not involved in the mutiny, and was sent as planned to Wardour Castle. A rather ineffectual siege continued until March, though Paulet and his men were brought back to Hopton's field army in time for the spring campaign, with Paulet appointed as Hopton's Major General of Foot.

Both Appleyard's and Paulet's Regiments were present at Cheriton on 29 March, though specific references to their actions are scarce. Appleyard himself led 1,000 commanded musketeers in the earlier phases of the battle, which probably included some of his own men, and forced out his Parliamentarian counterparts. Appleyard himself was wounded later. At the rendezvous which followed, Appleyard's Regiment was transferred to the Oxford Army. Paulet became Governor of Winchester, where his regiment was henceforward mainly garrisoned, although detachments served with the Oxford Army on some occasions.

The next units from Munster to reach Bristol arrived in November, and consisted of 800–1,000 foot forming the Regiments of Nicholas Mynne and Sir William St Leger, and 300 horse of Lord Inchiquin's Regiment under Captain Bridges.

---

8   *Mercurius Civicus*, no. 24, 2–9 November, 1643 (ed. Jones, vol. I), p. 142.
9   P.R. Newman, *Royalist Officers in England Wales, 1642–1660: A Biographical Dictionary* (New York: Garland, 1981), p. 3, item 15.

Ormonde had attempted to quell some of Lord Inchiquin's concerns by telling him that the King had no wish for him to send so many troops from Munster to England that he was left unable to defend the area he still held, but Inchiquin remained pessimistic. On 23 November he informed Ormonde that as a result of delays of shipping intended to carry over the next 'wave' of troops :

> The loss is considerable his majesty has suffered by it, there being 500 men run away from their colours for want of means to subsist; and the rest were kept together with so much difficulty, that if the fleet had not come as it did, truly I think we had lost the whole army. And though we have sent 700 away with part of the fleet, and shipped the rest of those foot that could be found aboard the rest, yet I fear our ruin will not be avoided, the remaining part being much the greater, and windbound in the harbours, where they have spent all the provisions which they had for transportation to one pound of bread and a half of cheese per man; and if the wind carry them not away before they eat that, I expect their landing again here, and presently after, their disbanding, for I protest I have not any thing to give them.[10]

It is unclear to which units Inchiquin was referring. It may be the regiments of Inchiquin himself, and those of Lord Broghill and the Earl of Cork.

Of the regiments which reached Bristol in November Nicholas Mynne's Regiment of Foot had originally been commanded by Sir William Ogle, under whom it went to Ireland in May 1642, serving in Munster. Ogle himself apparently returned to England in October 1643 and secured Winchester for the Royalists. His regiment was handed over in Ireland to its lieutenant-colonel, Nicholas Mynne. Mynne was a highly experienced professional soldier. Born in about 1597, he was a lieutenant-colonel in the army of the Second Bishops' War, and in 1642 a member of the Council of War in Munster.

The second regiment had originally been commissioned in 1642 by the Merchant Adventurers of London for service in Ireland, and raised in the West Country before being shipped to Munster from Bristol and Minehead in August and September 1642. Originally possibly whitecoats, they were operationally commanded by their lieutenant-colonel, William St Leger, and according to Lord Inchiquin being sent unarmed. On their return to England they were still commanded by St Leger, 1615 to an Anglo-Irish family in Munster, the eldest son of Sir Wiliam St Leger, Lord President of Munster.[11]

Lord Inchiquin's Regiment of Horse had been raised in England in 1642 and arrived in Munster in March of that year. It saw action at Liscarroll in September and Bandonbridge in November 1642. Captain Bridges may have been Inchiquin's captain lieutenant.

Mynne and St Leger's men were initially clothed on arrival by Thomas Bushell, though once again coat colours are unknown.

---

10 Carte, *Life of Ormonde*, vol. V, p. 522.
11 Newman, p. 324, item 1250.

It was decided that Mynne and St Leger should reinforce Sir William Vavasour, who since the failure of the King to capture Gloucester in September and the subsequent stalemate of the First Battle of Newbury, had been tasked with blockading Gloucester. On the first stage of their march, the Anglo-Irish force arrived at Thornbury. Edward Massey, Parliamentarian Governor of Gloucester, promised 'entertainment' to any who defected. Corbett claimed that many responded favourably 'resenting the difference of the Cause', though shortage of funds evidently limited the effectiveness of Massey's appeal.

The most that Massey could do was harass the Royalist march, which he did with some success. Captain Backhouse, with 200 horse and dragoons from Gloucester attacked the Royalist advance party at Wotton under Edge and briefly captured four pieces of artillery, but were beaten back by superior numbers, claiming to have inflicted a number of casualties without loss to themselves.[12]

The Anglo-Irish marched on towards Tetbury, still harassed by the Gloucester horse. The Royalists were reinforced b Lord Chandos's Regiment of Horse from Sudeley Castle and, still skirmishing with the enemy, linked up with Vavasour.

These reinforcements enabled Vavasour to tighten his blockade of Gloucester, and took a major role in a skirmish at Painswick.

In February 1644 Nicholas Mynne and his Regiment was sent to fortify and garrison the town of Newent, whilst St Leger and Inchiquin's horse were retained as part of Vavasour's field force. At some stage, although its record is annoyingly obscure, the detachment of horse under Captain Bridges was apparently garrisoned at Berkeley Castle, dismissed by Corbett who commented that 'This enemy was no way formidable nor mischievous in anything but the plundering of the country', and was kept in check by a Parliamentarian outpost at Frampton on Severn.[13]

At some point at the end of 1643 or early in 1644, Inchiquin's horse seem to have been in Chepstow. Here, probably on 22/23 January, they were surprised in their quarters by a raiding party led by Massey and 'there was killed a Captain Carvine in his chamber and captured Sir Henry Talbot 3 Captains, 3 Lieutenants, 3 Irish reformadoes, Sergeant Major Moore Captain Roche Captain Barry, Captain Seabrook together with 60 common soldiers.'[14]

St Leger's Regiment had been moved into Worcestershire and when in April Vavasour rendezvoused with the King at Marlborough, the unit, renamed the Duke of York's Regiment of Foot, was absorbed into the Oxford Army.

Vavasour's lack of success had caused the Royalist high command to lose confidence in him, and when Prince Rupert took over command in the Welsh Marches his days were numbered. The King asked Rupert to appoint a new colonel general in the southern Marches. Charles evidently hoped that local man Lord Chandos would be appointed in order to mollify the Royalist gentry of the area. However Rupert chose Colonel Nicholas Mynne.

---

12 John Corbet, 'Historical Relation of the Military Government of Gloucester', in John Washbourne, *Bibliotheca Gloucestrensis* (Gloucester, 1825), p. 49.

13 *Ibid.*, p. 72.

14 *Ibid.*, p. 72.

Mynne proved an effective local commander: 'In the first entrance he began to lash out',[15] and raided close to Gloucester, appearing at Winmard Hall below the town, and capturing a number of the garrison who attempted a counter-attack by boat across the Severn. Mynne 'lay strong' at Newent and outlying minor garrisons, and Massey could do little more than establish his own outposts to watch Mynne. Constant minor skirmishing followed.

Mynne was briefly taken prisoner when Massey captured Tewkesbury on 4 June, but quickly exchanged. By the summer Mynne was being described as a 'serious and active enemy; a perpetual terror to the country'; he was ravaging the countryside around Gloucester 'with fire and plunder, running cattle and burning the countryside.'[16] However, his days were numbered.

Early in August Mynne was planning a major move, although there is some uncertainty regarding his precise aim, and indeed the precise date. One theory is that he was planning to join up with troops from Worcester and trap Massey on his way back from operations in the Forest of Dean. Corbett reported however the plan was for the Royalists to rendezvous at Corse Green and then attack Gloucester, possibly hoping to take advantage of Massey's absence, and that Mynne and his regiment had been joined by the Hereford troops though the Worcester contingent had yet to arrive.

It was probably on the evening of 2 August when Mynne reached Corse Green, and, as the Worcester contingent had yet to arrive, withdrew across the River Leadon at Highleadon, to 'lie close' in Hartbury Field, though some stragglers were taken by a troop of Parliamentarian horse, possibly from Tewkesbury. The Parliamentarians then lost track of their opponents in the dark.

Mynne 'with great speed marched that night unto Redmarley, by way of Upleadon and Payford'. Massey and his force, now evidently on their way back from the Forest of Dean 'after a tedious wandering to find them out, came to Eldersfield, two miles from Redmarley', where they rested until dawn.

At daylight, according to Corbet, Massey could hear Mynne's drums as the Royalists formed up for battle. Total numbers involved are difficult to estimate. Corbet says that Mynne had 160 horse, 640 musketeers and 210 pikes, which, if it was information obtained from prisoners, may be accurate. Massey's numbers are not stated, but appear to have been mainly horse. It seems most likely that fighting began soon after 6:00 a.m., on an area of common land between the enclosures near to the two villages. Corbet provides the only detailed contemporary account. The Royalists were:

> … all drawn up into battalions, and the hedges lined with musketeers. To beat them out of their advantages the governor [Massey] divided the foot into two bodies, and drew out the horse into single troops, because the frequent inclosures would not make room for a larger form (the enemy in the meanwhile plying us with small shot) and having disposed of his own troop, with the hundred musketeers from Tewkesbury newly come in, and many of the country inhabitants armed with muskets, and good resolutions, to one part of the town, he drew the Gloucester musketeers, about a hundred and sixty … and the greatest part of the horse to

---

15 Corbet, p. 107.
16 *Ibid.*

another place of best advantage. Himself advanced with this party, and led the van, which consisted of three troops; these were seconded with three other troops left to the command of Captain Backhouse. Some of the foot were placed in each flank of the horse, and one single troop with the rest of the foot brought up the rear. They were drawn out into this posture, marched up to the face of the enemy, the governor in the van, next unto him Colonel Harley in the head of his troop, gallantly, and in good order, gave the charge, beat them from their ambuscades, put their horse to flight, and in the instant of time, got into the van of their foot, cut down, and took them prisoners, that few escaped our hands. The horse and foot, both officers and soldiers, played their parts with resolution and gallantry. The enemy was left to our execution, and their whole body broken and shattered, many wounded and slain, but more taken. Major General Mynne was slain in the place with a hundred and seventy. Among the officers, Lieutenant-Colonel Passy then mortally wounded, Major Buller, seven captains, for lieutenants, five ensigns, twelve sergeants and near three hundred common soldiers were taken prisoners.

Some troops advanced in the pursuit five miles from the place of the fight, but upon the view of a strong party from Worcester that came to join with Colonel Mynne, they were enforced to leave the pursuit, and prepare for a second encounter. And a strange hand of Providence kept asunder the Hereford and Worcester forces, whose joining would have proved unto us an inevitable destruction. For Lieutenant-colonel Passie [Passey] who commanded the fresh party of an hundred and fifty horse, and five hundred foot, just upon the beginning of the fight was riding up to Mynne's brigade to bring news of their arrival, but happily intercepted, and wounded by our scouts, and left for dead, So that neither enemy had the knowledge of each other's condition; but the Worcester forces advanced within two flight shot of the place, whilst our men were scattered here and there in chase of a vanquished enemy, nor did the governor when the first brunt was over, expect an afterbirth.

The first discovery was made by Colonel Broughton [and] Captain Backhouse, upon whom a blunt fellow charged up from the head of the main body in the entrance of a cross-lane. Him they surprised by the name of friends; drew him aside from the view of the company, and informed us of the strength at hand. Forthwith they make a noise in the enemy's hearing pretending to fall on with a body of ours ready for a charge, by the sudden outcry daunted and drove back that strong party, and made, a way for the governor's retreat, and those with him, which were now dispersed, secure of the victory, and following the chase. Our straggling pursuers were gathered together, drew back to the place of the fight, and there expected the charge, choosing rather to make good the victory achieved upon so great hazard and disadvantage, than venture all by seeking out a fresh and doubtful enemy with our few and weary soldiers. Only three or four slain, five or six wounded, amongst whom Colonel Harley received a shot in the arm. The success of this design cut off the main strength of the King's forces in South Wales; and secured the country from our plundering neighbours on the Welsh side. The body of Colonel Mynne was brought to Gloucester, and vouchsafed an honourable burial. His death was by his own party much lamented, together with the loss of a brave regiment that was commanded from Ireland to fight here ...[17]

---

17 *Ibid.*, pp. 110–12.

Local tradition claims that Mynne was killed by one of the Tewkesbury contingent who recognised him. His regiment does not seem to have survived the defeat, and survivors were presumably incorporated into other units. Some of the prisoners later escaped, and others were probably sent to Ireland.

Whilst Mynne was campaigning in the Marches there were other landings in the West Country.

When the Cessation was reached and the decision taken to send Anglo-Irish troops to the mainland, Inchiquin, and to a lesser extent probably, Ormonde, assumed that they would form one army: under Ormonde, with Inchiquin as major general. It was an idea which the latter returned to with Ormonde after the first waves of troops from Munster had reached England. Early in January 1644 Inchiquin told Ormonde:

> I humbly desire you will be pleased to intimate unto me what you would have me say concerning the armies gone from this kingdom into England at my coming thither, which will be about a month hence …
>
> What I desire to know is how far you would have me engaged in commands there; whether you desire I should use means to bring both armies together; if so, whether you would have me interested in any command with them. For my resolution is to meddle no further in this, than according to what I shall find or have cause to think best pleasing unto your lordship …[18]

Ormonde replied on 17 January:

> My lord, I am so little able to direct you what to propound, when you come to court, that I am not yet satisfied why you should go, especially if you be so furnished for the maintenance of that place as I hear. …
>
> For the drawing together of those men that were sent hence, and thence into England, all I can say is, that if there be any thought of calling me over to command either, I shall desire your lordship to continue in the command you have.[19]

This did not please Inchiquin, who responded:

> Your lordship is pleased to think my going into England needless, and I could wish it were so; but indeed I cannot apprehend a possibility to set what I shall propound in a right course to be effected, if I be not personally present there…[20]

By 10 February Inchiquin was at Oxford, where he found to his evident displeasure, that the Presidency of Munster, which he had expected to receive, had been conferred on the Earl of Portland instead. His hopes of military command in England were also fading rapidly. He had been told that:

---

18 Carte, *Life of Ormonde*, vol. V, p. 2.
19 *Ibid.*, p. 12.
20 *Ibid.*, p. 27.

I shall be called to my charge here, and shall have the forces of Munster united against the spring, with a considerable body of horse joined to them, under my command. This my lord, I confess is a great honour, but how it is to be brought about I know not, for two of my regiments are a considerable part of my Lord Hopton's army, and it is thought he will as soon quit his command as part with them. The rest are divided under other generals, from whence there will be no small stir to get them. And lastly, when I shall get them together, I know no possibility to keep them so 2 days, if there be not a place of rendezvous appointed us, where I may have the command of a country which may yield a contribution that will afford them sustenance, which I do not yet find within his majesty's power to assign me, except he take it from some that has it now under their command; which cannot be without unmaking a general. So that, my lord, you may perceive I am like at last to be thought unworthy of any employment, (though I hope not by his majesty yet) I must needs fear the world, seeing me fall from the command of an army, to my troop and foot company in Ireland, will see that the ground to dismiss me.[21]

By 19 February Arthur Trevor was telling Ormonde that 'Lord Inchiquin is returning [to Munster] as full of anger as his buttons will endure...'[22] It was a significant step towards Inchiquin's defection to Parliament. An additional strain on Inchiquin's buttons was the arrival in England of the last major contingent of troops from Munster.

In January Inchiquin's Regiment of Foot (800 men), together with Lord Broghill's Regiment of similar strength, arrived in Weymouth. A suggestion that a third regiment, that of the Earl of Cork, arrived at Bristol in February seems to be inaccurate; Cork himself travelled to Oxford then, but there appears to be no record of his regiment in England.

Lord Inchiquin's Regiment of Foot was originally raised in Munster in 1640, as part of Strafford's 'new army', disbanded in May 1641 and re-mustered on the outbreak of the rebellion. At this stage, at least in theory, any Catholic rank and file would have been removed. How completely this actually happened is less certain. The original plan had been for half of the men to be raised in England the remainder in Munster, but in the event all were recruited in Munster, and it seems very likely that some 'native Irish' may have been among them. It may be significant that *Mercurius Aulicus* would call them 'Irish', a term not applied to the troops from Leinster.

The regiment was originally that of Sir William St Leger, then Lord President of Munster, but on his death in April 1642 it was taken over by Inchiquin. Operational command in England was exercised by Inchiquin's brother, Lieutenant-Colonel Henry O'Brian. The officers appear to have been either English or Anglo-Irish. The regiment had seen significant service in Ireland, most notably at the Battle of Liscarroll.

Lord Broghill's Regiment of Foot, also about 800 men, is more obscure. It was raised in Munster in 1642, and possibly fought at Liscarroll before unrecorded service in Munster in 1643.

---

21 *Ibid.*, p. 36.
22 *Ibid.*, p. 38.

Inchiquin's Regiment quickly made its presence felt in action in Dorset, as recorded by *Mercurius Aulicus*. On 17 February there was:

> '[A] skirmish [at Holmebridge] betwixt his Majesty's forces in Dorsetshire and the rebels, at a Bridge 4 or 5 miles from Wareham, where they were assaulted gallantly by the Lord Inchiquin's Regiment and some of His Majesty's Horse, where they killed divers, and brought 33 prisoners into Weymouth. In this action the Lord Inchiquin's Foot, both Officers and common Soldiers expressed most gallant courage; for (the straitness of the Pass hindering them from the Enemy,) they ran through a river almost up to the neck to assault the rebels, who flying fast after Sydenham their leader, were as swiftly followed by these Foot, who wounded divers of them in this pursuit; for had not Sydenham with eight score Horse run so fast, and by crossing a River recovered Wareham, this skirmish had made quick work with the Rebels of this County.[23]

On 27 February *Mercurius Aulicus* reported another encounter:

> The news of this day was of another skirmish in Dorsetshire, betwixt his Majesty's forces and the rebels; who peeping out of their nest at Wareham, were stopped by part of the Lord Inchiquin's Regiment at Holme Bridge, three miles from Wareham, where it was sharply disputed above four hours, until Captain Purdon and his Lieutenant, (two most valiant and incomparable Officers) were both shot by the Rebels, so as their men began to give back. But here I must acquaint you with a piece of most gallant and matchless courage in this Captain Purdon and his Lieutenant, who though they had but 25 foot soldiers and 20 horse (not a man more) yet did they fight almost 5 hours at this bridge with above 300 Rebels horse and foot; and withstood all their Carbines and Musket shot, till 10 of the Captain's foot were sore wounded, himself and Lieutenant dangerously shot, so as they both fell down, yet would by no means be carried off, but caused his men to lay him and his Lieutenant at the brink of the Bridge, and commanded them not to leave the Place, or him, while he lived; and (if he bled to death as he lay) not to leave his body till some other friends might come to their relief; which the men performed most stoutly, the brave Captain himself (as he lay) charging and discharging his Pistol, three or four times against Rebels at five yards distance, by which unexpressable valour the Rebels were still kept off, though they pressed hard for the Captain, till at last the Rebels (some fresh forces from the Isle of Purbeck) ran their way to Wareham, leaving 40 Rebels dead behind them, whom the Captain had the pleasure to see stripped, and not only got their fine new Saddles, Carbines and Clothes (sent lately from London) but took also eight cartloads of Hay and other Provisions, which these Rebels had robbed from the Country people. The Captain had 12 men wounded, but not man killed, save the valiant Lieutenant who bled to death as he lay on the ground, though all the while he encouraged the soldiers with more cheerful expressions than you can easily imagine in a dying man. The Captain we doubt not will recover again, who with a good cause and 45 men is able to beat 300 Rebels, especially if they be led by perfidious Sydenham,

---

23 *Mercurius Aulicus*, (ed. Thomas, 1971), pp. 843–4.

who in this action commanded in chief, but (as 'tis confidently affirmed) is now dead of his wounds, being shot in the belly, either by this Captain or one of his brave company.[24]

Unsurprisingly, the Parliamentarian version of the incident was somewhat different:

We heard then also certain intelligence, that the Garrison forces belonging to Lyme and Poole in Dorsetshire had joined themselves together in a body and fallen upon the Lord Inchiquin's Regiment of Irish renegadoes, whom they have totally routed, took two pieces of Ordnance, fired their Magazine, slain many of them, and taken several prisoners…[25]

This claim which was derisively dismissed by *Aulicus*.

A report that Inchiquin's men were present at Cheriton on 29 March seems unfounded, and they apparently remained in Dorset, where, on 13 April, *Aulicus* reported their next exploit:

We can assure the Reader of an Express we had this day from Weymouth in Dorsetshire, wherein 'tis signified that Colonel Ashburnham's Lieutenant-Colonel Frowd, my Lord Inchiquin's Lieutenant-colonel O'brien, and his Major [Thomas] Pigot resolved to assault the Rebels' Garrison at Wareham on Thursday last [10 April], who so discreetly ordered the business, and so gallantly performed it with their brave Irish, that they made an onslaught upon the Town, scaled the Walls, and took it by break of day, with the loss of only two men, and five wounded. They found dead in the streets 25 Rebels, and 14 more were drowned. They took 6 Captains, and 150 Common Soldiers, the rest escaping by the shore to Poole whither Sydenham went over night. They took also 13 pieces of Ordnance and Murderers, 200 muskets, 40 pair of pistols, 5 barrels of powder and 20 skeins of match … A sergeant of Colonel Barnes that run away when they lay before Wardour Castle, and another who had run from Corfe Castle, were both hanged at Wareham, Where Lieutenant-colonel O'Brien is now Governor wit his incomparable Musketeers, who, though they took the Towne by escalade, yet 'twas got more easily than they'll part with it again …[26]

Mercurius Civicus took another view of the operations of the Anglo-Irish in Dorset:

Another pressing motive for the sending some Forces to the west, is the freeing of Dorsetshire and other western parts from the cruelties and inhuman useages of the bloody Irish, who (as is certainly informed by those who were lately beholders of many such sad spectacles) do daily ravish and deflower all the Maids and women that they can find in those parts, murdering such as refuse to satisfy their lusts, yea many times before their husbands' faces; and at Beaminster thirteen

24 *Ibid.*, pp. 853–4.
25 *Mercurius Civicus*, no. 41, 29 Feb–7 Mar 1643[4] (ed. Jones, vol. I), p. 66.
26 *Mercurius Aulicus*, (ed. Thomas, 1971), pp. 934.

of them, after they had successively lain with one maid, most cruelly thrust her through with their Skeins. They have also burned to the ground the greatest part of Shaftesbury, and two other Market Towns in the county of Dorset.[27]

When, early in April, Prince Maurice and his forces moved against Parliamentarian-held Lyme, they were joined by 'the Irish regiments'. In practice this seems to have been Lord Broghill's, with possibly a detachment from Inchiquin's.

The records of the siege make few mentions of the Irish troops. On 30 April the garrison made a sally and 'clogged one of the enemy's ordnance lying within pistol shot of Marsh's ford and the line, slaying 50 or 60 men and 2 or 3 women of the Irish'.[28]

On 14 June at the end of the siege, 'Lieutenant Phayre of Broghill's Regiment' with his wife, servant maid, 25 officers and common soldiers, who having delivered up 17 arms desired they might keep their swords, which was granted', and defected to the garrison.[29] They were more fortunate than an elderly Irish woman, left behind as the Royalists raised the siege and withdrew on 15 June:

> An act of cruelty was committed by the mariners this day who finding an old Irish woman of the enemy's looking out her friends, not supposing them to be gone, drove her through the streets to the seaside, knocked her on the head, slashed and hewed her with their swords, robbed her of 20 or 40 shillings, cast her dead body into the sea which was cast on shore between Lyme and Charmouth, where her carcass lay until consumed.[30]

The Earl of Warwick's Secretary however said that she was slain and pulled to pieces by the townswomen, or in another version was placed in a hogshead barrel stuck with nails and rolled into the sea.[31]

O'Brien and his Regiment continued to garrison Wareham into the summer. The Parliamentarians claimed that the inhabitants of the area suffered severely from O'Brien's depredations. On 11 July *Mercurius Civicus* reported:

> I might here also tell you of the usurpations and oppressions of Lieutenant-Colonel O'Brien, who commands his brother the lord Inchiquin's Regiment, and is now Governor of Wareham, as far as his bounds reach, which are not far, and I hope will not be long; but in the meantime (like him whom he most desires to serve) he now rages the more furiously in regard he thinks he shall have but a short time to command there …[32]

---

27 *Mercurius Civicus*, no. 49, 25 Apr–2 May 1644 (ed. Jones, vol. II), p. 111.
28 Nathan Drake, *Diary*, in A.R. Bayley, *The Great Civil War in Dorset 1642–1660* (Taunton: Barnicott and Pearce, 1910), pp. 149–50.
29 *Ibid.*, p. 186.
30 *Ibid.*, p. 188.
31 *Ibid.*, p. 188.
32 *Mercurius Civicus*, no. 60, 11–17 July, 1644 (ed. Jones, vol. II), p. 182.

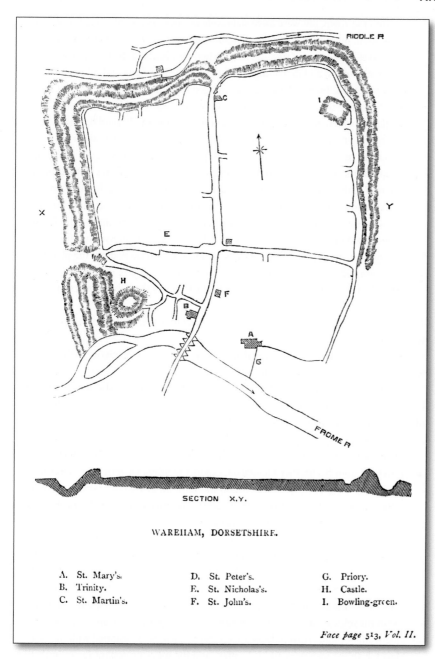

WAREHAM, DORSETSHIRE.

A. St. Mary's.
B. Trinity.
C. St. Martin's.

D. St. Peter's.
E. St. Nicholas's.
F. St. John's.

G. Priory.
H. Castle.
I. Bowling-green.

Face page 513, *Vol. II.*

18 A Victorian plan of the remains of Wareham Castle. (From G.T. Clark, *Mediaeval Military Architecture in England* (London: Wyman & Sons, 1884), facing p. 513).

On the same date *Civicus* also related that:

> Lieutenant-Colonel O'Brien governor of Wareham sent forth a party of 240 horse and foot towards Dorchester, who came about 8 of the clock that morning within 3 miles of the Town, and continued facing it till 2 of the clock in the afternoon, of which when the Town had intelligence they sent to the parliament's Garrisons at Aderbury, Weymouth and other places near them, and also immediately gathered themselves to the number of 3,000 men, women and children; upon the Enemy;s first return into the Town, they fired the Courts of Guard, and came up a little

way into the Town, but were there so bravely received by the Inhabitants not only of the Men, but also the women thereof, who did now the second time behave themselves as gallantly as they did lately, when they beat out the trench by pelting them with stones, and defending themselves with their Spits and other suchlike weapons, that although the enemy discharged furiously amongst them, yet they forced them to retreat out of the Town as far as Fordington, by which time Col. [William] Sydenham … came in with their foot for their relief, and having forced the enemy to fly. Pursued them to their works at Wareham, and in that pursuit slew of them 12 of them took 60 horse and 160 prisoners, whereof 8 were a company of natural Irish commanded by a captain formerly employed by the Parliament in Ireland, 7 of these 8 were presently executed and the other spared, for in regard he did execution among his fellows … The intention of the Enemy;s coming was (as confessed by the Capt of the Irish and others) first to have summoned the Town to pay £1000 or upon refusal to have plundered them and afterwards have fired their houses. They pressed divers Wagons and Carts to carry away the plunder, which were all taken with 3 barrels of powder and some store of shot and above 80 Cattle, which they had plundered from the Country thereabouts rescued.[33]

The hanging of some 'native Irish' was a new feature, and a foretaste of what was to come.

Walker says that Maurice reinforced the Wareham garrison with 500 foot, which may have been Broghill's men.

In August the Parliamentarians with 1,200 men from the local garrisons laid siege to Wareham. In the event the outcome was resolved by the defection of Lord Inchiquin to Parliament that summer:

The occasion of the surrender was upon a Letter sent from the Lord Inchiquin in Ireland unto his brother Lieutenant-Colonel O'Brien, Governor of Wareham, wherein he declared 'That his resolution was to stand firm to the parliament, and to live and die in the defence of their Cause, and therefore desired him that he would seriously consider of the same, and to surrender, the said Town for the use of the parliament.' Which Letter being read unto the soldiers in the Town, they were for the most part willing to have the Town surrendered, only some few Irish rebels, as seemed averse, and upon the obstinate denial of it were soon dispatched by the other Soldiers, in requital of so much Protestant bloodshed by them and other their inhuman brethren in Ireland. And the said Lieutenant-colonel and the rest of his soldiers hath declared themselves for the parliament; and also the said Lieutenant-Colonel hath prevailed with 500 of them to be shipped with him for Munster, to the assistance of his brother, and the other protestant forces in that Province.[34]

The terms of surrender were:

That officers and soldiers are to march away with colours flying, drums beating, bullet in mouth, and freely to enjoy arms, horses bag and baggage.

---

33 *Ibid.*, p. 186.
34 *Ibid.*, p. 226.

That immediately after the rendition of the town the said officers and soldiers shall be maintained at the charge of King and Parliament, and a timely provision made for carrying them over to Ireland, they to receive one month's pay.

That the inhabitants of Wareham and such as hath repaired thither are to be at liberty to enjoy and dispose of their estates according to the law of the land, paying contribution proportionable to the same as other places do under the obedience of Parliament.

That there shall be no plundering all inhabitants who desire to depart shall be at liberty so to do with time to carry away their goods, and all prisoners on either side shall be released.

And that such of the garrison, being Irish recusants, as are unwilling to go with the Governor into Ireland to fight against the rebels shall have safe conduct to Bristol, or any part of the King's army, without arms.[35]

On 7 September 500 of the Irish were billeted at Hayling Island. Here they were to receive £1,200 and 300 old muskets with ships to carry them back to Ireland. Some allegedly offered to help at the siege of Basing House.[36] With the departure of Inchiquin's Regiment, the Royalists had lost the services of one of the most capable Anglo-Irish units, whose career in England, though short, had been very effective. It is often stated that Broghill's Regiment was included in the surrender, but there seems to be a possibility that some of its men continued to serve with the Royalists in the west until Hopton's surrender in 1646.

A list of the Western Army, dated around 27 July 1644, includes a unit simply described as 'Irish'.[37] These may be as, Stephen Ede-Borrett suggests, 'Irish' waiting to be allocated to other units. However, if the list does indeed predate the defection of the Munster forces, it could refer to Broghill's Regiment.

Any chance that further reinforcements might be despatched from Munster had been brutally ended in April. Early in January, Colonel Anthony Willoughby, who had been operating in Connaught, the King wrote on 4 February, 'hath proposed to us the present levy of 400 volunteers in any part of Ireland for our service here, and the transportation of them to Bristol by the end of March next.'[38]

Willoughby met with a slow response, but by April had mustered 150 men, and embarked with them in April. However his ship was intercepted by Parliamentarian warships under Captain Richard Swanley, operating out of Milford Haven. And Willoughby and his men carried prisoners to Pembroke. *Mercurius Aulicus* reported furiously on the outcome;

This day we were certified from a very good hand, that that barbarous Mariner Captain Swanley lately took some small vessels coming from Ireland, which he brought into Pembroke, Swanley tendered the Covenant to all the Prisoners, upon

---

35 Quoted in Bayley, p. 209.
36 British Library Harleian MS 6804, f.199.
37 HMC, Report on the MSS of the Marquis of Ormonde, London, 1899, p. 17.
38 *Ibid.*

pain of death; some few took it, but most refused. But this bloody fellow took the refusers, bound them back to back, and cast them into the Sea. Those few that took it to avoid death were not all set at liberty, for the Officers were imprisoned, and threatened that if the common Soldiers who had taken the Covenant should afterwards revolt to his Majesty, he swore he would see their Officers hanged and quartered.[39]

A London newsletter said with delight that as the Irish were supposed to be good swimmers, Swanley 'caused [them] to use their natural art, and try whether they could tread the seas as lightly as their Irish bogs … and binding them back to back, cast them overboard to swim or drown.'[40]

Ormonde told Archbishop Williams that 70 men and two women were drowned, 'making the men also very fearful to venture upon the voyage, it being very well known to them that most of the men so murdered had served with them against the Irish, and all of them lived during the war in our quarters.'[41] This event, and growing Parliamentarian control of the Irish Sea spelt the effective end of troops being sent from Munster.

There is evidence of the continued presence of Irish troops in the Western forces. On 27 January 1645, Goring, using apparently only horse, beat up Parliamentarian quarters at, among other places, Farnham and Aldershot. Reporting the action on 29 January to George Digby, Goring added that the Irish soldiers 'gave no quarter to any man, which I can hardly blame them for, considering the inhuman useage of the other party to their countrymen upon cold blood, which I am very confident we shall make them weary of.'[42]

The context suggests that these Irish were either cavalry or at least mounted troops of some kind, but their exact identity remains illusive. The probability that on his occasion they were mounted infantry is however strengthened by a reference by Goring to his Irish foot regiments in the bungled attempt to intercept Parliamentarian forces near Ilminster on 20 May.[43]

The 'Irish' in the Oxford Army

With the approach of the summer campaign, it was decided that elements of Hopton's Army, including his 'Irish' regiments, should reinforce the Oxford Army. Symonds does not list any of them among the units present at the rendezvous on Aldbourne Chase on 10 April, though the Duke of York's 'full regiment'[44] was nearby at Marlborough.

By the time active operations began, The Oxford Army had been joined by the Duke of York's Regiment, Appleyard's and possibly part of Sir John Paulet's. They probably remained in the same tertias throughout the summer.

39 *Mercurius Aulicus*, ed. Thomas, 1971), pp. 965–6.
40 Peter Gaunt, *Nation Under Siege: The Civil War in Wales 1642–48* (Cardiff: HMSO Books, 1991), p. 44.
41 Carte, *Original Letters*, vol. I, p. 48.
42 Bodleian Library, Firth MS. C7, ff.298–9.
43 British Library, Harleian MS 986.
44 *Ibid.*

The Duke of York's was in the tertia commanded by Thomas Blagge, whilst those of Paulet and Appleyard formed part of Sir Bernard Astley's largely 'western' tertia.[45]

Probably because of their relatively small numbers, and perhaps because they had not the same impact as the Leinster veterans when serving with the more experienced troops of the Oxford Army, there are few references to the specific actions of the Munster units. At Cropredy Bridge (29 June) Astley's tertia is noted as supporting the cavalry brigades of the Earls of Northampton and Cleveland, and one of Appleyard's ensigns captured an enemy dragoon guidon.[46]

Appleyard is mentioned in action during the hedge fighting of the operations around Lostwithiel, where he was probably commanding a 'commanded' body of musketeers as at Cheriton.[47]

The same organisation, though with depleted numbers, probably maintained during the operations which resulted in the Second Battle of Newbury (27 October). Once again references to the individual units are few, with the exception of the Duke of York's Regiment, still strong enough to operate independently. It was sent to support the Western foot tasked with holding the position around Church Speen village on the eastern flank of the Royalist position, and was committed in a counter-attack against Skippon's advancing foot. Sir William St Leger was killed, but his men were able to hold their ground in the hedgerows east of the village until nightfall.[48]

---

45 Symonds, p. 41.
46 *Ibid.*, p. 15.
47 Edward Walker, *Historical Discourses Upon Several Occasions* (London, 1705), p. 75.
48 *Ibid.*, p. 115.

8

Montgomery

Whilst Rupert and the Marches Army headed for York, the situation which Byron had feared was unfolding on the Welsh border.

Rupert was probably aware of the risks he was taking in stripping the Marches of so many troops, and did what he could to minimise the danger. His main concern was for the key garrisons of Chester and Shrewsbury, and the small town of Oswestry which lay between them. In a command shake-up, Rupert had appointed professional soldiers as Governors for each of them. William Legge was at Chester, Sir Fulke Hunckes at Shrewsbury, whilst Sir Abraham Shipman, a career soldier from Nottinghamshire who had been deputy governor of Chester, was given command at Oswestry.

The main problem was a shortage of experienced troops. The only 'first line' horse available was John Marrow's Regiment. At Chester the bulk of the garrison was formed by Sir Francis Gamull's town regiment, which would be of limited value in field operations. The main source of infantry would be the Anglo-Irish at Shrewsbury. These consisted of a detachment, probably one company, of Sir Michael Earnley's Regiment and that of Sir Fulke Hunckes. Both, as we have seen, had suffered badly at Nantwich, though possibly had been recruited to some extent since.

Oswestry was defended mainly by raw Welsh levies. On 22 June a combined Midlands Parliamentarian force under the Earl of Denbigh appeared before Oswestry, and after brisk fight captured both town and castle. The capture of Oswestry was seen as a notable regional success for the Parliamentarians. Easy communications between Chester and Shrewsbury had been severed, and the way opened for a further advance into Mid Wales. For now Denbigh established Colonel Thomas Mytton, commanding the Parliamentarian forces in Shropshire, as governor.

From the Royalist viewpoint it was vital to recover Oswestry. Operations were directed by Sir Fulke Hunckes Governor of Shrewsbury, who drew in contingents from already depleted Royalist garrisons over a wide area. According to Parliamentarian reports, contingents came from both Wales and the Marches and as far away as Derbyshire, and probably totalled around 1,500 foot and 600 horse.

Details of Royalist operations around Oswestry are sketchy, but it seems that the vanguard of their force, including John Marrow's Regiment of Horse, began to close in on the town around 28 June, and retook St Oswald's Church outside the town. However they were still preparing for a major attack when a Parliamentarian relief force under Sir Thomas, including his own regiment of horse and Cheshire and Shropshire foot, approached on 2 July.

Next day at about 2:00 p.m. the Parliamentarians came in sight of Oswestry. Sir Fulke Hunckes claimed later in a somewhat sketchy report to Prince Rupert that he had ordered Marrow 'to discover their strength, but expressly forbade him to engage himself, yet contrary to my knowledge and direction, he took with him the whole body of horse, and was routed before I knew anything of it.'[1] How true this was is open to question: certainly it seems that Marrow attempted to hold the crossing of the little River Perry near Whittington, and, said a Parliamentarian account:

> … very firmly assaulted and charged up, but were repulsed, and forced to retire through the courage of our horse, who most courageously entertained the enemy. Three several times the skirmish was doubtful, either side being forced so often to retreat; but in the end, our foot forces coming up relieved the horse, beat back the enemy and pursued them with such force that the horse, thereby encouraged, which indeed was formerly weary, joining with the foot, they put the enemy to absolute flight.[2]

Whatever the rights and wrongs of Marrow's action, he had at least given Hunckes, who claimed only to have left Shrewsbury with his main force on the previous day, time to begin his retreat. Hunckes said that the first news of Marrow's defeat came when 'the first man I met with was Marrow, all alone.'[3] However Sir Fulke certainly had enough time to withdraw his foot substantially intact, together with two heavy guns, though the Parliamentarians claimed that 'We killed of their men, about forty, and some of them proper handsome men, and very well clad.' They claimed to have captured 200 common soldiers, and seven carts carrying powder and match, as well as, strewn along the Royalist line of retreat, 'some whole veal and muttons newly killed.'[4]

The Earl of Denbigh now arrived on the scene, and called a council of war with the victorious Parliamentarian commanders. This decided to press on to Shrewsbury, in the hope of triggering an uprising among Parliamentarian sympathisers in the town.

On Thursday 4 July, rendezvousing on Knockin Heath, the Parliamentarians advanced to Montford Bridge, about four miles north-west of Shrewsbury. One arch of the bridge had been replaced by a drawbridge, guarded by 40 Royalist musketeers and some horse, but Denbigh's foot gained the bridge after 'a little dispute', the horse meanwhile crossing by a ford a couple of miles to the south-west. The Parliamentarians kept up the

---

1   J.R. Phillips, *Memoirs of the Civil War in Wales and the Marches*, vol. II (London: Longmans et al., 1874), p. 187.
2   *Ibid.*, p. 180.
3   *Ibid.*, p. 187.
4   *Ibid.*, p. 183.

pursuit to within one and a half miles of Shrewsbury, surprising Colonel Ranulph Egerton's Regiment of Horse in their quarters, and taking a number of prisoners.[5]

Suspecting, correctly, that the Royalists might be preparing an ambush, Denbigh called a halt to the pursuit about a mile from the town and drew up his forces on a heath. Here he received word that Marrow had advanced out of Shrewsbury and lined all the hedges between the heath and the town with musketeers. Denbigh reported:

> Immediately I ordered the horse and foot to give on, who killed some on the place, drove the rest into the gates of, the town, and my troop which led the van took Major Manley, major to the Lord Byron and Governor of Bangor, within little more than pistol shot of their works.

He claimed to have taken a number of arms and about 20 troopers and common soldiers, and that Marrow himself only escaped through the goodness of his horse.[6]

Denbigh decided that the defences of Shrewsbury were too strong to assault, and withdrew, Hunckes claiming that he had beaten off the attack, and blaming the debacle on Marrow. Prince Rupert was evidently not convinced. At the end of July Sir Michael Earnley had been exchanged, though Warren and Monck were denied this. As *Mercurius Civicus* related:

> Col. Monk and Col Warren, lately sent from Hull, were this week brought to the House of Commons, and by them committed to the Tower, the main charge against them was, for that 'they being employed by the Parliament against the Irish Rebels had deserted that Kingdom, and taken up Arms against the Parliament here in England'.[7]

Lieutenant-Colonel Hammond, taken at Marston Moor, was not exchanged until September 1645, and the wounded Henry Tillier was also confined in the Tower. It was further evidence of an increasingly hard Parliamentarian attitude towards troops from Ireland.

Earnley may have been exchanged because of ill health, but Rupert on 18 August dismissed Hunckes as Governor of Shrewsbury, and replaced him with Robert Broughton. Earnley was made area commander for Shropshire. Reporting to Ormonde on Hunckes' departure, Royalist Daniel O'Neill said that there had been a number of defections to Parliament, and 'Sir Fulke Hunckes was put from his command for fear he should run the same way: now that he is alone, 'tis no matter whether we have him or no.'[8] At the end of the war Hunckes was serving in the West Country as a reformado with Hopton.[9]

---

5   *Ibid.*, p. 180.
6   *Ibid.*, pp. 183–4.
7   *Mercurius Civicus*, no. 59, 2–11 July, 1644 (ed. Jones, vol. II), p. 178.
8   Carte, *Life of Ormonde*, vol. VI, p. 204.
9   Newman, p. 205, item 788.

Clearly the Anglo-Irish foot had suffered heavily at Marston Moor, though no regiment seems actually to have ceased to exist. Many of the foot who Rupert rallied after the battle must have included them, and they retreated with the Prince to Chester, arriving on 28 July. By early August the remains of the Marches Army were quartered in and around the town and in north-east Wales. They were in no condition for active operations. As Brereton reported to the Committee of Both Kingdoms on 3 August: 'We conceive they are in much want of ammunition and arms, because they are so little active.'[10]

Rupert set to work to try to rebuild his forces, including the Anglo-Irish, but recruitment efforts met with little success. The Prince's legend of invincibility had perished at Marston Moor, and conscripts displayed even less enthusiasm than usual to join his ranks. A Parliamentarian report of 12 August said:

> Prince Rupert is in Chester, his horse are quartered in the several counties of Chester, Flint and Denbigh and Montgomery … none of them to durst bring any of his forces of horse over the hills beyond Ruthin or Flint … As for the foot, by reason of his wants thereof and daily recruital out of those further parts of Wales beyond the mountains, that are compulsorily brought in daily for recruits, run away as fast back upon the first opportunities.[11]

Another report commented 'Prince Rupert is in Chester, he is diligent to make recruits, some he gets, and some he loseth, for many are gone from him lately.'[12] On 20 August, having replaced Hunckes, Rupert quit the area and headed for Bristol, where he made his headquarters, effectively throwing up his command, and leaving Lord Byron, as his deputy, to cope as best as he could. Arthur Trevor, never at a loss for a colourful phrase, told Ormonde at the end of the month that Rupert was 'without arms, a general without an army, of ordnance without cure, not a gun too, less money, much mutiny.'[13]

Byron was faced with a rapidly deteriorating situation. On 20 August the Lancashire Royalists, with only half-hearted support from the Northern Horse, were defeated by Sir John Meldrum near Ormskirk. Meldrum was able to follow up his victory with an initially loose blockade of Lathom House and Liverpool. And on the same day the Royalists suffered another blow when John Marrow was mortally wounded in a skirmish with Brereton's forces. This was followed on 26 August by a reverse for the Northern Horse at the hands of Brereton at Malpas in Cheshire.

Byron reported gloomily to Rupert:

> Lancashire [is] thus destitute of all forces, but what is left in the garrisons, the enemy quarters near Liverpool; and this night 4 of the biggest of those ships, which were formerly there, are come into the harbour, so that now I believe they

---

10 *Calendar of State Papers, Domestic Series, 1644*, ed. W.D. Hamilton (London: Eyre & Spottiswoode for HMSO, 1888), p. 417.
11 *Ibid.*, p. 424.
12 *Ibid.*, p. 426.
13 Carte, *Life of Ormonde*, vol. V, p. 349.

will make that Town their business. The soldiers are all very hearty, and so long as ammunition and victuals last will not give it up I am sure; but unless the King's affairs be so prosperous in the west that he may send some forces this way, and that your Highness return in convenient time, these countries with all the North of England, will be undoubtedly lost.[14]

Byron also had news of Sir Michael Earnley's Regiment. Henry Slingsby had noted that '100 soldiers of Sir Michael Earnley's Regiment' under a Major Palmer had marched out of York on its surrender on 14 July, and had made their way to Furness with orders to recruit.[15] However Byron now reported to the Prince:

> Sir Michael Earnley's Regiment, which I had expected to have come along with Sir Marmaduke Langdale, is left in Furness; the fault is laid upon Sir Francis Mackworth [the Earl of Newcastle's Major General of Foot] who would not suffer Sir Marmaduke to dispose of them, so that unless they make their retreat to Carlisle I know not what will become of them.[16]

19 Sir Thomas Myddelton of Chirk, Denbigh. Sergeant Major General of the Parliamentary forces in North Wales. (From reprint of John Vicars, *England's Worthies*, 1647 (London: John Russell Smith, 1845))

This is an interesting indication of the possible scale of Anglo-Irish losses at Marston Moor. It will be remembered that De Gomme illustrates Earnley's and Gibson's Regiments being in a combined division at the battle, suggesting a total of around 500 men. If we make the possibly rash assumption that each regiment had around 200–250 men, then Earnley's had apparently lost, at least temporarily, half its number.

The regiment itself was apparently at least partially reformed when Earnley became governor of Shrewsbury. As for Palmer's detachment, it seems most likely that they did take refuge in Carlisle, and after its garrison joined the King on their surrender in July 1645, this may be the company of Earnley's noted that autumn in Bridgnorth garrison.[17]

On 3 September Sir Thomas Myddelton advanced into Montgomeryshire, his first objective being an ammunition convoy from Bristol on its way to resupply Byron at Chester, who was critically short of powder. If he succeeded in capturing it, Myddelton intended to continue and attempt to surprise Montgomery Castle.

The ammunition convoy reached Newtown on 3 September. Early next morning Myddelton's men surprised the town, capturing a number of

14   John Lewis (ed.), *Your Highness' Most Obedient Servant* (Newtown: Jacobus, 1996), p.25.
15   Sir Henry Slingsby, *The Diary of Sir Henry Slingsby* (London: Longman et al., 1836), p. 124.
16   Lewis, op. cit.
17   Symonds, p. 80.

officers and men of Prince Rupert's Regiment of Horse. They also took the convoy of four wagons, with 36 barrels of powder, 12 barrels of sulphur, a particularly serious loss for Byron's powder mill in Chester, and a quantity of shot and match.

From here Myddelton moved on to Montgomery Castle, whose owner, the eccentric Lord Herbert, was intimidated into surrendering early on 6 September after the Parliamentarians breached the outer gate with a petard.

Strongly positioned on high ground, the castle dominated the Vale of Montgomery and the nearby crossing of the Severn. In enemy hands it was another serious threat to Royalist communications and opened the way for a further advance into Mid Wales.

The news was carried to Sir Michael Earnley, senior commander at Shrewsbury, who had already been preparing – with Sir Lewis Kirke, Governor of Bridgnorth, and Sir Michael Woodhouse, Governor of Ludlow – to lead a relief force to Montgomery. In all about 1,400 foot from the Shropshire garrisons and a mixed contingent of horse were despatched. The Royalists reached Montgomery early on 8 September, and forced Myddelton's foot to take refuge in the castle whilst Myddelton himself and the horse headed for Oswestry.

The Royalists, under the command of Colonel Robert Broughton, set about besieging the castle, hoping to starve the poorly provisioned garrison into surrender fairly quickly.

Myddelton meanwhile appealed to Sir William Brereton and Sir John Meldrum for help; the latter abandoned operations against Liverpool to go to the relief of the castle. Lord Byron reacted by preparing to reinforce Broughton from Chester.

20 The ruins of Montgomery Castle. (Photo: Jonathan Worton)

21 The likely battlefield landscape of Montgomery, looking north towards valley of Camlad. (Photo: Jonathan Worton)

The core of the Royalist foot remained the Anglo-Irish. Rupert had initially salvaged 2,000 foot after Marston Moor, though how many of them were the veterans from Ireland is impossible to estimate with certainty. No doubt other stragglers rejoined later. At Montgomery five regiments were named by the Parliamentarians as being present: those of Warren, Earnley, Hunckes, Broughton, and Tillier. Gibson's seems to have concentrated mainly on the defence of Chester. It seems likely that after Marston Moor attempts were made to rebuild the regiments around cadres which had been left behind in the Marches garrisons. This must particularly have been the case with Earnley's unit, and Tillier's also had suffered heavily. It seems that this favourite regiment of Rupert's may have been given some priority in recruits, given that green cloth stored at Powis Castle was earmarked for new clothing for this unit.[18] Jonathan Worton suggests that none of the Anglo-Irish mustered more than about 300 men, a significant proportion of whom may have been new recruits.[19] It is possible that a detachment of Lord Byron's Regiment of Foot may also have been present.

Strengths of the individual regiments must be hypothetical, but Warren's and Earnley's may both have had about 200 men, Hunckes', Broughton's and Tillier's perhaps 300 each, Byron's Regiment of Foot perhaps 100.

On 17 September Byron joined Broughton before Montgomery, and the combined Parliamentarian forces arrived later the same day. The Royalists with drew to the nearby high ground centred on a pre-Roman hill fort, Fridd Faldwyn.

On the morning of 18 September the main Royalist force was stationed on Fridd Faldwyn, with a detachment continuing to hold the siege lines around the castle. A Royalist Council of War, perhaps urged on by Sir William

---

18 Phillips, vol. II, p. 195.
19 Jonathan Worton, *The Battle of Montgomery 1644* (Solihull: Helion & Company, 2017), p. 43.

Vaughan, seems to have decided to mount a full-scale attack, possibly triggered at dawn when they observed that a large part of the Parliamentarian horse were absent foraging for supplies to attempt to run into the castle. To Byron and his commanders, particularly as their own horse were variable in quality, it must have seemed too good an opportunity to miss. Rather as at Nantwich in January, Byron decided on an immediate general attack.

There were probably a number of reasons for this. There are indications that the Royalist foot were still short of muskets after Marston Moor, and had a higher proportion of pikes than usual. It also seems likely that the Parliamentarian Cheshire foot were mainly musketeers, who might be at a disadvantage in hand-to-hand fighting. The Royalists for their part would probably not fare well in a prolonged firefight.

If as seems likely that the Royalists totalled in the region of 4,500 men; they had a distinct numerical advantage against Meldrum's force, reduced by the temporary absence of most of their horse to less than 3,000. It was a gamble by Byron, but one which seemed to have good prospects of success.

Meldrum described how 'Their horse and foot came on with great courage, resolving to break through our forces.'[20] It seems that the Royalist horse, who seem to have been deployed entirely on Byron's left with the aim of turning the Parliamentarian line and cutting their line of retreat over the River Camlad, were initially successful, though the Parliamentarians pushed back and did not break.

The Royalist foot led by Robert Broughton and Henry Washington were also initially successful. The Cheshire foot seem to have fired their three-rank salvo at too great a range, allowing the Royalists to close in before delivering a return salvo and then closing in, in hand-to-hand fighting. Sir William Brereton admitted that, 'It came to push of pike, wherein they were much too hard for us, having many more pikes.'[21]

However the Royalist assault did not result in the hoped-for collapse of the opposing foot. The Parliamentarian first line fell back on their supports, and stood firm. Meldrum paid tribute to 'the Cheshire Foot, with their officers, [who] carried themselves more like lions than men.'[22] Even so, as a Parliamentarian newsbook put it: 'The enemy put by our pikes and the day seemed very doubtful, they being encouraged, crying "the day is ours, the day is ours."'[23] Brereton agreed that 'it was very dubious and uncertain which way the Lord would incline the victory.'[24]

However the Parliamentarians were saved by the poor performance of the Royalist horse. At least according to Arthur Trevor's account, his brother Marcus's Regiment fought well, but was not supported properly by the Lancashire horse in particular, who had been defeated by Meldrum at

20 Phillips, vol. II, p. 205.
21 *Ibid.*, p. 202.
22 *Ibid.*, p. 205.
23 Phillips, vol. II, p. 205.
24 *Ibid.*, p. 209.

22 The view towards the town of Montgomery, showing the possible Royalist start line on the furthest ridge seen ascended by road. (Photo: Jonathan Worton)

23 The view looking north from Montgomery from the area suggested as Parliamentarian lines. (Photo: Jonathan Worton)

Ormskirk on 20 August, and Sir William Vaughan allegedly 'contributed not much to the action.'[25]

With the probable return of their foraging parties, the Parliamentarian horse counter-attacked and Byron's cavalry collapsed and fled the field.

Thus left on their own, the Royalist foot began to lose heart. Byron claimed that Robert Ellice's Regiment, on his left, was the first to break. This was followed by a general Parliamentarian counter-attack, and the whole of Byron's foot, Anglo-Irish veterans and raw recruits alike, broke. Arthur Trevor wrote that 'our men ran shamefully, when they had no cause of so great fear.'[26] The panic was increased, rather as at Nantwich, when the castle garrison made a sortie, driving away the guards in the siegeworks and threatening the rear of the wavering Royalist foot. A mass collapse of the foot followed, with most of them surrendering on the spot or breaking in flight. Many of the fugitives will have fallen victim to pursuing Parliamentarian horse.

Parliamentarian claims of the numbers of prisoners varied between 1,200 and 1,500, added to around 500 other Royalists killed or wounded, and the capture of up to 1,500 weapons. The list of officers captured bears witness to the damage inflicted on what remained of the Army of Leinster ('I' refers to identified Anglo-Irish officers):

Colonel [Major General] Robert Broughton (I)
Sir Thomas Tyldesley
Lieutenant-Colonel Bladwell
Major Williams
Captains Boulton, Egerton, Bellamy, Lloyd, Dolben, Congreve, Bowman, Wright, Morgan
Lieutenants Sydney, Rowes, Griffith, Morgan, Thurland, Wilson, Lloyd, Lewis, Bowen, Bricham, Hager, Minchley, Lloyd, Oliver, Kavanagh, Perkins, Aldersley
Quartermaster Snelling
Cornets Parsons, Hackkison, Stagge
Ensigns Wallis, Williams, Dutton, Lampley, Parr, Edwards, Clanton, Harrison, Coutry, Hest, Lagden, Jones, Barker, Price, Roberts, Richardson, Prichard, Winn, Johnson, Roe, Wright, Erwin[27]

Some at least of Sir Fulke Hunckes' Regiment were reported by Meldrum as returning to Shrewsbury, and Byron and the horse to Chester, but as Sir John told the Committee of Both Kingdoms, 'by that blow given here the best of their foot are taken away.'[28]

Sir Michael Earnley sent the first brief Royalist report to Prince Rupert:

I am very sorry that I hath not better news to present you withal. Upon the delivery of the Castle of Montgomery to the enemy by the treacherous Lord of

---

25 *Ibid.*, p. 208.
26 *Ibid.*, pp. 206–8.
27 *Ibid.*, pp. 207–8.
28 *Ibid.*, p. 206.

Chirbury, for the regaining of it, and your Highness's powder, which was taken at Newtown, and brought thither, I drew out a considerable force of horse and foot, who marched thither, here they beat Sir Thomas Middleton, and forced both his horse and foot into the castle, and kept them in ten days, and upon intelligence of the enemy's drawing thither for their relief, my Lord Byron came thither with a considerable force on Tuesday last, where it was our hap to be beaten yesterday, and the castle relieved ...[29]

Arthur Trevor minced no words in his report to Ormonde:

My last letter to your Excellency left the business before Montgomery in the balance, and this will inform your Lordship that, both parties being weighed, we were found too light (of foot at least) for, in plain English, our men ran shamefully when they had no cause of so great fear, so that we here are ordained to be the mocking-stock of the War.

The first charge was made by my brother upon all their horse, who killed Sir William Fairfax at the head of them, and put them all in disorder. Broughton and Washington did as well with the foot. Sir William Vaughan was the occasion of fighting the enemy in that place; but as my lord Byron tells me, contributed not much to the action. All the Lancashire horse ran without a blow struck, which disheartened the foot so infinitely that, being in disorder with the pursuit of the enemy, they could not be persuaded to rally again, which the rebels did, and advanced and made good the place, relieved the castle, being the work they came for, and took some prisoners. Our party consisted of 1,500 horse, and 2,000 foot, being the regiments of Broughton, Tillier, Warren, Hunckes, Ernley and the Prince of Wales, and are all taken. There are not 100 foot come off, and all their officers which were not taken before, killed or taken. Col. Broughton was there shot and taken prisoner ...Lord Byron, who is here observed never to have prospered since his practice to supplant Capel, who is as prudent and valiant a person as the nation affords ...[30]

Trevor was being typically malicious, of course, though Byron's record in the field, other than as cavalry commander, was at best mixed. The Irish regiments, at least in theory, remained in being, but as a force capable of taking the field independently, the Army of Leinster had ceased to exist. What remained of it was largely confined to the garrisons of Lathom House, Liverpool, Chester and Shrewsbury, to which the Parliamentarians now turned their attention.

There was now a significant change in Parliament's attitude towards troops from Ireland. Hitherto, although there had been frequent claims in Parliamentarian newsletters and propaganda of the depredations of the 'bloody Irish rebels' said to have been brought over to England by the Royalists, there had been no officially sanctioned reprisals against any troops from Ireland taken prisoner, who indeed had been readily enlisted into the Parliamentarian forces. However on 24 October an ordinance was issued by

---

29 *Ibid.*, pp. 208–9.
30 *Ibid.*, pp. 208–9.

Parliament declaring that no quarter was to be given to 'any Irishman or to any Papist born in Ireland which shall be taken in arms against Parliament in England.'[31] It is not entirely clear why the ordinance was passed at this date, before there was any sign of direct military support from the Irish Confederates for the King. It was possibly intended to keep up the fear of the Irish among the English population, and as a warning to any Irish who might come over in the future.

In practice, most Parliamentarian commanders, either from fear of Royalist reprisals or because of the huge difficulty in distinguishing between 'an Englishman by descent but an Irishman born' and so-called 'native Irish', especially if there was no evidence of the prisoner's religion, were initially unwilling to take drastic action. But the threat presented by the new ordinance would have a major role in events at Liverpool.

On 29 September Sir John Meldrum explained to the Committee of Both Kingdoms his intention to resume operations against Liverpool, ordering the Lancashire troops of Richard Shuttleworth and George Dodding to join him before the town. He explained that:

> The enemy is stronger within the town of Liverpool than we are without, besides the advantage of very strong works. It is rumoured that the Irish here desire to return and serve in Ireland if they may have quarter. These propositions have been made by the Irish to Lieutenant-Colonel Coote, son of Sir Charles Coote. I shall forbear to meddle upon so ticklish a point without your approval, which I entreat may be done with all expedition, in regard I am resolved to make trial so soon as the forces are ready.[32]

The garrison of Liverpool, with Sir Robert Byron as Governor, consisted of Cuthbert Clifton's Lancashire regiment and what is usually described as Robert Byron's Regiment. It does seem that part of Lord Byron's Regiment of Foot was also present. What is less clear is the precise identity of the 'Irish' who were in touch with Lieutenant Colonel Coote. It may be that Robert Byron's men had heard of Brereton's plan to have the Montgomery prisoners take the Covenant and be shipped back to Ireland to fight the Confederates, but Lord Byron's reaction later suggests that the culprits (in his eyes) were men of his own regiment.

Meldrum was anxious to foster unrest and alarm among the men of the Liverpool garrison, as reflected in his summons on 30 September to Sir Robert Byron:

> If you will render up the Town of Liverpool, with such Ordnance, Ammunition, and Arms, as are within the town, for the use of King and Parliament, you may expect such conditions for yourself and your officers as is fitting for your several qualities, for your baggage, horse and arms. And for the soldiers (of what nation soever) a free passage to their Country or dwelling houses without molestation,

---

31 See Brereton, *Letter Books*, vol. II, Appendix 1.
32 *Calendar of State Papers, Domestic Series, 1644–1645*, ed. W.D. Hamilton (London: Eyre & Spottiswoode for HMSO, 1890), pp. 9–12.

> or to march to any part of the kingdom in safety (Chester excepted). Otherwise you may expect no other quarter but such as the subjects of this Kingdom (being sensible of the butcherly cruelties as have been practised in Ireland, and here in Lancashire and highly exasperated against such natives as have brought in strangers to rip up the bowels of their own country by invading England) will give …[33]

In fact Meldrum was worried by lack of supplies and the raiding activities of the garrison of Lathom House. But the situation of the Liverpool garrison was also far from good. On 7 October Lord Byron told Prince Rupert:

> The officers at Liverpool are desirous to endure all extremities rather than yield the Town, but the soldiers for want of pay grow extreme mutinous, and daily run away; so that unless relief come very speedily I fear they will be forced to make the best conditions for themselves they can, and to yield up the Town which being once in the enemy's hands, Chester will be immediately blocked up on all sides. My Brother writ me word Liverpool was victualled but for fourteen days, of which some are already spent.[34]

Meldrum was anxious to bring operations at Liverpool to a close before the onset of winter, and therefore renewed his offer of terms to the garrison. The ordinary soldiers could take service with Parliament, and might serve in England, or in Ireland under the personal guarantee of Lieutenant Colonel Coote. Alternatively they might return either to their homes or to any Royalist garrison chosen by their officers.

Meldrum's offer was dismissed by Lord Byron as 'an insolent summons', and also rejected by Sir Robert Byron and his officers, who demanded more lenient terms. This was a serious mistake which ignored the mounting discontent of their soldiers. The Royalist situation was worsened early in October when Brereton's forces occupied the northern part of Wirral, making it impossible to slip any supplies through the Parliamentarian blockade. By 17 October Brereton was reporting to the Committee of Both Kingdoms that many of the soldiers in Liverpool were deserting thanks to clandestine contacts with Lieutenant-Colonel Coote, though some of the 'native Irish' were understandably cautious, and Brereton admitted that 'the officers have very subtly spun out the time, as though they intended to attempt an escape and break through the leaguer. I hope a little time will produce much.'[35]

A few days later he admitted to Sir Samuel Luke:

> Liverpool is very obstinate, but I doubt not in a short time we shall be master thereof. It may be God has a purpose to reckon with them for the blood formerly shed there and at Bolton, and to that end to harden them and to possess them with an obstinacy which may work for their own absolute destruction, there being grand Papists and Irish rebels, most bloody persons. I have offered Sir John

---

33 *Calendar of State Papers 1644–1645*, p. 252.
34 Lewis, *Your Highness' Most Obedient Servant*, p. 28.
35 *Calendar of State Papers 1644–1645*, pp. 46–7.

Meldrum 500 men to storm the town in case they will not surrender speedily and on reasonable conditions.[36]

Fortunately for all concerned, Meldrum had a more pragmatic attitude than his Cheshire colleague; in any case, the Royalist defence of Liverpool was collapsing. At the end of October, 'the English soldiers therein … having combined together, came away out of the Town, and drove away with them the Cattle that was thereabout…' Some of these troops, about 60 in number, and probably of Robert Byron's Regiment, took service with Parliament. Now, 'the Irish, seeing themselves left, only with some few English Commanders, they also being in great straits, and knowing no quarter would be given them, if they stood it out, they therefore also voluntarily came forth of the Town and cast themselves at Sir John Meldrum's feet …' According to Lord Byron the soldiers, 'after they had set guards on my brother and all the officers … sent out two sergeants, one of mine, the other of my brother's regiment to make conditions with Meldrum.' The Parliamentarian commander granted the common soldiers, perhaps 600 in number, terms not dissimilar to those which had been offered to Robert Byron early in October. Claiming, just about plausibly, that negotiations were completed 'before the Ordnance of Parliament against the Irish came into his hands or knowledge', Meldrum gave the Irish soldiers safe passage back home on their oath that they would not take up arms again against the English. The English troops in the garrison could either change sides or return to their homes.[37]

For the Royalist officers, including Robert Byron and Major Robert Bembridge of Robert Byron's Regiment of Horse, 14 captains and other officers, there was no such generosity. They would be held captive until exchanged. For some it would be a long captivity. Sir Robert, despite increasingly angry demands from his brother, was not given high priority by the Royalist higher command, and was imprisoned in Manchester and York until April 1645.

Brereton added further details of the surrender: 'The Irish should be transported to Ireland and take an oath never to molest England any more. Those that are English were to be entertained if they pleased, or also take an oath not to bear arms, and to repair every one to their several dwellings.'[38]

Lord Byron was furious concerning the circumstances of Liverpool's surrender, telling Lord Ormonde:

I must give your Excellency a sad account of the loss of Liverpool. Through the treachery of the common soldiers, who (not pressed with any other want but of loyalty or courage) most basely gave up both town and their officers to the mercy of the rebels. I had furnished Captain Lloyd's frigate [the *Swan*] with a new supply of victuals for the town, (which might have passed in despite of all their ships) but before the relief could come they had set guards upon my brother and all

---

36   Samuel Luke, ed. H.G. Tibbutt, *The Letter Books of Sir Samuel Luke*, 1644–1645 (St Albans, for HMSO, 1963), item 862.

37   *Ibid.*

38   Luke, p. 348.

the officers and sent out two sergeants, one of mine, the other of my brother's regiment to make conditions with Meldrum, which were, to deliver up all their officers prisoners; themselves, either to take up arms for the rebels, or to be transported into Ireland for the service of the rebels there. Some few of them are since fallen into my hands, upon whom I have done justice: and if any of them hereafter shall be taken by your Excellency's forces, I humbly desire they may be made examples of disloyalty and Treachery; and the rather, because they were all natives of Ireland, and therefore the more trusted here, as not so apt to be seduced as the people of this country. My brother Robin is now prisoner at Manchester, with some of his officers, the rest being dispersed into other garrisons of the rebels; and I am so unfortunate, as at this time to have no exchange for him here. There is one Wemyss, a Scotchman who was General of the Ordnance to Waller, now a prisoner at Ludlow, who I believe would exchange for my brother, and his Lieutenant Colonel, Sir Francis Butler. I have written to Court about him; but what I shall say may perhaps be thought to proceed from the affection of a brother; and therefore do humbly desire your Excellency would be pleased to urge this exchange in your next letters to Court; which will infinitely add to those many obligations your Excellency has already been pleased to put upon me and my family.[39]

The fate of the soldiers who fell into Byron's vengeful hands was recorded by Randle Holme in Chester:

9 November 1644, being Saturday in the forenoon the gibbet was by the Lord Bishop's means removed from the Abbey Gate field to the side of the pillory by the cornmarket house. Four Soldiers with papers on their breast were hanged, whereupon was written in text letters, 'These men die for treachery in betraying Liverpool'.[40]

These were probably from Robert Byron's Regiment, which now ceased to exist, apart from perhaps a company remaining in Chester. Others, however, evidently from Lord Byron's Regiment, were shipped back to Dublin, where they were rounded up by Colonel Thomas Napier, Byron's recruiting agent, and sent back to serve with Lord Byron to the end of the war.[41]

The remainder of the Anglo-Irish remnant who escaped from Montgomery, except apparently for Gibson's Regiment, were in no state to take the field. Byron presumably made attempts to raise more conscripts to bolster their ranks, but had little success. His strongest Anglo-Irish unit was probably Richard Gibson's Regiment, possibly commanded by Lieutenant-Colonel George Vane. But Byron had little support from the war-weary population of North Wales, or from garrison commanders, anxious to preserve local resources for themselves.

---

39 Lewis, op. cit., p. 25.
40 British Library, Harleian MS 2135, quoted in Morris and Lawson, p. 68.
41 BCW Regimental wiki for John Byron's Regiment of Foot <http://https://wiki.bcw-project.org/royalist/foot-regiments/lord-byron>.

On 18 October Sir John Mennes reported to Prince Rupert that Gibson's men 'would not be suffered to enter into Conway, but had the gates shut on them'. Byron recalled them to Chester.[42]

From November onwards, Brereton steadily tightened his blockade of Chester, aided by lack of reaction from the Royalists. In part this was the result of the disasters at Liverpool and Montgomery, but also because of friction between Byron and Will Legge, the Governor of Chester appointed by Rupert in the summer. Legge blamed Byron for the defeat at Montgomery, Byron blamed Legge, for reasons which are obscure, for the loss of Liverpool The result was that there was evidently little cooperation between them.

The last offensive move by the Anglo-Irish whilst under Byron's command came on 18 January 1645 when Byron and Legge mounted an attack aimed at attacking and burning a new Parliamentarian outpost at Chrisleton and then move on to relieve Beeston Castle. It was an ambitious plan, even though the Royalists planned to surprise the enemy garrison at Chrisleton. The Royalists mustered around 600 horse and 800 foot, the latter including Gibson's men, Prince Rupert's Regiment of Foot, and Sir Francis Gamull's city Regiment. Speed was essential if the enemy were to be taken by surprise, but, perhaps because of friction between Byron and Legge, or the reluctance of Gamull's men to take part, the operation was mismanaged from the start.

There was considerable delay in the expedition setting out, in a dilatory advance 'rather for a May show than a warlike procession',[43] and by the time the Royalists had progressed down Foregate Street and out of the defences at Boughton Turnpike, they were considerably strung out. The enemy had had ample warning of their approach, and drawn out 700 foot to meet them.

The Royalist vanguard of 300 musketeers were engaged whilst their main body was still leaving the outworks, and attempted to occupy a holding position in the hedgerows along the lane between Boughton and Chrisleton until the main force could join them. But they were charged by the Parliamentarian horse led by Michael Jones and Jerome Zankey. The Royalist soldiers, some of them evidently raw recruits, or the citizen soldiers seeing their first serious action, were 'terrified', and many of them 'cast down their Arms'. Particularly to blame, according to Randle Holme, was Prince Rupert's Regiment: 'The Bluecoats ran ere they shot, and flung away their drums, wheeling towards the waterside [the Dee]'.

Jones and Zankey caught the Royalist horse still attempting to deploy, and drove them back towards the outworks, while the Cheshire Parliamentarian foot under Major General James Lothian cleared away the Royalist musketeers remaining in the hedgerows leading to Boughton.

Before any Royalist reinforcements could enter the fight, the Parliamentarians made an orderly withdrawal to Chrisleton, driving along with them some prisoners 'and whom we could not bring off we cut and slashed miserably, which caused many to supplicate themselves prisoners, that they might escape wounds.'

---

42 *Ibid.*
43 British Library, Harleian MS 2135, quoted in Morris and Lawson, p. 68.

Royalist casualties in this mismanaged affair were heavy. Though they lost relatively few dead, apart from 40 men said to have been drowned in the River Dee, large numbers were taken prisoner. The common soldiers captured were said to be 'most of them Chester men, as Shoemakers, Cobblers, Taylors, Barbers and the like ... to the great amazement of the Citizens, who vowed that they would never come out again.'

It is clear from the prisoner lists that there were also some of the Anglo-Irish ('I' refers to identified Anglo-Irish officers):

Colonel Robert Werden (successor to John Marrow)
Colonel George Vane (Gibson's?)
Lieutenant-Colonel Gough (I)
Majors Gray (I), Deane (I)
Captains Rory O'Neale ('a notorious Irish Rebel', Byron's Foot?),
　　　　Harrington, Ware, Pool, Ravenscroft
Captain-Lieutenant Marrow-Haggen
Lieutenants Humphreys, Goulborne, Wright, Davies, Dowdell, Balls,
　　　　Castleton, Brookes, Bryan, Dering
Ensigns Musgrave, Gorse, George and Chute
Sergeants Price, Moulton
Corporal Jackson

Of Major Mainwaring's Regiment [Gamull's Foot] were taken 36 men, 1 of Colonel Trevor's [Marcus Trevor, H]; 5 of Sir Robert Byron's Regiment of Foot [I]; 33 of Colonel Warden's [possibly Warren (I)]; 1 of Capt. Smith's, 11 of Capt. Morgan's, 2 of Lieutenant Col. Grosvenor [Gamull's Foot], 6 of Captain Lloyd, 1 of Capt. Rews, 2 of Capt. Pritchard's, 2 of Col. Russell's [Prince Rupert's regiment of foot] and of Legge, the Governor's own troop, 4.[44]

The defeat marked the end of Byron's ability to mount significant offensive operations, and left Chester under increasing threat. Byron appealed for aid to Prince Maurice, who had succeeded his brother Rupert in command in the Marches.

Maurice stripped the garrisons of Staffordshire and Shropshire, especially Shrewsbury, and mustered around 2,000 men. Joined by Welsh Royalist troops, he managed to open the Welsh side of Chester, but it was outweighed by disaster elsewhere.

Sir Michael Earnley, though in increasing ill-health, was still Governor of Shrewsbury, and on 25 January 1645 had written to Sir Francis Ottley, a Shropshire Commissioner of Array, and himself a former Governor of Shrewsbury:

Although you pleased to join with the gentlemen of this county to promise me contributions speedily to be brought in for the subsistence of this Garrison, yet, neither you nor they, have performed. By means whereof I am in extreme hazard of a Mutiny, which I can no less conceive to be the aim of those that have brought

---

44 *Perfect Passages*, no. 14, Jan. 22, 1645.

me to this distraction. Here is not now any money towards the pay of the Soldiers twelve pence. I shall desire you to give them notice hereof, and to take some present course that I may be presently supplied, or otherwise I must be enforced to suffer the Soldiers to live as they may.[45]

Earnley's difficulties were increased when Prince Maurice removed part of the garrison for his attempt to relieve Chester. The Parliamentarians were aware of the opportunity presented to them, and on 21 February the Shropshire Committee drew out from their garrisons 250 foot and 250 horse. They were reinforced by 250 Cheshire foot and 350 Staffordshire horse. The foot were under the command of Lieutenant Colonel Reinking, the Dutch or German professional soldier employed by the Shropshire Committee, whilst Thomas Mytton led the horse.

Shrewsbury was strongly fortified, and even against the weakened garrison surprise was essential. The Parliamentarians arrived before the town at about 3:00 a.m. on the morning of 22 February:

How to get over the work was both dangerous and difficult, being strongly pallisadoed and well fortified. We therefore, in a little boat that was provided for the purpose, conveyed eight carpenters up the river, and landed them within the enemy's breastwork under the castle hill. On the east side were the sentinels, [who] after some pause gave fire upon them, but they soon sawed down so any of the pallisades as gave our men free passage. The first that stormed were 40 troopers dismounted, with their pistols and about as many firelocks … After these followed some other musketeers along Severn side, under Castle hill, and near Sir William Owen's house, entered the town. After these marched 350 foot under the command of Lieut Col Reinking. These having gained the streets part of them marched to the market place, who after some exchange of shot gained the main court of guard there. The rest marched to the castle foregate, which within quarter of an hour was gained, the gates opened, the drawbridge let down, at which our horse, under the command of Col. Mytton and Col. Bowyer, with the gentlemen of the Committee, entered. It was now about break of day. The shrieks of the town was such strange kind of cock-crowing as I believe you never heard the like. Being thus entered, the castle and a strong outwork at Frankwell held out, but by twelve o clock the castle was delivered upon these conditions: 'That the English should march to Ludlow, but the Irish be delivered up', which we shall hang with authority. The strong work at Frankwell was surrendered upon bare quarter.[46]

Most of the officers were taken in their beds, among them Sir Michael Earnley, sometimes stated incorrectly to have been killed. He remained in custody, and died, probably of consumption, in April, and was buried in St Margaret's Church.

The other prisoners included:

Major Earnley (Sir Michael's brother)

---

45 *The Ottley Papers*, vol. V, p. 270.
46 Quoted in *The Ottley Papers*, vol. II, pp. 235–6.

Lieutenant-Colonels Edward Owen, Thomas Owen

Major Ranger

Captains Rainsford, Lucas, Cressy, Collins, Long, Pontesbury Owen, Henry Harrison

Lieutenants Charles Smith, Edward Palmer, Matthew Wightwicke[47]

The Shropshire Committee carried out their threat and hanged 13 'Irish' prisoners. They were claimed to be 'native Irish' and so executed under the terms of Parliament's ordinance. Rupert, however, thought otherwise, and retaliated by hanging the same number of Parliamentarian prisoners. These were apparently soldiers of the Shropshire Committee, taken in March during his operations in Cheshire. The incident is described in a Royalist account:

> Monday 17. The Princes met at [Fenn's Moss] and that night quartered at Whitchurch. Mytton came in our rear. We took 12 prisoners.
>
> Wednesday 19. The rendezvous at Bunbury Heath where the Prince [Rupert] having intelligence of 1500 of the rebels to be near Whitchurch drew a large party thither but the enemy, having notice of his advance, hastened to Shrewsbury. Our men followed in the rear, killed one and took some few prisoners. This day at the rendezvous we hanged the 12 prisoners taken on Monday all on one crabtree, they having formerly served his Majesty and we being invited142 thereunto by their examples at Shrewsbury.[48]

Rupert explained his decision in a furious letter of 15 April to the Earl of Essex:

> I cannot see why the Houses should think it strange that I have used some prisoners I have taken in the same way that some of my soldiers have been used. Those executed, after having been granted quarter at Shrewsbury, had served the king well against the Irish rebels, and, after the Cessation, were by his command brought over here, where they again performed their duty. I would not be doing my duty if I had not let those that massacred them know that their own men must pay the price for their inhumanity…
>
> That all good men must abhor the circumstances of blood and cruelty caused by the rebellion in Ireland (and all other rebellions) is not applicable to this argument. Many of your soldiers served the King in Ireland, yet when they are taken, they are given quarter by this side and it is observed. If you do not do the like, and quarter is denied to all who are proclaimed traitors and rebels by act of Parl. the war will become more merciless and bloody than it hath been or any good man or true Englishman could desire it to be so. Nor can the threat in your letter to use all prisoners taken from the King's army in this manner make any impression on me other than that of grief at such contrary to the rules and customs of war in the Christian world. If such an ordnance be made, would you expect I should submit to it and continue to allow quarter to your men. I have taken prisoners, among those that have taken up arms against the King, men of all

---

47 *Ibid.*

48 Brereton, *Letter Books*, vol. I, item 242.

nations – English, Scotch, Irish, French, Dutch, Walloons – and of all religions and opinions averred by Christians, and have always allowed them free quarter and free exchange. I will continue to do so, hoping that God will open the eyes of those who have been so strangely deceived into arms against the King to the scandal and destruction of the Protestant religion (in which I was born and in which I will die) and of the Parl. of which the King is head, and that they will subdue those who out of ambition and malice have made the paths in which they all tread. But, if the contrary course shall be held and those under my command are murdered in cold blood when taken prisoner, under what senseless and unjust pretensions whatsoever, I will cause for every officer and soldier of mine so treated, the same number of yours that are taken prisoner to be put to death in the same manner. Their blood, together with that of those murdered under your ordnance, will be required at the hands of those who by their actions force others to observe the rules they lay down. And since they have not listened to the King's gracious offer of peace, the English nation seems like to be in danger of destroying itself.[49]

Rupert's threatened reprisals did not end the killings of the 'Irish'. Because of the location of the Anglo-Irish troops, the focus was naturally on Cheshire and Shropshire, and in fact executions had taken place before the Shrewsbury incident. There was variation in how rigorously and with what degree of enthusiasm the terms of Parliament's ordinance were applied. Sir William Brereton seems to have been in favour of enforcing the ordnance, but as we have seen, Sir John Meldrum at Liverpool had taken pains to avoid doing so, even though some of the enemy he was dealing with were clearly 'native Irish'.

Some of Brereton's officers were reluctant to carry out death sentences. When Major Croxton, Governor of Nantwich, was asked by Brereton to execute some soldiers captured from the Beeston Castle garrison, he responded that, 'I could have wished that no quarter had been given to them that were first taken, but having quarter given them I know of no order or ordnance that authoriseth the taking away of their lives.' Croxton's motivation was not concern for the prisoners but the fear of reprisals. 'The castle soldiers have taken divers of our men prisoners since theirs were taken, who must expect no more mercy than we intend to them. I refer this to your further order.'[50] The most infamous episode, as we have seen, was the killing of Colonel Willoughby's men. There was no similarly large-scale killing until near the end of the war, apart from the killing of women at Naseby, which we look at below.

When prisoners were executed, both sides tended to find other reasons. Desertion from their own forces was often cited, even if the victim was also described as Irish. The Staffordshire Parliamentarian Committee attempted to shift responsibility for dealing with two 'Irish' prisoners by handing them over to Colonel Fox, who was known to have no hesitation in killing 'Irish' prisoners.

---

49 Brereton, *Letter Books*, vol. I, item 250.
50 *Ibid.*

On 19 March, having reinforced Prince Maurice, Rupert again forced Brereton to raise his 'leaguer' of Chester. Will Legge had been recalled to Oxford in January, and Byron was confirmed as Governor of Chester in his place. This gave him little comfort, for on leaving, the Princes took with them most of the remaining Anglo-Irish troops. Byron wrote bitterly of this on 26 April to Lord Digby:

> The business of Hereford interfering [a major rising by Clubmen] Prince Rupert was suddenly called away before either ammunition or victual could be brought into Chester, and together with his Highness marched away the remainder of the old Irish regiments with some other horse and foot to the number of at least 1,200, so that I was left in the town with only a garrison of citizens and my own and colonel Mostyn's regiments which both together made not above 600 men, whereof half were being Mostyn's men.[51]

It seems in fact that Byron was not entirely accurate. There is, as we shall see, evidence that some at least of Gibson's Regiment remained in the Chester area. The troops taken away by Rupert also included his own regiment of foot, and possibly his regiment of horse, if it had remained in Chester after the defeat at Montgomery. It seems likely that the remaining Anglo-Irish foot who left with Rupert numbered around 500.

---

51 *Calendar of State Papers 1644–1645*, pp. 78–79.

9

Naseby and After

The Anglo-Irish accompanied Prince Rupert into Herefordshire, where they took part in his ruthlessly effective operation to crush the Clubmen there. They were probably with the Prince and Astley at Ledbury, where Massey's Parliamentarian forces from Gloucester suffered a reverse, though no details of the part played by the Anglo-Irish are known.

Throughout these weeks, based mainly on Hereford, Rupert and Astley were endeavouring to recruit their forces, and orders had been given, for example, for 1,000 new levies from North Wales. Enlistments had mixed success, Matthew Appleyard, whose regiment was with Astley, is said to have commented of some of the Welsh levies: 'Shall I deliver muskets to such as these?'[1]

Parliamentarian reports emphasised Rupert's efforts to levy new recruits, but also suggest that many of them, especially, one suspects, the Herefordshire Clubmen forcibly conscripted, deserted at the first opportunity.

When Rupert joined the King at Stow-on-the-Wold at the start of the summer campaign, Symonds states that he brought 1,000 foot with him.[2] It is usually assumed that these comprised 500 men of his own regiment of foot, and the 500 men of the Shrewsbury Foot, as the Anglo-Irish were termed by De Gomme. This may well be so, especially as Rupert's Foot Regiment, in which he seems rather to have lost interest after Marston Moor, was still at Chester in January. However Symonds also includes the regiment in the separately listed force of 3,300 foot under Lord Astley. Although such recruits as Rupert had been able to retain were evidently used to fill out existing units, it is very unlikely that the Anglo-Irish obtained more than a few of them.

Based on the identity of officers captured at Naseby, it is evident that all of the units which came over from Ireland in the winter of 1643/44 (with the exception of the foot regiments of John and Robert Byron), were represented in the Shrewsbury Foot. Any regimental structure must have been theoretical rather than actual, and Peter Young's suggestion that they were organised into

---

1   Rev. J. Webb and Rev. T.W. Webb, *Memorials of the Civil War Between King Charles I and the Parliament of England as it Affected Herefordshire and the Adjacent Counties* (London: Longmans, 1879), vol. II, p. 225.
2   Symonds, p. 80.

10 companies, each averaging 50 men, seems quite likely. Even more than most of the Royalist units in the spring of 1645, the Shrewsbury Foot were evidently over-officered, including men who had been captured at Nantwich and/or Montgomery, and subsequently exchanged.

The Shrewsbury Foot were commanded by a Lieutenant-Colonel Smith, who has so far defied certain identification. Newman suggests a Colonel Robert Smith,[3] who had served in the West Country in 1644, but has no apparent links with the Welsh Marches or the Anglo-Irish. Perhaps more likely is a Lieutenant-Colonel George Smith, listed as a Royalist activist in Flintshire in 1658, and who may be the Lieutenant-Colonel 'Smyth' recorded by Symonds as being in command of 600–700 foot in the Marches in December 1645.[4]

The Shrewsbury Foot were now added to George Lisle's tertia. Serena Jones points out the coincidence here, that Warren's Regiment had been commanded by Lisle's younger brother at Marston Moor, where he had been killed.[5] George Lisle's tertia, partly because of the losses suffered by Lisle's own regiment during Cromwell's recent raid into Oxfordshire, began the campaign as the weakest of the Royalist foot.

The Shrewsbury Foot would have taken part in the fierce fighting on 28 May at Leicester when Lisle's tertia spearheaded the assault on the Newark breach. *Mercurius Aulicus* described how:

> The hottest and most desperate service was at the breach in the Newark-wall, which the Rebels had within fortified, having cast up a work against the breach, and bestowed there the most and best of their men; here Colonel George Lisle with his Tertia of tried Soldiers forced his entrance in despite of all the rebels Pikes, Cannon and Muskets, which poured thick upon him; the Rebels' advantage was here so great, that twice the Colonel was forced back, the Colonel himself being knocked down into the Ditch, but he and his brave men (sworn never to yield) went on the third time, and inexpressable valour beat down the Rebels and entered the Breach … Those that first Entered opened the Ports and let in the Horse which instantly entered the Town.[6]

Symonds said that Lisle was backed by the King's Regiment of Foot, but had cleared the breach before they arrived.[7] A more important role was played by Henry Bard, Richard Page and the Newark Horse, which broke through on the other side of the town, and took Lisle's opponents in the rear.

In all the Royalists lost 200–300 dead.[8] Lisle's men, including, it can be assumed, the Anglo-Irish, took part in the sacking of Leicester which followed, with quarter being denied to some of the defenders.[9]

---

3   Newman, p. 349, item 1335.
4   Symonds, p. 80
5   Serena Jones, *No Armour But Courage* (Solihull: Helion, 2016), p.271.
6   *Mercurius Aulicus*, (ed. Thomas, 1971), p. 1053.
7   Symonds, p. 51.
8   Glenn Foard, *Naseby: The Decisive Campaign* (Barnsley: Pen & Sword, 2004), p. 120.
9   *Ibid.*, pp. 119–20.

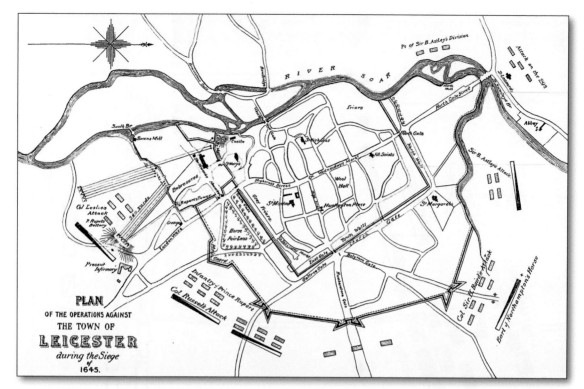

24 A nineteenth-century street plan of the Royalist assault on Leicester. (From *Glimpses of Ancient Leicester*, Mrs T. Fielding Johnson (Leicester: Clarke and Satchell, 1906), facing p. 217)

Astley's foot also included the three Anglo-Irish Regiments which had been serving with the Oxford Army foot since April 1644. Appleyard and his men were said by Symonds to have been the first to break into the town, and Appleyard was knighted and made Deputy Governor of Leicester under Lord Loughborough. A detachment of his regiment, and possibly some of Sir John Paulet's, would remain in Leicester as the core of its garrison.

It is unclear whether the Duke of York's Regiment was involved in the assault on Leicester, but with a probable strength of 500–700 men it was possibly the largest Royalist foot regiment at Naseby. Unlike some of the others it was still equipped with both pikes and muskets.

Most of our knowledge of the Royalist order of battle at Naseby is based on De Gomme's well-known plan.[10] However this needs viewing with some reservations. Its original was drawn up no later than 4 June (it includes Sir Richard Willys and some of the Newark Horse who returned to Newark that day). It will have been produced by Lord Astley, as Major General, no doubt with input from Prince Rupert, and although it certainly seems to have represented the Royalist deployment at least to a great extent, the possibility exists that there were changes in deployment before battle was joined on 14 June.

For example, the plan does not include either Appleyard's or Paulet's Regiments. Some of Appleyard's remained with him in Leicester, and it was plausibly suggested by Young that the remainder and Paulet's men formed

---

10 Young, *Naseby 1645: The Campaign and the Battle* (London: Century, 1985), pp. 101–5.

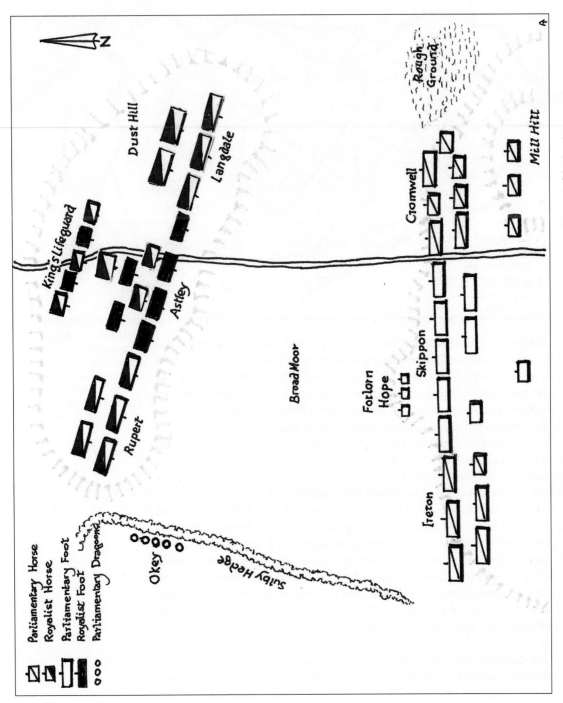

Map 5 Naseby, 14 June 1645. The defeat of the King's Oxford Army at Naseby was to signal the end of the Royalist cause.

the detached bodies of musketeers who supported the Royalist horse during the battle. Both were probably all-musketeer units.

The Shrewsbury Foot formed the second line of Lisle's Tertia during the battle. After the initial clash between the foot, the Anglo-Irish were brought up in support with the rest of the second line. There are no surviving details of their role in the battle. Like most of the Royalist foot, they were overwhelmed and the survivors forced to surrender. They were probably among the foot who came under attack from Cromwell's horse and Fairfax's Regiment of Foot.

On the right of the Royalist foot, the Duke of York's Regiment repelled an attack by Ireton and some of his horse. Ireton was wounded in the leg by a halberd and briefly captured.

Several units made a last stand, and although this extract from *The Kingdom's Weekly Intelligencer* is normally thought to refer to Prince Rupert's Regiment, it is possible that it could refer to the Shrewsbury Foot:

> The Blue Regiment of the King's stood to it very stoutly and stirred not, like a wall of brass, though encompassed by our Forces; so that our men were forced to knock them down with the butt end of the Musket. It is conceived that a great part of them were Irish, and chose rather to die in the field than be hanged.[11]

The most notorious episode in the aftermath to Naseby was the massacre of a number of women found in the Royalist baggage train. There has been considerable debate regarding their identity. One theory is that they were Welsh, mistaken because of their language for Irish. This seems rather unlikely, and the evidence suggests that although killing and maiming in the aftermath of battle may have been indiscriminate, some of the victims were Irish.

> The Irish women Prince Rupert brought on the field (wives of the bloody Rebels in Ireland), his Majesty's dearly beloved subjects our soldiers would grant no quarter to, about 100 slain of them, and most of the rest of the whores that attended that wicked Army are marked in the face, or nose, with a slash or cut.[12]

Some of these unfortunates may have been among the Irish wives recorded of some of the King's Lifeguard of Foot who had served in Ireland prior to the war, but others may well have been attached to men of the Shrewsbury Foot.

Although Colonel Smith, being mounted, apparently escaped from the field, few of his officers and men were as fortunate. There were no other officers of the rank of colonel with them, and the bulk of the other officers were taken prisoner.

Sir Matthew Appleyard's Regiment
Captain Hubbard
Captain King

---

11 *The Kingdom's Weekly Intelligencer*, no. 104, 10–17 June 1645, p. 838.
12 *Ibid.*

Captain Masters
Captain Montague Sanderson
Captain John Tirwhyt
Lieutenant Baker
Lieutenant Lewen
Lieutenant Alexander Middleton [Drayton, Somerset]
Lieutenant James Thomson [Palmer's Company]

Robert Broughton's Regiment
Major Robert Broughton [Marchwiel, Denbighshire]
Captain Freestone
Captain Hill
Captain George Lisle[13]
Captain Hugh Polden
Lieutenant Darrenfield
Lieutenant Duppey
Lieutenant Oliver

Ensign Thomas Johnson [Freestone's Coy]
Ensign Porter
Ensign Thomas Pritchard
Ensign Vaughan

Sir Fulke Hunckes' Regiment
Lieutenant Perrin
Lieutenant Rewes
Ensign Smith

Sir John Paulet's Regiment
Captain Mason
Lieutenant Birkwhit
Lieutenant Bradford
Lieutenant Burling
Lieutenant Kirkman
Lieutenant Wynne
Ensign Cooke
Ensign Glascock
Ensign Hutchins
Ensign Rice
Ensign Yate

Henry Tillier's Regiment
Captain Church
Captain Dykes
Lieutenant Busbridge

---

13 Not to be confused with Colonel George Lisle, who was severely wounded and carried from the field at some point during the battle.

Ensign Bowen
Ensign Dillon
Ensign Harrison

Henry Warren's Regiment
Major Daniel Moore

Duke of York's Regiment
Captain James Dyer
Captain Fitzmorris
Captain Hill
Captain Widman
Captain Lieutenant Hawksworth
Lieutenant Curtys
Lieutenant Rossey
Lieutenant Riley
Ensign Bennet
Ensign Bradshaw
Ensign Rosley
Ensign Young[14]

It seems likely that after the fall of Shrewsbury, Earnley's Regiment, other than the company noted at Bridgnorth later in the year, had disappeared. Gibson's now only consisted of whatever remained at Chester, and Warren's probably had no more than one weak company.

It was certainly the case that virtually all of the Shrewsbury Foot, including most of the junior officers and NCOs were killed or captured. A handful may have escaped en route to London, but they were few.

Fairfax had originally asked rather unenthusiastically for the death penalty to be inflicted, according to Parliament's ordinance, on any 'Irish' prisoners; but in the event, probably because of the usual problems in differentiating between 'native Irish' and other categories, they were imprisoned instead.

Parliament was determined that the King should not have the means to rebuild and retrain his broken infantry, so no exchanges were offered. About 800 men accepted the option of serving in Ireland, others were recruited by the French and Spanish, but the majority would remain prisoners until the end of the war.[15]

Leicester surrendered on 18 June, and the detachment of Appleyard's Regiment with him was allowed to march out and rejoin the King.

Henry Tillier, in the Tower, was exchanged in June for Colonel Sir Robert Pye, captured during the storm of Leicester. Tillier's captivity had not been easy. It is unclear whether he had been wounded at Marston Moor before capture, but once a prisoner he encountered problems detailed in his petition to the House of Lords. The House had previously ordered that, 'the Order of

---

14 Edward Peacock, *The Army Lists of the Roundheads and Cavaliers* (London: Chatto & Windus, 1874), p. 65.
15 Foard, p. 308.

this House, for Major General Tillier continuing near his Surgeon, shall be in Force until the Pleasure of this House be known.' Tillier's deposition asserted:

> That he had received a Command from the Lieutenant of the Tower, by one Mr Yeates, or his Remove out of the Chamber where he then was, to one Mr Sopis, one of the other Warders of the Tower being formerly kept by one Delayfield, who, conceiving himself damnified by this his intended Removal, threatened the aforesaid Tillier with great Strictness and Severity, though at that Time he was close Prisoner, using him with base Language and incivility, not permitting him to stir out of his Chamber, or anybody to come to him; so that, the Day before the said Tillier was hurt, Mr Yeates being present with him in his Chamber, and was an Eyewitness to the Rudeness and Misbehaviour of the said Delayfield, both in his Carriage and Language, he was desired, by the aforesaid Tillier, to command the said Delayfield from thence, which he at that Time did. The Day after, this Delayfield coming to his Chamber about Two of the Clock to open the Door, where he was still Prisoner, that he might have his Victuals brought in, being Two of the Clock in the afternoon, the aforesaid Tillier being extremely troubled to see himself neglected by his Keeper, this Delayfield, of whom he had so well deserved, desired him Three several Times to Depart the Chamber, and to lock the Door, and leave him to his own Quiet, which the said Delayfield refused to do; and making his Approach to the Table where he sat at Dinner, replied, 'He would stay there in Despite of him.' Whereat the said Tillier rose arose from Table, and entreated him to forbear the Chamber, for that his insolencies were not to be endured; and desiring him thus to leave his Chamber. The said Delayfield violently laid Hands on him, striking him with the Key of the Prison Door on the Forehead, to the great danger of his Life, for which he hath been in Cure ever since the Two and Twentieth of January last, there being several Pieces of the Skull taken out, the Wound remaining yet uncured. Upon his Examination, he will set forth the whole Particulars; in the meantime he doth most humbly submit himself with this his Business to the most honourable House of Lords.
>
> Henry Tillier.[16]

The Lords' response was:

> General Tillier not to be removed back to the Tower, his wound not being cured.
>
> The deposition of Major General Tillier was read. And Mr Dixon, his Surgeon, certified this House at the Bar. 'That his Wound is not cured, and it will be dangerous yet to remove him to the Tower, though he be sent for by the new Lieutenant of the Tower.'
>
> It is Ordered That the Lieutenant of the Tower be sent to, to know the Reason why he sent for Tillier to be remanded to The Tower; he having been permitted by Order of this House to lie near his Surgeon, for the better curing of his Wound.[17]

It may be that Tillier's injury was the reason that, unlike other Anglo-Irish senior officers, an exchange was agreed for him.

---

16 Journal of the House of Lords, 1 May 1645, vol. 7, p. 346.
17 Journal of the House of Lords, 1 May 1645, pp. 345–6.

… the lords and commons do approve of, and agree unto, the Exchange of Colonel Henry Tillier, Prisoner to the Parliament, for Sir Robert Pye Junior, Prisoner to the King's Forces. And it is further Ordered, That the Manner of expediting this Exchange, and returning the Prisoner exchanged, be referred to the Committee of Both Kingdoms.[18]

If Tillier was still affected by his injury, he seems to have recovered rather quickly. He rejoined the King, who was now in the southern Welsh Marches, full of schemes to rebuild the Royalist foot, and in need of every experienced officer he could obtain. For much of the summer the Royalist Council of War was absorbed in ambitious plans to recruit men.In June the King and Rupert were planning to raise 8,300 men, in 17 regiments. But war-weary South Wales and the Marches produced nowhere near the numbers of men demanded, and many of those who were levied quickly deserted. On 4 July a revised list was produced of 3,700 men in 10 regiments. Among the colonels of the new regiments were to be Sir Matthew Appleyard, Henry Tillier and Sir John Paulet.

The new units were evidently expected to have an initial establishment of 400 men, including officers, and most probably never approached this figure. The Royalist 'New Model' in any case never took the field as a distinct entity. John Belasyse recounted that the King:

[Went] to Hereford and Raglan Castle to recruit himself with a new foot army in South Wales, but those which were raised there were otherwise disposed of being sent over the Severn, some to supply the garrisons in the West, others to Prince Rupert at Bristol, who was gone thither [on 4 July] to his Government to defend the place during His Majesty's residence in South Wales.[19]

Appleyard's Regiment may still have included the small number of Anglo-Irish troops who had been with him in Leicester, but Tillier's is likely to have been entirely formed from raw Welsh and Marches recruits. Both units were among the troops sent by the King to reinforce Rupert at Bristol.

On 26 July Charles wrote to the Prince:

Nephew this messenger coming out of France is in such haste to go to you that I shall only tell you that you will find I have been better than my word in my last letter, for yesterday I gave order for Tillier's and [Colonel William] Pretty's Regiments to march to you with all possible speed…[20]

Appleyard and Tillier were members of Rupert's Council of War in September during the siege of Bristol by Fairfax, and concurred with his decision to surrender. Disarmed (though Rupert's Firelocks were permitted to retain their muskets), they and the remainder of the garrison were permitted to march to Oxford, where a Parliamentarian spy noted:

---

18 Journal of the House of Lords, 10 June 1645, vol. 7, p. 421.
19 British Library, Harleian MS, 6852, f.275.
20 Warburton, vol. II, p. 148.

Oxford is strong with soldiers, there being more now in that Garrison than hath been all this summer, occasioned by divers Garrisons surrendered to us, the soldiers whereof went thither. And besides there is come in of late a company of Major General Tillier's, they have no Ensign flags, instead whereof every Company carrieth (upon the head of a pike) about a yard of Green Taffeta.[21]

It is a last glimpse of Tillier's Regiment of Foot. Both Tillier and Appleyard would be in Oxford on its surrender in June 1646, when whatever remained of their men were disbanded.

Apart from a stray company of Earnley's Regiment in Bridgnorth, most of the remaining 'Irish' foot serving with the Royalists were with Lord Byron in and around Chester.

Byron's own Regiment of Foot was reinforced in April by 100 new recruits from Ireland under Lieutenant-Colonel Little, who henceforward served with the regiment in that capacity.[22] The regiment in April now mustered around 300 men and in the early hours of 20 September the Parliamentarians, spearheaded by Finch's firelocks who had changed sides after Nantwich,[23] surprised the Chester suburbs. During the months of siege which followed Byron's foot would be a mainstay of the garrison, regarded by Byron as more reliable than the citizen soldiers and Welsh troops who made up the bulk of the garrison.

Several officers from Richard Gibson's Regiment served with Byron, probably as reformadoes, though as we shall see, there are suggestions that some of the men were serving in North Wales towards the end of the war. Major Sydenham was a 'chief instrument' in repairing the breach in the medieval walls made by Parliamentarian guns before the abortive assault on 22 September.[24]

By early October, Byron wrote that his regiment consisted of 'about a hundred Irish, under the command of Lieutenant-colonel Little'.[25] It is unclear what had happened to the remainder of its men.

On 8 October, the besiegers made their most determined assault of the siege. An understrength company of Byron's Regiment, under Captain Norris and Lieutenant Lane, took part in the defence of the 'north breach'. Byron related that:

[The] enemy stormed the new breach with great disadvantage, having both a very steep bank to ascend, and when they were got up, a precipice to come down and withal were flanked by two towers (the Goblin's Tower on the one hand the New Tower on the other) from whence our musketeers were not sparing of their shot. Notwithstanding all such disadvantages they both assaulted it and brought their ladders to the walls, and began to scale with a great fury. The line was filled with

---

21 BCW Regimental wiki for Henry Tillier's Regiment of Foot <http://wiki.bcw-project.org/royalist/foot-regiments/henry-tillier>.

22 John Barratt, *The Great Siege of Chester* (Stroud: Tempus, 2003), p. 108.

23 See Appendix III.

24 Barratt, *Chester*, p. 89.

25 *Ibid.*, pp. 118–20; Little may the captain of that name who served with the forces in Ireland.

halberdiers where I had likewise caused heaps of stones to be laid in convenient distances, which when the Enemy came under the walls, did more execution than muskets could have done, the shot was placed upon the flankers of the wall, where it was most useful. Our men for a good space were at handy blows with them on top of the wall. The Enemy (as fast as their ladders were thrown down and their men knocked off) raring up others in their stead, and bringing up fresh supplies ...[26]

The assault was eventually beaten off, with, according to Byron, considerable loss to the attackers.

Sir Edmund Verney (of Gibson's Regiment) who seems at some stage to have been Byron's Deputy Governor (or at any rate effective second in command, as Sir Francis Gamull was in theory deputy Governor) was in command of the defenders at the 'old breach', where the attackers were also repulsed.

By January 1646, the combination of starvation and bombardment, and dwindling hopes of relief had brought both citizens and Byron's Welsh troops to the brink of mutiny. Whilst he tried desperately to play for time, Byron moved his family to the castle, garrisoned by his Irish troops under Colonel John Disney, another officer of Gibson's. On 30 January surrender terms were agreed. Among the clauses was, 'That such Irish as were born of Irish parents, and have taken part with the rebels in Ireland, now in the city, shall be prisoners.'

This should of course have included at least some of Byron's Regiment of Foot. Byron made particular efforts to exempt them from this clause, which would in effect condemn them to death under the terms of Parliament's ordinance. Although the Parliamentarian commissioners could not officially agree, Byron's men were quietly allowed to depart with the rest of the garrison, whilst Brereton told the Speaker of the House of Commons that he still had to verify the number of Irish in the town.

With the fall of Chester, Byron's aim was to hold the strongholds of North Wales for as long as possible, with the increasingly forlorn hope that reinforcements from the Irish Confederates might yet arrive. He established his headquarters at Caernarvon, leaving part of his regiment with Sir John Owen, Major General and Governor of Conway. However Owen reported that they deserted daily for lack of arms, so Byron ordered them to join him at Caernarvon.[27] Byron also refers to a supply of arms sent by sea to Beaumaris for Major Sydenham's company. This could have been what remained of Gibson's Regiment, though this cannot be confirmed;[28] however Byron told Owen that they could not be spared for the Conway garrison.[29] On 10 April he told Owen, 'By cause you have part of Little's men already I shall send the rest to you ...'[30] He had already ordered Colonel Vane, possibly now in

---

26 *Ibid.*, p. 163.
27 National Library of Wales, Clennau MS 603.
28 *Ibid.*, 608.
29 *Ibid.*, 609.
30 *Ibid.*, 611.

25 Colonel Thomas Mytton. Following the resignation of Sir Thomas Myddelton in compliance of the Self-Denying Ordinance in April 1645, Mytton, of Shropshire, was appointed regional commander of the Parliamentary forces. He was frequently titled 'Major-General Mytton'. (From reprint of John Vicars, *England's Worthies*, 1647 (London: John Russell Smith, 1845))

command of Gibson's to return to Caernarvon with his men from Merioneth. If Gibson's men were with Byron at Caernarvon, they would have been included in his terms of surrender on 4 June. His regiment of foot would suffer a grimmer fate.

The fall of Caernarvon enabled Thomas Mytton, commanding Parliamentarian forces in North Wales, free to turn his main attention to Conway, the last place where troops from Ireland might theoretically land. On 9 August Mytton's troops stormed the town, surprising the guard, and took a number of prisoners, including Irish who were bound back to back, and taken down to the harbour and 'cast overboard and sent by water to their own country.'[31]

Sir John Owen held out in the castle until November, when he sent Mytton draft articles of surrender. These included a clause that 'all Irish men shall have your passes to go into Ireland to have free quarter in their march and shipping provided with free transportation.'[32] The articles finally agreed on November make no mention of the Irish, so it seems most likely that Mytton tacitly allowed these last Irish soldiers of King Charles to return to their homeland.

---

31 Quoted in *The Ottley Papers*, vol. II, p. 326.
32 National Library of Wales, Clennau MS 624.

Afterword

The impact of the troops from Ireland has remained a subject of controversy and debate among historians. The main arguments relate to the numbers involved and the proportion of 'native Irish' among them.

Estimates of numbers range between 21,000 and 8,000, with 15,000 often suggested. The higher figure however can only be supported if a large number of troops recruited in Ireland are added to the men of the returning Anglo-Irish Regiments. The numbers of these who actually landed were the subject of fierce debate between Parliamentarian and Royalist propagandists. It was of course in the interest of the Parliamentarians to maximise claims of an influx of the hated Irish rebels in order to stir up anti-Royalist feelings among the population in general. In the same way the Royalists sought to minimise the numbers of native Irish, even denying that there were any.

The actual definitions of English born in Ireland, and Native Irish were frequently as unclear to contemporaries as they are to modern historians, and any clear estimate is impossible. Certainly to troops sent over from Leinster in late 1643/early 1644 were predominantly English or Welsh. They may have recruited a small number of English settlers in Ireland, but probably included few 'native Irish'. Despite attempts to prevent their embarkation, they were accompanied by a fairly small number of female wives and camp followers, again initially made much of in Parliamentarian propaganda, but quickly fading from view.

The unfortunate women killed or wounded in the Royalist baggage train after Naseby were claimed to have been Irish, though the more generally accepted view is that most of them were Welsh. In fact it is equally possible that unfortunates caught in the path of adrenalin-charged troopers were struck down regardless of nationality.

It has been suggested that Welsh or Cornish-speaking Royalist soldiers were sometimes, deliberately or otherwise, taken to be Irish. This may have happened in some cases, though Welsh speakers would have been fairly widely recognised as result of such factors as cattle-droving.

There was more evidence of popular opposition to the troops from Ireland among the civilian population of southern England. It was probably the case that units raised or recruited in Munster contained a higher proportion of local men, both settlers and native Irish. And two of the three units to reach England, those of Lord Inchiquin and Lord Broghill, which were definitely largely 'native Irish' in composition, served there. The third, Lord Byron's Regiment of Foot, serving in the Welsh Marches and the North, and latterly in the Chester garrison, does not appear to have generated a great deal of comment until the closing stages of the war.

Although the Parliamentarians proved ready enough to enlist captured or deserting Anglo-Irish troops in the same way as they did other Royalist troops, the same attitude was not extended to actual or alleged 'native Irish'. Killings of such soldiers began from the early stages of the war, and was formalised by the ordinance of 1644. This was certainly motivated by fears of intervention the side of the King of the Irish Confederates, and certainly if it had materialised would have met with a ruthless response.

In practice, as we have seen, Parliamentarian commanders interpreted the legislation with a good deal of discretion, reasoning that its implementation would invite similar treatment of their own men, as demonstrated by Prince Rupert. And in the summer of 1644, following the defection of Lord Inchiquin to Parliament, his troops hitherto reviled as bloodthirsty savages, were shipped back to Munster and the service of Parliament.

Although the actual numbers of 'native Irish' troops serving the Royalists in England Wales can. never be known, an examination of all listed arrivals of troops from Ireland makes it unlikely that there were more than a couple of thousand.

It remains to consider the impact of the troops from Ireland on the war. It was never as great as the Royalists and hoped and the Parliamentarians had feared. If the original intention to employ the Irish troops as a united force had been feasible and they had been employed in the north of England as planned as a 'sure cure for the Scots', they might well have tipped the balance of the war there. As it was, the problems of sufficient shipping and naval control of the Irish and Celtic Seas meant that they arrived in uncoordinated detachments over a dispersed area, and could never be utilised as planned.

As it was, even after the defeat at Nantwich, which severely mauled the Leinster troops, they remained a potent force in the Welsh Marches. They salvaged the Royalist position in North East Wales in 1643, and consolidated control of the northern and central Marches in the spring of 1644. Without his Anglo-Irish foot, Rupert could not have launched his invasion of Lancashire and the 'York March' in the summer of 1644. It was not until after their defeat at Montgomery in September that the Leinster foot ceased to be a viable independent field force.

Elsewhere the impact of the troops from Ireland was more mixed. In the winter of 1643–44 units from Munster enabled Sir William Vavasour to maintain the initiative against the Parliamentarian garrison of Gloucester, and Appleyard and Paulet's Regiments provided some much needed infantry strength to Hopton's army in his operations in Hampshire.

The part played by the troops from Ireland when serving with the Oxford Army is less easy to quantify. Serving with the already relatively experienced foot of Jacob Astley, they seem to have made less of an impression, though the strong foot regiment of the Duke of York had an active role at both Second Newbury and Naseby.

Inchiquin's and Broghill's regiments extended Royalist control in Dorset, but, along with the remainder of Maurice's Western Army, could make no impression at the siege of Lyme.

It remains to consider what impact the Irish had on tactics and the nature of the war. The latter stages of the war did see some developments in Royalist infantry tactics. There seems to have been greater reliance on 'salvee' fire and close quarter hand-to-hand fighting. Whilst it is the case that George Monck advocated the 'salvee', there is no evidence that this was a particular feature of the war in Ireland, and was probably an unrelated development intended to avoid a prolonged firefight in a situation with inferior Royalist numbers.

The leading Anglo-Irish military theorists were George Monck and Henry Tillier. Neither would have opportunity in the brief intervals when they were not prisoners to significantly influence Royalist infantry tactics.

The question of whether the arrival of the troops from Ireland made the conduct of the war harsher is still the subject of debate. The 'massacre' at Bartholmley Church was certainly the work of Robert Byron's Regiment, though its exact circumstances are open to interpretation. In general, however, more notorious episodes, such as the Hopton Castle killings, and the Bolton and Liverpool 'massacres' of 1644, cannot be directly attributed to the troops from Ireland, but to individual circumstances.

On balance, though the 'King's Irish' were never utilised to their full potential, they almost certainly prevented a Royalist collapse in the Welsh Marches and parts of the north of England for much of 1644, and provided a useful reinforcement for the Oxford Army. It is not in fact clear that their use actually lost the King any significant support, as most hostility towards them was from areas already Parliamentarian in sympathy.

Appendix I

Sir William Vaughan's Regiment of Horse

This unit was one of the most successful arrivals from Ireland, and had a considerable impact in the Welsh Marches and a significant role in the wider war.

William Vaughan's origins have so far defied identification. He is usually assumed to have been a member of one of the numerous Vaughan families of the central Welsh Marches, possibly from Herefordshire or Radnorshire, although there is also a possibility that he was from one of the branches of the family which had settled in Ireland, in 1644.

However Vaughan's admission in 1596 to Shrewsbury School tends to support a Marches or Welsh origin, and suggests that he as born in 1584/5, making him almost 60 years old.

Vaughan seems to have begun his military career as a professional soldier in 'foreign arts', and may have been the 'Captain Vaughan' listed in Cromwell's Regiment in Mansfeld's expedition of 1624.[1]

In 1641 Vaughan commanded the 6th troop of the Earl of Carnarvon's Regiment of horse, and his officers were:

Lieutenant Thomas Crofts (son of Cornet Richard Tailey?)
Quartermaster James Vaughan (brother of William)

Vaughan commanded Sir Richard Grenville's horse in his victory over the Irish rebels in February 1643 at Rathconnell, and was knighted by Ormonde on his bringing news of the victory to Dublin. It was a success which bore Vaughan in good stead, when after the Cessation he was chosen to command the regiment of horse sent from Leinster to England.

Ormonde encountered considerable difficulties in equipping this unit. He told Sir Edward Nicholas:

The truth is, I have much ado (at so low an ebb in present is this revenue) to provide for their passage, and furnish them for their service in that measure they

---

1   John Rushworth, *Historical Collections* (London, 1721), vol. I, pp. 153–4.

are, being enforced to take up of some merchants here upon my own engagement, a provision of great saddles and arms for them.[2]

The regiment under Sir William Vaughan's command sent to England in February 1644 consisted of four troops, drawn from the units in Ireland of Captain Povery, Sir Thomas Armstrong, Lord Leicester, and Sir Adam Loftus, all of Sir Thomas Lucas's Regiment, which was to be reduced.

The troops so formed were commanded by:

Sir William Vaughan
Captain John Devalier (Giovanni Devalier, evidently a Florentine professional soldier]
Captain Thomas Crofts (son of Sir Christopher Crofts)
Captain John Bonner

The establishment of each troop was to be:

1 Captain
1 Lieutenant
1 Cornet
1 Quartermaster
4 'other officers' (probably including a trumpeter and a saddler)
40 mounted troopers and 10 unmounted (owing to a shortage of horses)

The regiment thus in theory totalled 244 men, although it appears that the total sent from Ireland was approximately 350.[3]

Other personnel included:

Lieutenant Bernard
Cornet Collins
Quartermaster Lyneker.

And among the troopers:

John Bembricke
Arthur Bembricke
Richard Bembricke
Phelim Dempsie
William Whittinge
John Fitzgerald
George Tayler
William Mandeville[4]

---

2   HMC Ormonde, MS N.S., vol. I, p. 12.
3   *Ibid.*, p. 146.
4   *Ibid.*, p. 148.

This suggests that were a number of men born in Ireland in the regiment's ranks.

On arrival in England Vaughan's Regiment needed additional horses before it could take the field. With sufficient mounts, Vaughan and his horse were quickly in action. On 24 March they joined with Robert Ellice's Regiment of Foot in taking Apley Castle, and next day defeated the Shropshire Parliamentarian commander, Thomas Mytton, near Longford. Mytton reportedly lost 245 out of 410 horse and foot. The Royalist casualties included Captain Thomas Crofts, who was killed.

Vaughan rapidly began establishing his regiment. In the early spring it had been expanded to seven troops:

Sir William Vaughan (Captain Lieutenant Beverley Usher)
Lieutenant-Colonel Henry Slaughter (Keighley, Yorkshire)
Major Radcliffe Duckenfield (Duckenfield, Cheshire)
Captain Thomas Crofts
Captain John Devalier
Captain John Bomer

A seventh troop under Captain George Hosier also joined the regiment. This apparently had been raised independently in Shropshire prior to Vaughan's arrival.[5]

Vaughan and his Regiment were on the right wing of the Royalist horse at Marston Moor. By then the unit was probably around 500 strong. Nicholas Armourer, who had been a lieutenant in Ireland, had taken over Thomas Croft's Troop. Vaughan's losses at Marston Moor are unknown, but may have been heavy enough to contribute to a poor performance in September at the battle of Montgomery.

However, Prince Rupert's departure to Bristol gave Vaughan an opportunity for greater independence, and for the kind of small-scale fighting at which he was particularly proficient. In September he established himself at Shrawardine Castle, west of Shrewsbury. At around the same time he raised a regiment of foot which was intended primarily to garrison Shrawardine and the other strongholds which Vaughan now occupied. These included as well as Shrawardine – where Vaughan's brother, Dr Charles Vaughan, a clergyman, was made Deputy Governor – Dawley House (Major Radcliffe Duckenfield), Lilleshall Abbey (Captain Henry Bostock, under Captain Devalier), Caus Castle (Captain John Devalier) Leigh Hall (Captain David Lloyd under Devalier), High Ercall (Captain Nicholas Armourer, Vaughan's Regiment of Foot).[6]

Not surprisingly, the Shropshire Parliamentarians did not welcome the new arrival, and in September Thomas Mytton made a raid on Shrawardine. Sir William Vaughan and a number of his officers were captured whilst attending a service in the parish church. Sir William agreed to order the surrender of the Castle, and Mytton allowed him to ride up to it to order

---

5   Young, *Naseby*, p. 52.
6   *Ibid.*

his men to yield. However he garrison had lowered the drawbridge, and Sir William quickly rode inside, the drawbridge was raised and the Parliamentarians left helplessly outside.

Vaughan's men quickly earned a mixed reputation for their activities. On 24 October Vaughan surprised Montgomeryshire Parliamentarian troops under Sir John Price at Welshpool and took a number of prisoners.

In the cut and thrust of raid and counter-raid the Royalists had their own casualties. More than 50 years later when Richard Gough was writing his *History of Myddle*, the fate of Cornet Collins, who had come over with the regiment from Ireland, was still remembered:

26 The site of Caus Castle, near Westbury in Shropshire. A Norman castle built on a hill fort, the site at time boasted a parish church and many streets. By the seventeenth century the castle was in poor condition but was garrisoned by Captain Devalier of Vaughan's cavalry. (Photo: Charles Singleton)

> There happened no considerable act of hostility in this parish during the time of the wars, save only one small skirmish, in Myddle, part of which I saw, while I was a school boy at Myddle, under Mr. Richard Rodericke, who commanded us boys to come into the church, so that wee could not see the whole action, but it was thus. There was one Comet Collins, an Irishman, who was a Garrison soldier for the King, at Shrawardine Castle. This Collins made his excursions very often into this parish, and took away Cattle, provision, and bedding, and what he pleased. On the day before this conflict, he had been att Myddle taking away bedding, and when Margaret, the wife of Allen Chaloner, the Smith, had brought out and showed him her best bed, he thinking it too coarse, cast it into the lake, before the door, and trod it under his horse feet. This Cornet, on the day that this contest happened, came to Myddle and seven soldiers with him, and his horse having cast a shoe, he alighted at Allen Chaloner's Shop to have a new one put on. There was one Richard Maning, a Garrison soldier at Morton Corbett, for the Parliament. This Maning was brought up as a servant under Thomas Jukes, of

Newton, with whom he lived many years, and finding that Nat Owen, (of whom I spoake beefore,) did trouble this neighbourhood, he had a grudg against him, and came with seven more soldiers with him, hoping to find Owen at Myddle with his wife. This Maning and his companions came to Webscott, and so over Myddle Park, and came into Myddle at the gate by Mr. Gittin's house at what time the Cornet's horse was a shoeing. The Cornet hearing the gate clap, looked by the end of the shop and saw the soldiers coming, and thereupon he, and his men mounted their horses; and as the Cornet came at the end of the shop, a brisk young fellow shot him through the body with a carbine shot, and he fell down in the lake at Allen Challoner's door. His men fled, two were taken, and as Maning was pursuing them in Myddle Wood Field, which was then unenclosed, Maning having the best horse overtook them, while his partners were far behind, but one of the Cornet's men shot Maning's horse which fell down dead under him, and Maning had been taken prisoner had not some of his men came to rescue him. He took the saddle under his arm, and the bridle in his hand, and went the next way to Wem, which was then a garrison for the Parliament. The horse was killed on a bank near the further side of Myddle field, where the widow Mansell has now a piece enclosed. The Cornet [Collins] was carried into Allen Chaloner's house, and laid on the floor; he desired to have a bed laid under him, but Margaret told him, she had none but that which hee saw yesterday; he prayed her to forgive him, and lay that under him, which she did, Mr. Rodericke was sent for to pray with him. I went with him, and saw the Cornet lying on the bedd, and much blood running along the floor. In the night following, a Troop of horse came from Shrawardine, and pressed a team in Myddle, and so the Cornet to Shrawardine, where he died the next day.[7]

Vaughan's raids were having a notable impact, as *Mercurius Aulicus* related, tongue in cheek:

Why didst though suffer that Castle [Shrawardine] which was the seat of holiness to be possessed with profaneness and Popery?? O curse with a heavy curse the Great Devil of Shrawardine, what doth torment Thy children and let all the righteous and holy say Amen.[8]

Vaughan was able to maintain the strength of his Regiment with more success than many commanders. In part this was the result of success in action. This not only enhanced the reputation of the unit and its commander, but was also a source of weapons, equipment and horses. In December 1644, for example, in an action near Welshpool, Vaughan's men captured 22 pairs of pistols, and on 4 July 1645, in one of his greatest exploits, Vaughan raised the siege of High Ercall, capturing gunpowder, bullets and muskets.[9]

Following the Parliamentarian capture of Shrewsbury in February 1645. Vaughan's territory came under increasing pressure. On 26 March 1645

---

7   Richard Gough, *The History of Myddle*, 1701, ed. David Hey (Harmondsworth: Penguin, 1981), p. 70.

8   *Mercurius Aulicus*, 1 February 1644 [45] (ed. Thomas, 1971), p. 1369.

9   *Ibid.*, p. 1119.

the Parliamentarians captured Leigh Hall, and the Shropshire Committee reported it as:

> A place which formerly being possessed by some of sir William Vaughan's commanders did much impoverish the country. For prevention thereof, we sent a party of horse and foot, and with the loss of one captain surprised the enemy in the house, their number being 18, some whereof were Irish and executed according to the ordinance.[10]

The latter presumably were among the troopers who had come with Vaughan from Ireland, and correctly or otherwise identified as 'native Irish'.

When Captain Devalier lost his base of Caus Castle, he 'took his troop to Ludlow, and is now colonel'.[11] Nevertheless, Vaughan raised a replacement troop, which he put under the command of his brother, James. With the beginning of the summer campaign of 1645, Vaughan, accompanied by his wife and her servants in a coach and six, mustered most of his Regiment and rode out to join the King, en route defeating some Parliamentarian Shropshire horse at Much Wenlock.

At the siege of Leicester at the end of May Vaughan's Regiment was 400 strong, making it, with Prince Rupert's Regiment, the strongest regiment of horse in the Royalist army. At Naseby, Vaughan's Regiment was in the first line on the Royalist right, and had notable initial success, breaking right through Ireton's horse, and possibly threatening the flank of the Parliamentarian foot. However Vaughan suffered a number of casualties in the ensuing defeat. Taken prisoner were:

Lieutenant-Colonel Henry Slaughter
Captain George Hosier (acting major, Duckenfield was probably besieged in Dawley House)
Lieutenant Armstrong
Cornet Edmonds
Quartermaster Nurse[12]

In Shropshire the Parliamentarians took advantage of Vaughan's absence; on 24 June Shrawardine Castle surrendered. However, Vaughan quickly struck back. After Naseby his regiment were among the horse which accompanied Prince Maurice to Worcester. Sir William, with 400 horse, still mostly his own regiment, left Worcester on 3 July, and moving via Bridgnorth, possibly picking up reinforcements, entered Corvedale, which had recently been occupied by the Parliamentarians, and surprised seven troops of Parliamentarian Shropshire horse quartered in the area of Broncroft Castle.

---

10 F. Stackhouse Acton, *The Garrisons of Shropshire During the Civil War* (Shrewsbury: Leake and Evans, 1867), p. 57.

11 Symonds, p. 85.

12 Young, *Naseby*, p. 85.

27 The fields before High Ercall, site of Vaughan's dramatic relief of the house there. (Photo: Charles Singleton)

The enemy lost in all, by their own admission, about 80 men. The Royalists claimed that two officers and 47 troopers were captured, and five killed.[13]

In the next stage of what seems to have been a carefully planned operation, Vaughan rendezvoused with troops from a number of local garrisons as far away as Lichfield, crossed the River Severn in the Buildwas area, and next morning fell on the besiegers of High Ercall with 900 horse and 40 dragoons. The Parliamentarians were taken by surprise, and suffered around 500 casualties, including most of their foot.

At the end of August Vaughan burned most of the town of Bishops' Castle, probably as punishment for the anti-Royalist attitude of the townspeople.

Sir William and his regiment were present at the Royalist defeat at Rowton Heath (24 September), but no members are identified among the lists of prisoners. In October the Regiment still had seven troops:

Colonel Sir William Vaughan (Captain Lieutenant Beverley Usher)
Major Radcliffe Duckenfield
Captain John Bomer
Captain Nicholas Armourer

---

13 *Mercurius Aulicus*, 13–20 July 1645 (ed. Thomas, 1971), pp. 1661–2.

Captain James Vaughan

Captain Dixie (Dixie had been a corporal in Ireland, and had risen from
the ranks)

Captain Bartholomew Brookes

Vaughan was evidently still maintaining the strength of his regiment, which Sir William Brereton, regarded as being as 'good as any horse' in the Royalist forces.[14]

Appointed general of horse in Wales, Shropshire Worcestershire, Staffordshire and Herefordshire, Vaughan was tasked with attempting he relief of Chester, but was defeated on 1 November at Denbigh Green. A number of his regiment are listed among the prisoners:

Tho. Norbury (trumpeter)

Allex Shelton (corporal)

Troopers:

John Coale

John Tidder

Oliver Beddowes

Rich Shetrliffe

Wm. Farrer

John Mitton

Olover (Hughes)

Rich. Davies

John Sissin

Edw. Hopkin

Rich Pierson

Tho. Steephen[15]

On 3 November, back in Herefordshire, two of Vaughan's troops were surprised and beaten up at Pembridge by local Parliamentarian forces.

There is some evidence of Vaughan's unpopularity among fellow commanders, probably mainly because of the vigorous foraging carried out by his men. In December the governor of Ludlow, Sir Michael Woodhouse, refused Vaughan's men admission to the town, and there were rumours that the two commanders were preparing to fight a duel.

Vaughan next fell on the village of Wrockwardine, used as a base by the Parliamentarians who were again besieging High Ercall. He burned the village, but failed to capture the Parliamentarian strongpoint of the church.

February saw Vaughan's men plundering Clun, Presteigne and Leintwardine, and one Richard Jones of Trevern in Gladestry complained

---

14 Brereton, *Letter Books*, vol. I, pp. 130–1.

15 *Ibid.*, item 802.

28 The remains of part of the earth work defences at High Ercall. Sir William Vaughan went to Ireland, serving firstly as captain of a frigate, and then major general of horse to Ormonde, and was killed leading a charge at the battle of Rathmines in 1649. (Photo: Charles Singleton)

he had lost property worth £400–500, including the rings from his wife's fingers.[16]

Vaughan's reign of terror in the Marches came to an end in March 1646, when he was involved in the Royalist defeat at Stow-on-the-Wold. Vaughan himself was wounded, but escaped to Oxford. Captain John Bomer was among the prisoners. Most of what remained of the regiment were probably in Oxford at the time of its surrender in June.

Nicholas Armourer held High Ercall until its surrender on 28 March. Described as 'good, plucked, brave fighting men', the garrison made their way to Worcester, on whose surrender only 17 men remained in Armourer's troop of horse.

Officers of Sir William Vaughan's Regiment of Horse

IO = Indigent Officers' List, 1663
Lieutenant-Colonel John Slaughter (Slaughter, Gloucestershire; POW Naseby)
Major Radcliffe Duckenfield

---

16 Webb & Webb, *Memorials of the Civil War*, vol. II, p. 65.

Captains

Nicholas Armourer
John Bomer (Bommer; POW Stow-on-the-Wold)
Thomas Crofts (K. Longford)
Wolstan Dixie (Market Bosworth, Leicestershire)
Giovanni Devalier (Florence, Italy)
Thomas Fox (I.O. Montgomery)
George Hosier (POW Naseby; I.O. Shropshire)
Johnson (Dragoons, Shrawardine)
Edward Jones (St Martins, Shropshire; I.O. Shropshire)
Roger Ranakers (I.O. Chester)
James Vaughan
Capt. Lieut. Beverley Usher

Lieutenants

Armstrong (POW Naseby)
Billingsley (Reformado)
Thomas Moon (Lieutenant-Colonel Slaughter; I.O. London)
William Sugar (Captain Dixie's Troop; I.O. Shropshire)
Morgan Vaughan (Captain Fox's Troop; I.O. Radnor)

Cornets

John Cotton (I.O. York)
Edwards (POW Naseby)
William Ling (I.O. London)
Henry Lyon (Captain Ranakers' Troop; I.O. Lancaster)
Thomas Sherwood (I.O. Somerset)
George White (Captain Armourer's Troop; I.O. London)
Thomas Wright (Capt Jones' Troop; I.O. Durham)

Quartermasters

Thomas Aston (Duckenfield's Troop; I.O. Lancaster)
Huntingdon Crossman (Bomer's Troop; I.O. London)
John Newton (I.O. Chester)
Nurse (POW Naseby)
Alexander Shelton (I.O. London)

Prince Rupert's Firelocks

This is one of the more intriguing of Royalist units. As we shall see, there is strong evidence of a significant Irish element in its ranks. Clues to its origins may be found in two letters from the King and Prince Rupert to Jan van Haesdonck.

Haesdonck has been aptly described as a 'military entrepreneur'.[1] A Flemish merchant, Haesdonck seems to have had involvement in pre-war drainage projects in East Anglia. On the outbreak of the Civil War, he organised large-scale arms imports for the Earl of Newcastle's northern Royalist Army, an activity which he expanded to include the remainder of the King's forces. He also operated privateers in the Royalist interest.

On 18 November 1643 the following agreement was made:

> Articles of agreement made by and with his Majesty's consent, the 18th of November 1643, between his Highness Rupert Prince Palatine, on the one part, and John Van Haesdonck on the other, concerning bringing over from beyond seas into England 200 soldiers, more or less, such as are experienced and practised 'in party and buyting [*sic*]' in the Low Countries between the King of Spain's side and the United Provinces, who are to be joined with as many English soldiers as shall be necessary to complete a whole regiment of foot to be employed for his Majesty's service to compel the rebels and malignants to a contribution.
>
> 1 It is agreed that the said 200 soldiers shall be landed in England by the said John Van Haesdonck, and joined with English soldiers having knowledge of those parts where his Majesty shall employ them, and they shall be contented with the pay his Majesty allows his other soldiers. And whereas charge of bringing them over is proportionably to be borne between the Prince and Van Haesdonck: his Majesty is pleased that the said Prince shall be Colonel over the said Regiment, and the said John Van Haesdonck, Lieutenant-Colonel thereof, and have a company in the said regiment; and that Haesdonck, for better encouragement of the said soldiers to come over, shall have the recommendation of two captains and half the number of lieutenants and under officers of the said regiment.

---

1   Mark Stoyle, *Soldiers and Strangers, an Ethnic History of the English Civil War* (London: Yale University Press, 2005), p. 292.

And his Majesty is pleased that all booty from the rebels, as also the common prisoners taken by any of the said regiment shall be divided as follows: one-half thereof shall be equally shared amongst as many of the said soldiers as shall assist in taking the booty; his the commander of the party to have a double share, according to the usual custom beyond seas; the Prince is to have a fourth part of the booty, at the rate of 5s in the pound; the said Jan Van Haesdonck an eighth part at the rate of 2s 6d in the pound; the sergeant-major of the regiment a twentieth part, the captain of the company of such soldiers as assist in taking the booty is to have, according to the number of the soldiers, a twentieth part being one shilling in the pound; and the clerk, or whosoever shall be appointed to make the said partition, to have sixpence in the pound.

And as the charge of bringing over the said soldiers is to be disbursed by John Van Haesdonck, it is agreed between the said parties that it shall be repaid out of the half part to be divided between the Prince, Van Haesdonck and the other officers, before any distribution be made to any of them,

And, lastly, Prince Rupert for himself doth covenant and promise to and with the said Van Haesdonck that his Highness will well and truly observe and fulfil all the articles before mentioned, as well on his part as on behalf of his Majesty.[2]

On 24 November Prince Rupert wrote from Oxford to Van Haesdonck:

Whereas by consent of our Sovereign Lord, King Charles you are obliged, by articles in writing agreed upon between myself and you to raise and bring from beyond seas to my regiment for his Majesty's service 200 expert soldiers, more or less; these are to authorise you to bring them with the utmost speed to Weymouth in Dorsetshire, or any other port in his Majesty's possession where you may safely land them, and whence you may convey them to my regiment, in case, by wind, weather, or other occasion, you cannot bring them into Weymouth. I do hereby and in his Majesty's name, strictly charge all governors of any such his Majesty's ports and garrisons peaceably to suffer you and the 200 soldiers to come ashore, and accommodate you and them with meat, drink, and lodging, and, if occasion require, with a sufficient convoy from garrison to garrison in their march towards my regiment in his Majesty's army, always provided that you make no longer stay in any garrison than occasion require.[3]

These communications raise a number of questions. Rupert of course already had a regiment of foot (ex Thomas Lunsford) under Lieutenant-Colonel John Russell. Van Haesdonck had already received commissions as a captain of horse from the Earl of Newcastle and the King, but apparently never took up command in the field. So was Rupert in fact referring to his original regiment, or an entirely new one? He was shortly to take up his independent command in Wales and the Marches, so may well have felt the time to be right to have an independent Lifeguard of Foot. At around this time Rupert's

---

2 *Calendar of State Papers, Domestic Series, 1641–1643*, ed. W.D. Hamilton (London: Eyre & Spottiswoode for HMSO, 1887), pp. 500–501.

3 *Ibid.*, pp. 501–2.

original regiment of foot totalled 509 common soldiers,[4] so it may well be that the foreign contingent was intended to reinforce them.

In February 1644 the Regiment was issued 'by a former warrant', with 700 muskets and bandoliers,[5] suggesting that it had received new recruits. Soldiers raised, Van Haesdonck would have been recruiting during the winter of 1643/44 after active campaigning had ceased.

Regarding the likely nature of the recruits. The Spanish Army of Flanders had received a serious defeat in the previous summer at Rocroi, which may have inclined some professional soldiers to seek a more promising employer. Among them, given such considerations as language, the Irish would have been a likely preferred choice. This is supported by the relatively few names of the firelocks' officers preserved in I.O.:

Major Aeneas Lyne (London)
Lieutenant Owen Carty (Lyne's Company; I.O. London)
James Hinane (Lyne's Company; I.O. London)
Ensign Mortaugh O'Donoghue (Lyne's Company; I.O. London)[6]

The other question is when and indeed if Van Haesdonck's men arrived. The Royalist Ordnance Papers for the spring of 1644 record the steady arrival at Weymouth of ships from the Continent carrying cargoes of munitions. There is therefore no reason to suppose that a relatively small number of troops raised by Van Haesdonck could not have arrived in the same way. It is clear from the record of his other activities that Van Haesdonck did not take up his position as lieutenant-colonel.

Assuming that the reinforcements did arrive, they will have marched to join Rupert on the Welsh Border. The firelocks are not specifically mentioned as taking part in the Marston Moor campaign. However there is evidence that they may have been added to Rupert's Regiment of Foot as a firelock company, of 150–200 men. That this may have been the case is supported by an episode at the capture of Bolton on 28 May. The first Royalist assault, in which Rupert's Regiment of Foot took part, was repulsed with significant losses. The defenders hanged a captured 'Irish' officer in full view of the attackers, an unwise move which infuriated Rupert and played a part in the so-called 'Bolton Massacre'.

If the firelocks were indeed present, they were also probably at Marston Moor, although no account of their action there seems to have survived.

Rupert's Regiment of Foot was stationed in the Chester area until the spring of 1645, but the company of firelocks evidently joined Rupert on his return to Bristol and Oxford, and now, if not before, became known as his Lifeguard of Firelocks. They were with the Prince and Sir Henry Gage in their unsuccessful attempt on 11 January 1645 to surprise Abingdon. The

---

4   *The Royalist Ordnance Papers*, vol. II, p. 377, item 34.
5   *Ibid.*, p. 392, item 51.
6   Reid, *Officers and Regiments* vol. 4, pp. 152–153. Reid also includes Major Bunnington, Gentleman Pensioner killed at Leicester in 1645, but this is the result of a misreading of Richard Symond's rather confused text.

attackers were repulsed in a counter-attack, and a number of prisoners taken, among them some Irish, who were hanged.

The firelocks are next noticed by Richard Symonds in the assault on Leicester on 31 May: 'Colonel John Russell, with the Prince's regiment of blue coats, and also the Prince's Firelocks, assaulted. They set the Prince's black colours on the great battery within ... We lost ... 28 or 30 officers. Major of Prince Rupert's firelocks.'[7]

Once again, it is unclear whether the firelocks were present at Naseby. If they were, they apparently escaped relatively intact, as in September they were with Rupert at his surrender of Bristol. On 11 September the defeated Royalists marched out, and a Parliamentarian newsletter reported that 'He [Rupert] drew out part of his foot and horse before his waggons, and part following, himself next, with his Lifeguard of Firelocks came forth, all in red coats before him, and his Life Guard of horse following...'[8] Unlike the remainder of the surrendered Royalist foot, the firelocks were allowed to retain their weapons.

The firelocks accompanied Rupert to Oxford, and his disgrace and removal from command. But with fears that the Prince might attempt a coup, they were sent to the Royalist garrison at Worcester.

They were present at Sir William Vaughan's defeat at Denbigh Green, several of them being among the prisoners. None of the names are apparently Irish, suggesting that the firelocks had received new recruits at some stage:

Rob. Wigge	Wm. E[d]wards
Rand. Malpas	Abraham Tipps
David Williams	Nicholas Foster

However the firelocks were soon in action again. On 19 December the Shropshire Committee reported to Brereton an unsuccessful attempt by 2,000 Royalist horse and foot to relieve High Ercall: 'the forlorn were all Irish. Prince Rupert's Firelocks, all red coats.'[9]

The firelocks, probably no more than 100 strong at most, must certainly have been among the troops which Lord Astley led on his last desperate campaign which ended in defeat at Stow-on-the-Wold on 21 March 1646. These men may well have been the firelocks who briefly rescued Sir Charles Lucas, lieutenant general of horse, when he was captured during the battle.

None of their officers can be identified with certainty among the prisoners, but it can safely be assumed that Rupert's Firelocks as a unit did not survive the defeat.

---

7 Symonds, pp. 51–2.
8 Warburton, vol. II, p. 181.
9 Brereton, *Letter Books*, vol. II, item 1054.

Appendix III

What Sandford's Firelocks Did Next

It is not known who succeeded to the command of Sandford's company after he and his lieutenant were killed in the attempted storming of Nantwich on 17 January 1644. They may have been merged with Langley's company, but any successor's tenure office may have been brief, as apparently all of the firelocks were taken prisoner at the Battle of Nantwich on 25 January.

Perhaps 600 out of the total of around 1,500 Royalist prisoners took service with Brereton's forces. Most of them were apparently dispersed among various units, being 'listed under several captains,'[1] but the Firelocks, as elite troops with an already formidable reputation, were an exception, and retained a separate identity.

The fate of Captain Langley is unclear, though he was still with the Royalists in May, but Sandford's men at least came under Brereton's command. Probably reinforced by Sir William's existing dragoons, they formed three companies of Brereton's Regiment of Foot, and were later described by him as 'firelocks which were soldiers in Ireland'.[2] They were commanded for the remainder of the war by three captains, Simon (or Syon) Finch, Geoffrey Gimbart and Joseph Hoult. Nothing is known of Gimbart or Hoult, though they were most likely professional soldiers from outside Cheshire, and Norman Dore suggests that they may have been among the officers from the English forces in Ireland who came over in the summer of 1644 to take service with Parliament.[3]

Finch, however, is better documented. He was one of the Royalist officers from Ireland serving with Sir Michael Earnley's Regiment, taken at Nantwich. It is possible that he may have been in command of at least some of the firelocks at the time of his capture. Finch's defection was publicly condemned by his brother in a declaration:

---

1   Malbon, p. 115.
2   Brereton, *Letter Books*, vol. I, item 610.
3   *Ibid.*, vol. II, pp. 594–5.

Know all men by this proclamation. That I Captain John Finch under the Regiment of Colonel Henry Warren do inform the Mayor of Chester and Elizabeth his wife the several goods hereafter named which said goods were left there in the custody of the said Elizabeth, being late the goods of Captain Symon Finch under Sir Michael Earnley's Regiment; which said Symon was taken prisoner at Nantwich in the County of Chester, in his Majesty's service. But since that time, have forfeited the said goods by taking up Arms against his Majesty under the command of Sir William Brereton as it doth appear upon Oath taken before the said Mayor and others, as also by good testimony to the Right Honourable Lord Byron, Lord Field Marshal General, who by his warrant under his hand seal hereunto annexed, hath given to me the said John Finch all the said goods so remaining in their custody. An old pair of spurs,15 points, a little white pitcher, a plush jump with silver clasps, a taffeta doublet and cloth breeches, a cloak lined with plush, a pair of shammay sleeves, a Red scarfe, three coarse linen towels, an old trunk and £16 in money, which said goods were all appraised to £3 13 shillings and 2 pence, besides the money, which made up in the whole £19 13 shillings and 2 pence. All which said goods and money, I say, I John Finch do acknowledge to have received, of the said Randle Holme, and Elizabeth his wife, by virtue of the said warrant from the said Lord Byron and thereof every part and parcel thereof. I do hereby acquit and discharge them the said Randle Holme and Elizabeth his wife and their and either of their executors and administrators from the said goods. And I do promise and assume thereby, both for myself and Robert Finch Lieutenant under Captain Edmund Langley who is to have part thereof, both by my Lord Byron's direction and my promise to the said Lord Byron …

This fourteenth day of May anno dom 1644

John Finch[4]

By the late spring of 1644 Finch and his firelocks were operating with Brereton's troops in reducing minor Royalist garrisons in Cheshire. They saw action at Oswestry in early July, at Malpas against Langdale's Northern Horse in August, and were probably at the Battle of Montgomery in September.

By the beginning of 1645 Captain Finch had evidently made something of a name for himself, for on 31 January, the Shropshire County Committee, planning their assault on Shrewsbury, wrote to Brereton, asking for reinforcements, and saying 'we desire Captain Finch and his company to be in the party you send, for he is well known to us'.[5] On 22 February, guided by a Captain Wyllier, a recently deserted Royalist firelock officer, about 40–50 of Finch's firelocks played a major role in surprising Shrewsbury, and opening the way for the capture of the town.[6]

By the spring of 1645, references to Brereton's other two 'firelock' or 'dragoon' companies begin to occur, although they had quite likely been formed earlier.

Gimbart's company was present for a time during the spring at the leaguer of Beeston Castle, with Gimbart apparently then in command of operations

---

4   HMC Portland MS, I, p. 458.

5   Brereton, *Letter Books*, I, item 645.

6   Jonathan Worton, *The Battle of Montgomery, 1644* (Solihull: Helion, 2017), p. 41.

there, during which he indulged in an acrimonious exchange of letters with the Royalist governor, Captain William Vallett.[7]

In May, Brereton gave the total strength of his firelocks/dragoons as 210 men, whilst a muster of 30 April gives the following details: Finch's company, about 70 men, Gimbart's Dragoons 60 men, Captain Holt's Firelocks, 80 men.[8] The firelocks were referred to a few days previously, on 21 April, when Lieutenant-Colonel Michael Jones reported that he would have marched earlier that day 'if the firelocks' arms had been fixed. Smiths are in hand with them.'[9]

Finch's company was reported in May as being at the siege of Hawarden Castle,[10] and all of the firelock companies had an important role in Brereton's plans later in the month to rendezvous with the Scots and Lord Fairfax in order to oppose the northwards march of the main Royalist field army. In a letter of 21 May to the Committee of Both Kingdoms, Brereton reported that he was preparing to march to join his allies, with a force which included 'some choice dragoons, which are firelocks mounted',[11] and next day added that they were 'firelocks which were soldiers in Ireland lately mounted'.[12] The regard in which Brereton obviously held the firelocks is the more striking considering that throughout this period he was enforcing the Parliament's ordinance regarding the execution of captured 'native Irish'.

It seems likely that Gimbart and Hoult's companies were among the Cheshire troops detailed to shadow the King in his march on Leicester.[13]

September saw one of the most notable exploits of the Cheshire firelocks. In June Brereton had been recalled to Westminster under the terms of the Self-Denying Ordinance, and in his absence control was exercised by the Cheshire County Committee. In practice, day-to-day military affairs were managed by Lieutenant General Michael Jones and Major General James Lothian. At the end of July, the Parliamentarians had recommenced the leaguer of Beeston, but their main objective remained the capture of Chester.

On the night of 19 September, amidst great secrecy, the Parliamentarians drew off from Beeston a picked force, including 200 dragoons, presumably all three companies. Marching through the night along unfrequented by ways – 'a tedious march' – they appeared before the outworks of Chester at dawn on the 20th. They were spotted by a sentry, who, according to the Parliamentarians, asked 'if we had brought our dear bretheren (meaning the Scots) with us to take the city'. This may well have been a useful distraction, under the cover of which Gimbart's firelocks, carrying scaling ladders, slipped along under the cover of the bank of the River Dee up to the fortification nearest the river, known as Gun Mount. Lord Byron, the Royalist governor, claimed later that he had warned of the vulnerability of the defences at this point, but the more immediate weakness seems to have been that the

---

7   Brereton, *Letter Books*, vol. I, items 459–60.
8   *Ibid.*, item 385.
9   *Ibid.*, item 552.
10   *Ibid.*, item 552.
11   *Ibid.*, item 607.
12   *Ibid.*, item 610
13   *Ibid.*, vol. II, item 897.

outworks were largely manned by the citizen soldiers of Sir Francis Gamull's Chester Regiment, who lost their nerve:

> [Captain Gimbart] was the first that entered, his ladder being too short, he lift up his man to the mount [near the riverside] from the top of it his man drew him up by the hand, and then they cried 'A Town, A Town', immediately they cleared that Mount, slew Lieutenant Aldersley, the Captain of the Watch, and put the rest, about six men, to flight, then others set to their ladders, possessed themselves of all the Mounts on that side of the City, and with the instruments we brought with us, broke open the gates, then all the Horse entered, with the remainder of the Foot, with loud shouts, which utterly daunted the enemy.[14]

The Royalist defence collapsed as panic-stricken soldiers and civilians fled behind the protection of the medieval walls of the inner city, whose gates were closed only just in time, leaving most of the suburbs of Chester in Parliamentarian hands.

On the evening of 22 September, after an artillery bombardment had opened a breach in the walls near the New Gate,[15] and the Parliamentarians launched a full-scale assault. It was between 7:00 and 8:00 p.m., just after dark, though with 'fair moonshine', that the attack began.

It was spearheaded by Gimbart and Finch's companies, who were supposed to be supported by the remaining Parliamentarian foot. Byron claimed that the firelocks had been fortified before the attack with a mixture of aqua-vita and gunpowder to drink, which seems quite possible. He admitted that the attackers:

> [Came on] with great boldness, but were received with as much courage by Sergeant Major Thropp's men [City Regiment] … Those in the Newgate and in the houses adjoining the breach, annoyed the enemy with their Shot, as did the granadoes and the firepikes, which were used by very stout men, and placed upon the flanks of the breach Captain Crosby (who commanded the Chirk horse) did good service there, and the Rebels pressed on so resolutely that I caused more forces to be drawn down to assist Major Thropp's men. Thrice that night the Enemy was upon the top of the wall, but at last quite beaten off, seven of them were killed upon the top of the wall, who afterwards fell into the street, and were the next day buried by us …[16]

The attackers were apparently driven back after fierce hand-to-hand fighting, by Captain Crosby's dismounted troopers, armed with sword and pistol.

The Parliamentarians placed part of the blame for their repulse on the failure of the reserves who included many trained band troops, to support the firelocks, though they also admitted that 'if five hundred of them had

---

14 Lancaster, p. 23.
15 Traces may still be seen in the 'Roman Garden'.
16 Lancaster, pp. 23–4; John Byron, 'Account of the Siege of Chester' in *Cheshire Sheaf*, 1971, pp. 12–13.

then entered, they had all been cut off, they were so ready and well-provided in the city.'[17]

The Royalists admitted to only nine dead, including Crosby's lieutenant, cornet and corporal, but Byron claimed that the Parliamentarian lost 'for certain their Regiment of Firelocks to a very small number, besides divers others.'[18]

The attackers reported that Gimbart, Finch and his Lieutenant, and 'some others' were wounded. This is likely an underestimate, but the firelocks evidently did not suffer as heavily as Byron claimed, for they were soon in action again.

They were almost certainly present at the battle of Rowton Heath (24 September) though no details of their actions have yet been found. However, both Finch's and Hoult's companies, described by Michael Jones, their commanding officer on that occasion, as 'stout and resolute men' played a major role in the Parliamentarian victory at Denbigh Green on 1 November, holding a lane until the main Parliamentarian force came into action.

The firelock companies continued to serve during the remainder of the long leaguer of Chester. Brereton's *Letter Book* for 18 December records the payment to the Cheshire dragoons 'as appears under the hands of Captain Finch, Gimbart and Holt the sum of £416 16.00'[19] and on 12 January 1646 a further payment of £466.6.00 is entered.[20]

With the fall of Chester the firelocks joined Brereton and part of the Cheshire forces in the siege of Lichfield. The dragoon companies of Finch and Gimbart were paid £102 18s by Brereton as the promised gratuity for the capture of Chester. It has been suggested that the payment by Sir William himself, rather than, as was the case of the rest of the troops, by the Cheshire County Committee, may indicate the high value he placed on them. For a time Gimbart's company was detached to the siege of Holt Castle, but it is probable that Finch's men took part in the battle of Stow-on-the-Wold on 21 March.[21] Five of Finch's men were wounded in a Royalist sortie from Lichfield on 23 May.[22]

The eventual fate of the firelocks is unclear, but there are some interesting clues. One of Brereton's colonels, Robert Duckenfield, was appointed Governor of Chester on its surrender, and commanded a garrison regiment in 1648, responsible for Cheshire and Shropshire. This may have been a composite force drawn from Brereton's old army, but it seems very likely that it consisted mainly of troops from Brereton's Regiment. Finch was Lieutenant-Colonel, and in 1651 led it with distinction at the Battle of Worcester. He sat on the court martial of the Earl of Derby afterwards. It was disbanded shortly afterwards, apart from five companies which Finch took over to Ireland to complete Hardress Waller's Regiment. By 1656 Finch had joined Richard

---

17 Lancaster, op. cit.
18 Byron, op. cit.
19 Brereton, *Letter Books*, vol. II, item 981.
20 *Ibid.*, item 1042.
21 *Ibid.*, III, p. 53.
22 *Ibid.*, item 224.

Lawrence's Regiment (ex Robert Hammond) and was still lieutenant-colonel in 1659, though evidently not confirmed at the Restoration. However in 1666 he was granted 4,000 acres at Tullimore in Co. Tipperary, the family remaining in the area at the present day. So it may be that some of Sandfords old firelocks ended their careers back in Ireland.[23]

---

23 Charles Firth and Godfrey Davies, *The Regimental History of Cromwell's Army* (Oxford: Clarendon Press, 1940), vol. II, pp. 357– 8, 446.

Colour Plate Commentaries

Plate 1 Musketeer, Irish Confederate Army

Dressed in the traditional white trews of the Irish, this musketeer is well equipped with the equipment expected of a contemporary professional soldier. Irish soldiers had seen experience through out the ongoing European wars of the late sixteenth and early to middle seventeenth centuries and witnessed the latest developments in military technology and practice. As news of the Irish Rebellion spread across the Continent, many veteran officers and soldiers chose to return home. They brought with them arms and equipment and used their experience to train and lead the newly raised armies. The Confederacy was also able to gain support from abroad. France, Spain and the Papacy were able to contribute significant sums of money and logistical support to the Catholic cause.

Plate 2 Ensign, Tillier's Regiment

Henry Tillier was a professional soldier with experience in the expeditions to Cadiz in 1626 and the Île de Ré in 1627. Sometime in the 1630s he became the captain of the Military Company of Westminster before becoming the captain of the Society of the Artillery Garden. He became the lieutenant-colonel of Sir Fulk Huncke's infantry regiment, whilst serving in Ireland. In late 1643, he was promoted to the rank of colonel with his own regiment and arrived with Broughton's regiment and Vaughan's cavalry contingent back in England. Colonel Tillier and his regiment served with Prince Rupert at Newark, at the siege of Liverpool and at Marston Moor. The regiment was mentioned as wearing green soldiers' coats whilst on the 'Yorke March' on June 1644. Later in the summer Sir Thomas Dallison, in command of Prince Rupert's regiment at Welshpool, informed the Prince on 4 August 1644 that 'I have had 113 coats and caps for foot soldiers in the house of my Lord Powys, a hundred of which are blue, which will serve very well for your Highness's regiment of foot. The rest are green, which may be for Colonel Tillier's regiment. There are also three or four hundred yards of cloth, which may serve to make coats for your Highness's regiment of horse.'[1] For further comments on the colours, see the notes for plates G and H.

Plate 3 Pikeman

Surviving warrants[2] detail the issue of munitions and equipment to the newly raised infantry regiments of the Irish Expedition. Some 8,948 muskets, with equivalent numbers of bandoliers and rests were ordered between November 1641 to February 1642. A total of 3,982 pikes were ordered over the same period. This would imply an issue of one pike for just over every two muskets. However, the numbers delivered, 4,750 muskets and 1,500 pikes suggest a somewhat higher ratio of one pike for just over every three muskets. The caveat must be considered that not all the equipment ordered was planned for issue, and very likely a large percentage was held back for replacement and recruitment once in Ireland.

Plate 4 Cavalry Trooper

The bulk of the Royalist reinforcements to sail from Ireland were infantry. However, Captain Bridges of Lord Inchiquin's Cavalry Regiment landed with some 300 troopers in Bristol. In February 1644, some 160 men formerly of Lord Lisle's Regiment of Cavalry landed on the Wirral Estuary under the command of Sir William Vaughan. This trooper is well equipped with a sleeved buff coat, which is based on an example of one currently within the Shropshire Museum's collection.

Plate 5 Senior Officer

Professional officers were readily available to lead the army upon its creation. Over half the captains that received commissions for Ireland had seen service in the army that fought against the Scots. From pay warrants, it is possible to see that most of the infantry regiments sent to Ireland seemed to have a full complement officers. The return of those officers that survived conflict in Ireland, saw a dramatic impact on the decline of the 'grandee' Royalist officers, who has served the King in the regional armies from the start of the war. The pace of replacement picked up when Prince Rupert established his command along the Welsh Borders. Aristocratic officers such as Lord Capel and Sir Francis Ottley were replaced by pragmatic and tough veterans of the Bishops' Wars and the campaign in Ireland.

---

1 *The True Informer*, 17 August 1644; Phillips, *Memoirs of the Civil War in Wales and the Marches*, vol. II (London: Longmans et al., 1874), p. 19.
2 Ryder, 1987.

Plate 6 Musketeer

Despite the defeats of 1644, the Anglo-Irish foot was able to be reformed and re-equipped. For the 1645 campaign, many of the survivors were drawn into an amalgamated battalion of some 500 soldiers. This formation has been frequently referred to as the 'Shrewsbury Foot'. Some secondary sources refer to an issue of grey soldiers' coats, however a primary document relating to this has yet to be confirmed. This musketeer, having survived the defeats of 1644 and the disaster at Naseby, finds himself once more in a garrison along the Welsh Marches awaiting a bleak and uncertain future. Dedicated to the memory of the artist's friend, Boyd Rankin, 1946–2019.

Plate 7 Colours carried by Lord Inchiquin's regiments

Plate 8 Colours carried by Tillier's and Talbot's regiments

Notes to Plates 7 & 8 by Dr Les Prince

When illustrating flags from the English Civil Wars, one is faced with several challenges. The first is that we know practically nothing about the vast majority of flags used, whether infantry or cavalry. The second is that of the flags we do know from contemporary sources are overwhelmingly London biased, especially with regards to the infantry. For example, the two primary systems which have been identified for differentiation between the various captains in a regiment, sometimes called Venn A and Venn B, or Venn and LTB,[3] are derived mostly from London usage. It is a reasonable assumption that these systems, particularly the latter, were used by the field armies, but in the absence of direct and *complete* evidence, it remains an assumption, although there is some partial supporting evidence available from various accounts, especially Symonds' *Diary*.[4] Even when partial evidence is available, further challenges arise. We know from Symonds, for example, that at the Aldbourne Chase muster on Wednesday 10 April 1644, several Royalist regiments were woefully understrength and therefore carried at most two colours rather than an entire set. Furthermore, some of these understrength units were brigaded together and carried mixed stands of colours, as was the case for Jacob Astley's and Colonel Stradling's combined regiment. We also know from the account of Fairfax's progress through the West Country, that flags were often kept in storage, suggesting regiments routinely used only partial stands. Moreover, in this case, Fairfax distributed the colours he found willy-nilly to groups of ex-Royalist soldiers

---

3   Stuart Peachey and Les Prince, *English Foot* (Partizan Press: Leigh-on-Sea, 1990).
4   Harl. MS 986.

who had turned up to volunteer for the New Model, suggesting scratch units of, probably, short duration.[5] Add to this the known exotics, such as Rupert's well known infantry designs, and the various known stripey flags, neither of which appear to be systematic, and we have a melange of confusion. Finally, despite its prominence and importance, we know practically nothing of the flags carried by the New Model Army, which is a source of great frustration to those of us who are proud flag anoraks.

The flags which are illustrated here for Tillier's and Inchiquin's Foot, have been identified by a system of elimination from flags captured at Naseby.[6] Henry Tillier's (Tilyard's) regiment was known to have worn green coats, and although there is no necessary link between coat colour and flag colour, it seems reasonable to conflate the two here.[7] But it is worth realising that a London newsbook purporting that Inchiquin's Foot were at Cheriton asserted that they wore red coats,[8] and yet it seems that his foot colours were watchet (light blue) and white with unknown devices.

We are on firmer ground with Talbot's and Inchiquin's Horse. Talbot's regiment of yellow coats was seen by John Symonds at the Aldbourne Chase muster in 1644, carrying nine colours, six white and three yellow. Of these two are plain and three bear only the St George Canton. The rest have one to four black charges.[9] From Symonds' sketch, which is the size of a small postage stamp, it is not clear what this charge is, certainly he gives no written description and his sketchy character could be one of several heraldic beasts. There are two reasons for supposing it to be an heraldic dog (Talbot) however. First Symonds sketch has the same general shape and appearance of a dog, although the same could be maintained had the charge been a lion. Second, the heraldic dog, or Talbot, could have been adopted by Colonel Talbot as a fortuitous pun to adopt what is technically called a canting device. However, it should be noted that various coats of arms borne by several members of the Talbot family in the Middle Ages bore lions. The posture of the charge is also unclear; it could be passant or statant, but from the prominence of the forepaw on Symonds' sketch, passant seems more likely.

Inchiquin's cavalry cornets for Ireland are well known, and recorded in the Williams manuscript. Murrough McDermod O'Brien, 1st Earl of Inchiquin, 6th Baron Inchiquin, also known as Murchadh na dTóiteán ('Murrough of the Burnings') commanded 100 horse raised in England for service in Ireland. In July 1642 he was appointed commander of the Army in Muster. Although technically a Royalist at this point, he was in fact part of the army to defend Protestantism against the Irish Catholics, some of whom were, ironically Royalist as well. He went over to Parliament in July 1644, but in 1648 went back into the King's service. He was defeated by the New Model Army at Arklow in 1649. His cornets followed a systematic pattern, much like infantry ensigns, with the troop captains' seniority indicated by the number

5   Joshua Sprigge, *Anglia Rediviva*, 1647.
6   Williams MS; British Library E.288[45].
7   Harl. MS 986; E.6[23].
8   British Library, E.40[20].
9   Harl. MS 986.

of harps, except for the major who bore only a pile wavy with no St George canton. Each cornet bore the legend *Concordes Resonem da deus Alme Sonos*: Grant, O kindly God, that I may send forth Harmonious Sounds. It is curious to note that all the words begin with a capital letter except da deus.

Bibliography

Manuscript Sources

Carte MS 15; *Firth* MS C.6–8 (Bodleian Library)
Additional MS 16370, 18981, 18982, 18983; *Harleian MS,* 986, 2135, 6804 (British Library)
Portland MS, I (The University of Nottingham)

Printed Primary Sources

'An Exact Relation of the Bloody and Barbarous Massacre at Bolton', in *Tracts Relating to the Military Proceedings in Lancashire* (Preston: printed for the Chetham Society, 1844)

Brereton, Sir William, *The Letter Books of Sir William Brereton*, ed. R.N. Dore, 2 vols (Record Society of Lancashire and Cheshire), vols 123, 125, 1984 and 1990

Byron, John, 'Account of the Siege of Chester' in *Cheshire Sheaf*, 1971

Calendar of the Manuscripts of the Marquis of Ormonde, [formerly] preserved at the castle, Kilkenny. New Series. Royal Commission on Historical Manuscripts, 36 (1902–20)

Calendar of State Papers, Domestic Series, 1641–1643, ed. W.D. Hamilton (London: Eyre & Spottiswoode for HMSO, 1887)

Calendar of State Papers, Domestic Series, 1644, ed. W.D. Hamilton (London: Eyre & Spottiswoode for HMSO, 1888)

Calendar of State Papers, Venice, 1640–1642, ed. A.B. Hinds (London: HMSO, 1923–24)

Carte, Thomas, *A Collection of Original Letters and Papers … found among the Duke of Ormonde's Papers*, 2 vols (London, 1739)

Cholmeley, Sir Hugh, 'Sir Hugh Cholmeley's Account', in *The English Historical Review*, vol. V (1890)

Clarendon, Edward Hyde, Earl of, *History of the Rebellion and Civil Wars in England*, ed. W.D. Macray (Oxford: Clarendon Press, 1888)

Corbet, John, 'Historical Relation of the Military Government of Gloucester', in John Washbourne, *Bibliotheca Gloucestrensis* (Gloucester, 1825), p. 49

Fairfax, Lord Thomas, *Short Memorials of Thomas Lord Fairfax. Written by Himself*, (London, 1699; reprint London: Pallas Armata, 1985)

Historical Manuscripts Commission (HMC), 10th Report

Gough, Richard, *The History of Myddle*, 1701, ed. David Hey (Harmondsworth: Penguin, 1981)

Hogan, J., *Letters and Papers Relating to the Irish Rebellion between 1642–1646* (Dublin: The Stationery Office, 1935)

Hopton, Ralph, *Bellum Civile*, ed. C.H. Chadwyck Healey (Somerset Record Society XVIII, 1902)

Journal of the House of Lords, vol. 7

Lancaster, Nathaniel, *Chester's Enlargement* (London, 1647)

Lewis, John (ed.), *May It Please Your Highness* (Newtown: Jacobus, 1995)

Lewis, John (ed.), *Your Highness' Most Obedient Servant* (Newtown: Jacobus, 1996)

Luke, Sir Samuel, ed. Tibbutt, H.G., *The Letter Books of Sir Samuel Luke, 1644–45* (St Albans, for HMSO, 1963)

Magnalia Dei, in Atkinson, J.A. (ed.), *Tracts Relating to the Civil War in Cheshire* (Manchester: Chetham Society, 1844)

Malbon, Thomas, *Memorials of the Civil War in Cheshire*, ed. James Hall (Lancashire and Cheshire Record Society vol. 19, 1889)

Mercurius Aulicus, Oxford 1643–1644. In Peter Thomas (ed.), The English Revolution III: Newsbooks, 4 vols (London: Cornmarket Press, 1971). Vol. 1, Oxford Royalist.

Mercurius Civicus, London's Intelligencer, 1643–1644, ed. S.F. Jones, 2 vols (Reading: Tyger's Head Books, 2013, 2014)

The Ottley Papers, ed. William Phillips, in *Transactions of the Shropshire Archaeological and Natural History Society*, 2nd Series, vols 6–8 (Shrewsbury: Adnitt and Naunton, 1894–96).

The Pythouse Papers, ed. W.A. Day (London: Bickers, 1879)

Parkinson, R. (ed.), *Autobiography of Henry Newcombe* (Manchester: Chetham Society old series 26, 1852)

Peacock, Edward, *The Army Lists of the Roundheads and Cavaliers* (London: Chatto & Windus, 1874)

Roy, Ian (ed.), *The Royalist Ordnance Papers,* 2 parts (Oxfordshire Record Society, 1963 and 1975)

Rushworth, John, *Historical Collections* (London, 1721)

Slingsby, Sir Henry, *The Diary of Sir Henry Slingsby* (London: Longman et al., 1836)

Symonds, Richard, *Military Diary*, ed. Stuart Peachy (Southend-on-Sea: Partizan Press, 1989)

Walker, Sir Edward, *Historical Discourses Upon Several Occasions* (London, 1705)

Warburton, Eliot, *Memoirs of Prince Rupert and the Cavaliers*, 3 vols (London: Bentley, 1849)

Washbourne, John, *Bibliotheca Gloucestrensis*, 3 vols (Gloucester,1823)

Webb, Rev. John, and Webb, Rev. T.W., *Memorials of the Civil War Between King Charles I and the Parliament of England as it Affected Herefordshire and the Adjacent Counties*, 2 vols (London: Longmans, 1879)

Modern Sources

Barratt, John, *Cavaliers: The Royalist Army at War* (Stroud: Sutton, 2000)

Barratt, John, *Cavalier Capital: Oxford in the English Civil War, 1642–1646* (Solihull: Helion & Company, 2015)

Barratt, John, *Civil War Stronghold: Beeston Castle at War* (Birkenhead: Caracole Press, 1995)

Barratt, John, *The Great Siege of Chester* (Stroud: Tempus, 2003)

Bayley, A.R., *The Great Civil War in Dorset 1642–1660* (Taunton: Barnicott and Pearce, 1910)

Bull, Stephen, *A General Plague of Madness: The Civil War in Lancashire, 1640–1660* (Lancaster: Carnegie, 2009)

Carte, Thomas, *A History of the Life of James Duke of Ormonde,* 6 vols (Oxford: Oxford University Press, 1851)

Dixon, John, *The Business at Acton* (Caliver Books: Nottingham, 2012)

Farrow, W.J., *The Great Civil War in Shropshire* (Shrewsbury: Wilding & Son, 1926)

Firth, C., and Davies, G., *The Regimental History of Cromwell's Army*, 2 vols (Oxford: Clarendon Press, 1940)

Dictionary of National Biography, 40 vols (Oxford: Oxford University Press, 2004)

Foard, G., *Naseby: The Decisive Campaign* (Barnsley: Pen & Sword, 2004)

Gaunt, Peter, *Nation Under Siege: The Civil War in Wales 1642–48* (Cardiff: HMSO Books, 1991)

Gilbert, Sir John Thomas, *History of the Irish Confederation and the War in Ireland 1641–1643* (Dublin: M.H. Gill, 1882), 7 vols

Jones, Serena, *No Armour But Courage: Colonel Sir George Lisle 1615–1648* (Solihull: Helion & Company, 2016)

Hutton, Ronald, *Royalist War Effort* (London: Routledge, 2003)

Kenyon, J., and Ohlmeyer, J., *The Civil Wars: A Military History of England, Scotland Ireland 1638–1660* (Oxford: Oxford University Press, 1998)

Morris, R.H., and Lawson, P., *The Siege of Chester* (Chester: G.R. Griffith, 1923)

Newman, Peter R., *Royalist Officers in England Wales, 1642–1660: A Biographical Dictionary* (New York: Garland, 1981)

Phillips, J. R., *Memoirs of the Civil War in Wales and the Marches*, 2 vols (London: Longmans et al., 1874)

Reid, Stuart, *Officers and Regiments of the Royalist Army,* 5 vols (Southend-on-Sea: Partizan Press, n.d.)

Ryder, Ian, *An English Army for Ireland* (Partizan Press: Leigh-on-Sea, 1987)

Seacome, John, *The History of the House of Stanley* (Preston, 1793)

Stackhouse Acton, F., *The Garrisons of Shropshire During the Civil War* (Shrewsbury: Leake and Evans, 1867)

Stoyle, Mark, *Soldiers and Strangers, an Ethnic History of the English Civil War* (London: Yale University Press, 2005)

Terry, C.S, *Life and Campaigns of Alexander Leslie, Earl of Leven,* (London: Lonhmans et al., 1899)

Tucker, Norman, *Royalist Officers of North Wales, 1642–1660* (Colwyn Bay; printed for the author, 1961)

Wanklyn, Malcolm, *Decisive Battles of the English Civil War* (Barnsley: Pen & Sword Military, 2006)

Wedgwood, C.V., *The King's War* (London: Collins, 1958)

Worton, Jonathan, *The Battle of Montgomery 1644* (Solihull: Helion & Company, 2017)

Worton, Jonathan, *To Settle the Crown: Waging Civil War in Shropshire, 1642–1648* (Solihull: Helion & Company, 2016)

Young, Peter, *Marston Moor 1644, the Campaign and the Battle* (Kineton: Roundwood Press, 1970)

Young, Peter, *Naseby 1645: The Campaign and the Battle* (London: Century, 1985)

Young Peter, and Toynbee, Margaret, *Cropredy Bridge: The Campaign and the Battle* (Kineton: Roundwood Press, 1970)

Articles

Auden, J.E., 'Four Letters from Shropshire to Prince Rupert', in *Transactions of the Shropshire Archaeological and Natural History Society*, 4th Series, II (1910)

Auden, J.E., 'The Anglo-Irish Troops in Shropshire', in *Transactions of the Shropshire Archaeological and Natural History Society*, L, 1839–40

Dore, R.N., 'The Sea Approaches. The Importance of the Dee and Mersey in the Civil War in the North West', in *Transactions of the Historic Society of Lancashire and Cheshire for the Year 1986* (Liverpool: printed for the society, 1986), vol. 136

Gaunt, Peter, *Cheshire History,* No 5, 1995–6

Lowe, John, 'The Campaign of the Irish Royalist Army in Cheshire, November 1643–January 1644', in *Transactions of the Historic Society of Lancashire and Cheshire for the year 1959* (Liverpool : printed for the society, 1959), vol. 111

Lowe, John, And Dore, R.N. *The Battle of Nantwich, 25 January 1644*, in *Transactions of the*

Malcolm, Joyce, 'Caesar's Due: Loyalty and King Charles, 1642–46', THS Studies in History, No 38, London 1983